PERSPECTIVES ON SIGN LANGUAGE USAGE

Papers from The Fifth International Symposium on Sign Language Research

[VOLUME 2]

Perspectives on sign language usage

Papers from The Fifth International Symposium

on Sign Language Research

[VOLUME 2]

Held in Salamanca, Spain, 25–30 May 1992

[1994]

EDITED BY INGER AHLGREN, BRITA BERGMAN AND

MARY BRENNAN

THE INTERNATIONAL SIGN LINGUISTICS ASSOCIATION

 The Deaf Studies Research Unit | University of Durham | England

First Edition *1994*
International Sign Linguistics Association and Deaf Studies Research Unit,
Department of Sociology and Social Policy, University of Durham, Elvet Riverside 2,
New Elvet, Durham DHI 3JT, England.

ISBN 0-9519880-2-6

British Library Cataloguing-in-Publication Data.
A catalogue record for this book is available from the British Library.

Typeset in Fontshop Quadraat, 10.5 / 13 pt.
Printed and bound by Bailes Print, Houghton-le-Spring, Tyne and Wear, England.
Typography and cover-design: Ernst Thoutenhoofd.

Contents

VOLUME 1: Perspectives on sign language structure

VOLUME 2: Perspectives on sign language usage

Preface

The International Sign Linguistics Association (isla) was founded with the intention of supporting and encouraging research into the sign languages used by Deaf communities in many different parts of the world. One important way in which such support can be given is through the establishment of conferences, workshops and seminars, either for isla's own members or for a wider group. Moreover, isla seeks to collaborate with others—Deaf communities, linguistic organisations, educational groups and the like—in arranging appropriate forums for the exchange of information and the sharing of ideas. The Fifth International Symposium for Sign Language Research, held in Salamanca, Spain from the 25-30 May 1992 was one such forum. The Symposium resulted from direct collaboration between the *Centro Nacional de Recursos para la Educación Especial* and isla.

As Alvaro Marchesi, Director General de Renovación Pedagógica, Ministerio de Educación y Ciencia, stressed in his welcoming address to the Syposium, sign linguistic research not only furthers our understanding of the general nature of human languages, it can also help to deepen our understanding of the communities who use sign languages. The joint hope of the organisers that the Symposium would help to raise awareness of sign language issues in Spain and stimulate appropriate research appears to have been well placed. The period between the Symposium and the publication of these volumes has seen a number of events which have supported sign language research and teaching and, simultaneously, have raised the status of Deaf people and their language.

The presenters at the Symposium represented a variety of theoretical backgrounds and offered theories, descriptions and analyses relating to a considerable number of different signed languages. Given the breadth of the material, it was decided that it would be most appropriate to produce the proceedings of the conference in two separate volumes. The first volume focusses on studies of a structural nature and the second on studies relating to sign language usage. However, this distinction is clearly somewhat artificial, since authors of articles relating to such areas as sign language interaction, sign language acquisition and sign language lexicography, also present detailed descriptive analyses as well as theoretical perspectives. Similarly, those presenting a more structural perspective may also have provided observations on sign language usage. Nevertheless, we hope that readers will find the division into two volumes of practical help in accessing the material.

The publication of these two volumes has been undertaken in conjunction with the Deaf Studies Research Unit (DSRU) at the University of Durham, England. Special thanks are due to the DSRU and the Department of Linguistics at Stockholm University, Sweden which have dedicated considerable resources and staff time to the production of these volumes. Thanks are also due to Alvaro Marchesi, Marian Valmaseda and their colleagues in Spain; the interpreting co-ordinators, Esther de los Santos and Liz Scott Gibson and the team of interpreters and *isla* personnel who all worked so hard to make the Symposium a success. The *isla* executive would also like to thank the European Community Regional Secretariat of the World Federation of the Deaf for financial support for the Symposium.

PART 2

Use

Names in Québec Sign Language and what they tell us about Québec Deaf Culture [†]

COLETTE DUBUISSON AND JULES DESROSIERS *

1 INTRODUCTION

Numerous studies have been carried out on personal name signs in various sign languages, most of them dealing with ASL. Meadow [1977] mentions the interest that the study of name signs holds for our knowledge of Deaf American culture. Mindess [1990] et S. Supalla [1990, 1992] each describe numerous name signs in ASL. Mindess deals primarily with descriptive name signs whereas Supalla deals with arbitrary name signs.

As far as other sign languages are concerned, we have information on name signs in Swedish Sign Language and Chinese Sign Language: Hedberg [1989] and Yau & He [1989] describe the processes by which name signs are given under the particular conditions of a boarding school for Deaf children in China. The aim of this paper is to provide a description of personal name signs in LSQ. We will show that naming in Deaf families is characterised by the use of arbitrary initialized signs, but names given within the larger Deaf community are, in the majority of cases, descriptive in nature.

2 METHOD

In conducting this research, we compiled a corpus of 224 personal names expressed in signs. Our principal means of data collection was through a questionnaire, which gave us the following information:
whether the person bearing the name had deaf or hearing parents;
whether he or she was deaf from birth, had become deaf at a later age; or was hearing,
if an explanation for the name was known or whether it had been given arbitrarily;
if the person had one or several names and in the latter case, what the reason for the multiple names was;
at what age the person had received his or her name sign;
and where (at school, at home, etc.) the name had been attributed to him or her.

We transcribed the different name signs phonologically and took note of the explanations given by the Deaf respondents and any others involved in order to justify each name. We then analyzed the corpus and drew up a typology of name signs in LSQ.

The name signs that we have recorded correspond to the names used in the Deaf community for people known to our informants or to their friends, for members of our research team and various associates at our University as well as for numerous political, religious, historical and artistic personalities. We retained only a portion of the total collection of initialized names, which we will use as examples. We will return later to this type of name.

More than half of the name signs that we have identified belong to persons who were either born deaf or had become so at an early age (137 names out of 224). Table 1 gives a breakdown of the personal background of each person bearing a name sign. Some persons have more than one name.

Table 1: Distribution of subjects for the study

	Hearing parents	Deaf parents	Deaf relatives	total
Deaf from birth	104	9	24	137
Became deaf	6	1	-	7
Hearing	43	1	1	45
Celebreties	24	-	-	24
Total	177	11	25	213[1]

3 ATTRIBUTION OF A NAME SIGN

3.1 Differences between name signs and names in oral languages

Two characteristics distinguish name signs for oral language names. Unlike names in oral languages, name signs are not used to address an individual and they are not obligatory.

Unlike names in the majority of spoken languages, name signs are not used to attract somebody's attention; a name sign is used only in the absence of the person to whom it is attributed or when a signer refers to that person in a conversation (i.e. in the 3rd person).

It is rare that the creation of name signs is an absolute necessity such as in the situation described by Yau [1989], where monitors in the boarding school/home had to distinguish their 21 students by name in order to take roll call. In Québec, Deaf students are found only in a limited number of schools and the total of students per class is normally quite low.

3.2 Who has a name sign?

Sign names exist only in Deaf communities. The Deaf who live exclusively in hearing environments do not have name signs [Yau, 1989]. The Deaf living in Deaf families generally have at least two name signs: one for use within the family and one for use in the community.

Contrary to what one might think, it is not only the Deaf who have sign names. In fact, the majority of hearing people who have frequent contact with the Deaf community are also given a name sign. Political and religious personalities, major historical and artistic figures, as well as certain organizations also have name signs. The principle reason is undoubtedly cultural: for the Deaf, name signs are far more significant than are names which appear on a birth certificate. Another probable reason is that it is more economical to sign a name sign than to fingerspell it.

3.3 At what time is a name attributed?

The Deaf do receive a sign name in their home environment, often during childhood, but at differing periods depending upon the hearing abilities of the family. In families where the parents are deaf, it is most often an initialized name which is used (One of our informants told us, however, that in a family comprising four girls and one boy, the girls had a name sign based on the initial letter of their first names whilst the boy was simply signed GARÇON (boy). When a second boy was born, both boys had initialized name signs.) It is signed in neutral space by the dominant hand effecting a slight leftward movement, in a handshape representing the initial letter of the first name (in French). If several family members happen to have a first name with the same initial, then clarification is achieved by oralizing the names (i.e. the name is pronounced without voice at the same time as it is signed). As a general rule, Deaf children born to hearing parents do not have a name sign before starting school.

At school, Deaf children give each other short-lived sign names; a process which continues until adolescence, at about which time one name sign becomes more established and often permanent.

Hearing people acquire a name sign only if they have frequent contact with the Deaf community or if they are well-known personalities. Generally, when a hearing person is presented to a Deaf person, his or her name is fingerspelled. Afterwards, if the name is taken up in conversation, it is normally initialized and oralized. The attribution of a sign name does not generally occur until later, when the Deaf individual is better acquainted with the hearing person.

In the case of well-known personalities, their name signs are usually attributed at the moment when they come to prominence, at the same time as their names begin to appear more frequently in conversation. There are, however, exceptions, with certain individuals not receiving a name sign until after their death (for example, KENNEDY).

3.4 Multiple name signs for the same individual

A Deaf child of Deaf parents will almost always have two name signs. It is also possible that an individual's name sign may change in the Deaf community. This can happen if the physical, intellectual or behavioral particularity which had initially prompted the name changes or disappears altogether. Notwithstanding, such a name-change rarely occurs. Nor can an individual change his or her name for the simple reason of not liking it. On the contrary, in such an instance, it seems that the name may become even more firmly established. Yet, it can happen that separate groups give different names to the same individual, in which case the most recent name may replace the older name.

3.5 How is a name sign created?

LSQ name signs are most commonly in the descriptive category and we find it interesting to compare the process by which they are formed with that used to form other types of signs.

Klima and Bellugi [1979: 16-17] describe the process of creation of a nonce-sign by the deaf. Their aim was to analyze the distinction between miming and signing. In an experiment, they asked some ASL signers to recount the story of "The Unicorn in the Garden" (James Thurber). This story includes the mention of a "strait jacket", for which there was no unanimously accepted sign. At the beginning of their narrative, in order to illustrate this concept, each signer performed his or her own pantomime depicting the principal characteristics of a strait jacket and the act of being forced into one. But pantomime is not an economical procedure and the more the story advanced, the more the pantomime was curtailed. An evolution could be observed towards the formation of a sign, representing only one or two characteristics of the concept, as it gradually assumed the handshape, location and movement of a possible sign.

Our observations indicate that the creation of a name sign follows approximately the same steps as those described by Klima and Bellugi for everyday signs: in essence, only one of the characteristics of an individual is retained and used to name that person.

4 DESCRIPTION OF NAME SIGNS

Thus, sign names frequently represent only a single characteristic of the person to whom they are attributed. In this case, using the terminology of S. Supalla [1990] we will say that they are personalized or descriptive. They also may be initialized. Table II illustrates the different types of name signs of persons that we have recorded to date: the numbers in each box indicate the number of names found for that category.

4.1 Descriptive names

A descriptive name is attributed to a person according to either a physical feature, a character trait or a related characteristic.

Table 2: Different types of name signs

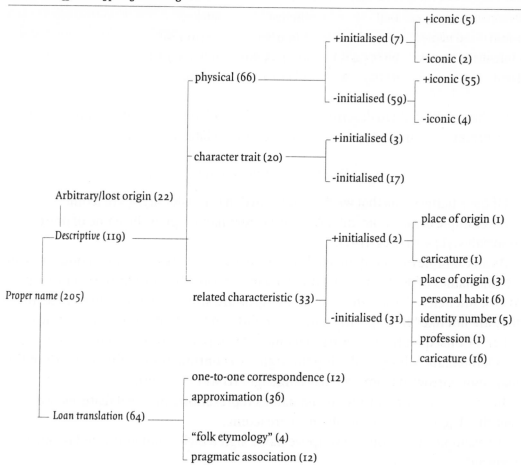

Mindess [1990] divided her corpus of descriptive name signs into two categories: a class of initialized names of more recent origin referring to behaviours, hairstyles or hobbies; and a class of more traditional names, older in origin, describing physical traits, and which are not initialized. According to Mindess, the form of the names belonging to the newer class may be attributed to an imperfect understanding/knowledge of Deaf culture.

In LSQ, name signs are found in both initialized and uninitialized form. In general, initialization is used to distinguish name signs from others with a similar form: nothing leads us to believe that initialization of name signs is due in any way to a lack of understanding of Deaf culture. The table 3 shows that initialized name signs make up only a small percentage of the total of descriptive name signs; we see in addition that they are given about as often to Deaf individuals as to hearing individuals.

Table 3: Distribution of initialization in descriptive names

Descriptive name signs	Deaf	Hearing	total
+ initialized names	5 (4.2 %)	7 (5.9 %)	12 (10.1 %)
- initialized names	66 (55.4 %)	41 (34.5 %)	107 (89.9 %)
Total	71 (59.7 %)	48 (40.3 %)	119 (100 %)

We have collected 119 descriptive names, of which 66 represent a physical feature, 20 represent a character trait and 33 represent a related characteristic.

4.1.1 Names representing physical features

Of the 7 name signs that we have identified in this category, 5 are iconic.

An example of an iconic initialized descriptive name sign is the name of one of our associates: /L/ + CURLY-HAIR.

As an example of an initialized descriptive name sign which is not iconic, we will cite the names of deaf twins: JUMELLE (twin) + N (for Nicole) and JUMELLE (twin) + M (for Michèle). Although these name signs are still based on a physical feature, they are not like "having curly hair" or "being big", but rather like "resemble each other". Consequently, they are not iconic. The initial, instead of being represented by a handshape while producing the sign, is a continuation of the first part of the loan sign borrowed from everyday language: JUMELLE (twin).

In the category of non-initialized names representing physical features, we have identified 59 name signs of which 54 are iconic.

An example of an iconic descriptive name sign which is not initialized is: BROSSE (crew cut).

In the same category, one finds the name signs of Adolph Hitler, Clark Gable and General de Gaulle.

A descriptive name sign representing a physical feature can also be non-initialized and non-iconic. We will cite here the name which is signed as AFRIQUE (Africa), given to a person who has black skin.

4.1.2 Names representing a character trait

These names may be either initialized or not. Of the 20 name signs that we have collected, only 3 are initialized.

As an example of initialized descriptive name signs representing a character trait, we will cite those of two persons having the forenames Julie and Colette, indicating someone who smiles often.

To illustrate the category of non-initialized descriptive names representing a character trait, we will cite LUNE (moon): this is derived from a French expression "dans la lune" (in the moon), meaning "day-dreaming".

Another example is a name sign which corresponds to PLEURER (cry), which is attributed to many people because when they were children they cried a lot. (It is possible that several people belonging to different social groups may have the same name sign, but as Mindess [1990] notes it is very rare that such a situation arises within the same group and, if it were to happen, there are ways that confusion could be avoided.)

4.1.3 Names representing a related characteristic

Certain name signs are given as the result of a related characteristic frequently observed in a person. These name signs can be either initialized or uninitialized. 33 name signs in this category were identified, of which only 3 are initialized.

Among the initialized names representing a personal characteristic, we draw a distinction between those which have been attributed according to the person's place of origin and those which are a caricature of some personal trait or habit.

In the first category, a person's place of origin, we will cite the name of one of our students, Laurence, who came from Belgium, whose sign is an initialisation with "L" of the sign BELGIUM (which is made with an outward movement of the /Y/ hand from the cheek).

In the second category, that of a caricature, we will cite the name of a professor whose surname began with a P: it was signed with a /P/-handshape above his watch, because he demanded, and rigidly enforced, strict punctuality on the part of his pupils.

Among the non-initialized names representing a related characteristic, we draw a distinction between those that have been attributed according to a person's origins, a personal habit, an identity number, a profession, and those which are caricatures of a personal trait.

As an illustration of a non-initialized name sign corresponding to a person's origins, we can cite the name Joliette. This name was given to a person who spent his childhood and adolescence in the town of JOLIETTE and then lived the rest of his life in Montréal. His name sign, nevertheless, did not change.

A name sign which reflects a habit is PIPE. This name was given to a person who smoked a pipe.

As examples of name signs based on identity numbers, we have found 3, 18, 75, 99 and III (This name is signed by an /L/-handshape effecting a rightward movement.) With the exception of 99, all these name signs were the numbers marked on the person's clothing at school. The number 99 comes from the shirt number of Wayne Gretzky a famous hockey player.

Certain names are given according to a person's profession. As an example, we can give BARBIER (barber), because this person had worked for a long time as a barber.

Other names represent a caricature or were given in order to tease the recipient. We have identified many examples of this type. A professor who habitually used a projector when giving his courses was given the sign name PROJECTEUR (overhead-projector). A hearing person received the name sign PAS-CAPABLE (can't) because when learning LSQ she always confused this sign with the sign COMIQUE (funny). Finally, Jerry Lewis' name is signed with an /A$_x$/-hanshape pinching and tugging at the ear, representing one of his trademark gestures.

4.2 Loan translation

We have identified 64 name signs which are loan translations. They were not, however, all borrowed in the same way. Consequently, we divide them into four categories: those which are in a one-to-one correspondence with a sign in everyday language, those which are an approximation of a sign in everyday language, those which can be attributed to "folk etymologies" and those which are based upon pragmatic association. None of the 4 categories either involve or imply an individual's personal characteristics. It is simply a question of a total or partial correspondence between the surname or first name in French and a sign in LSQ.

4.2.1 One-to-one correspondence

The French surnames Boucher, Boulanger, Drapeau, and Couture all correspond to everyday French words: "butcher", "baker", "flag", "sewing", respectively LSQ represents these surnames with the signs that translate the respective French words: BOUCHER/butcher, BOULANGER/baker, DRAPEAU/flag and COUTURE/sewing. Similarly, a girl named Aimée (beloved) has the name sign AIMER (to love).

4.2.2 Cross-linguistic approximations

Some name signs derived from everyday LSQ are given because their commonly accepted French gloss approximates the written or (visible) oral form of the person's French name or surname. A girl named Blanche has the name sign BLANC (white), and a boy named Jean-Guy has the name sign QUI (who) (confusion between voiced and voiceless segments is a frequent occurrence, as the distinction cannot be made through lip-reading). A person with the surname Lévesque has the name sign ÉVÊQUE (bishop), a person named Lajoie has the name sign JOIE (joy), a person named Ladouceur ("la douceur" translates literally as "softness) has the sign DOUX (soft) and a person with the surname Chalifoux has the name sign FOU (mad), etc.

In certain cases, although a sign in the language may correspond to a French name, it will be modified or even completely changed in the creation of the name sign. For example, a person named Leboeuf has a name sign BOEUF (bull), but the orientation of the palm is reversed. An individual with the surname Gariépy has a name sign which is iconic in form but based initially on an approximation of the oral form of the surname. Gariépy, when lipread, closely resembles the word Gaspésie, the name of a region covering the Gaspé peninsula in eastern Québec. A name sign was invented (a /C/ handshape on the dominant hand and a /I/ handshape on the non-dominant hand, pointing toward the inside of the /C/), which is a relatively accurate reproduction of the shape of this peninsula on a map. However, the everyday LSQ sign GASPÉ has no connection with the invented name sign.

4.2.3 "Folk etymology"

Certain longer names are broken into two signs. Thus, a person with the surname Bellefeuille has a name sign BELLE + FEUILLE (beautiful + leaf), the surname Laverdure is signed LAVER + DUR (wash + hard) and Rioux is signed RIRE + OÙ (laugh + where).

4.2.4 Pragmatic association

Some names are created as the result of an association made between a French word and an LSQ sign. Thus, a person whose family name is Pilote (pilot) has a name signed AVION (airplane) and someone else named Pépin (pip/seed) has the name sign GRAINE (seed). On occasion, the association is less direct. A person with the surname Saint-Pierre (Saint Peter) has the name sign CLÉS (keys) by association with the keys of Saint Peter, a person with the surname Sainte-Croix (holy cross) has the name sign ROUGE (red), through word association with the Red Cross, and a person with the surname Guillemette has the name sign RASOIR (rasor), by association with Gillette the rasor manufacturers. Finally, we should also mention Saint John the Baptist, whose name is signed MOUTON (sheep), by association with the sheepskin he is always depicted as wearing.

4.3 Initialized names

Initialized name signs are used in Deaf families to refer to a family member. The initial used is always that of the individual's first name.

When the Deaf give a name to hearing people, in the vast majority of cases, they begin by initializing the name and surname, together with oralization if there is a risk of confusion with some other person. In a small, close-knit group, only the first name will be initialized. Initialization is generally produced by the dominant hand, in neutral space.

5 ARBITRARINESS

In our corpus, there remain 22 name signs for which we have been unable to find an explanation. Their origin has probably been lost, although they all conceivably must have belonged to one of the categories of descriptive names. Some of these names are initialized. We have listed them in the category labeled "arbitrary", not because of a belief that they were attributed on an arbitrary basis, but rather because we were unable to find a satisfactory explanation for their origin[2].

For example, we were unable to explain why a person named Gauthier has his name signed in a /G/-handshape with the dominant hand, at the level of the navel, moving slightly inwards and downwards.

6 DIFFUSION OF SIGN NAMES
6.1 Inheritance

Within the same family, if the father has a descriptive name, it can be passed on to his son, or sons, and even to the whole of his immediate family; eventually, it will also be passed on to the extended family. For example, all Fortin's now have the name sign CHAT (cat); it was originally given to a boarding school teacher, who was sharp and alert like a cat, and always caught unawares any misbehaving pupils.

6.2 Enrichment of the everyday language

The process that borrows name signs from the everyday lexical stock of LSQ may also be reversed so that newly created name signs can enter LSQ as signs for everyday referents.

We have identified three examples of this type. A person named Champagne born around the turn of the century who was reputed to have smelly feet and was given a name sign produced by the dominant hand in a /B/-handshape making a leftward movement, in contact with the tip of the nose (i.e fanning one's nose). Nowadays, not only does everyone bearing the name Champagne have this name sign, but the sign has also come to refer to champagne, the wine. Another example comes from the name sign of Duplessis, a former prime minister of Québec, who had the habit of putting his hands in his waistcoat pockets. He was given a two-handed name sign, both hands in a /K/-handshape oriented downwards, at the level of the hips. Later, this sign entered the language with the meaning of DÉPUTÉ (member of Parliament). The third example that we identified is that of a school principal named Cadieux. He was given a name sign produced by a /C/-handshape, the palm oriented towards the chest, making a slight downward movement with the fingertips brushing against the chest. We have not found an explanation for this name sign, which we have listed in the category "arbitrary", but we do know that it is currently used in everyday language with the senses "Montreal Deaf Community Centre" or COLLEGE, when a small downward movement is added.

7 CONCLUSION

In conclusion, we have shown that the creation of name signs in LSQ follows the same process as the creation of certain new signs in everyday LSQ. Originally, these signs were iconic, in the sense that they were based on a characteristic of the object or the person being named. Later, as the situation changes, the iconic association between the sign and the object (or person) begins to fade away and the original association gradually falls into oblivion. We have no reason then, to believe that the names we have classified as "arbitrary" would have been arbitrarily attributed when first used.

We have also shown that initialization fulfils several roles. Firstly, within the framework of a Deaf family, it allows the use of a French given name. In addition, when it is used in a name sign based upon a physical, intellectual or behavioural characteristic, it often serves as strategy of disambiguation, if several people have the same characteristic.

The different names that we have collected also give us an insight concerning the absence of taboos in LSQ: any name can be given to an individual, even if it carries a negative connotation.

Footnotes

* Jules Desrosiers and Colette Dubuisson: ***ADDRESS***
†.This research has been financially supported by the Social Sciences and Humanities Research Council (SSHRC). We would like to thank Carole Pilon for her assistance in the analysis and classification of the data. We would equally like to thank Linda Lelièvre, Nathalie Madore and Louise Barrière for their help in collecting the corpus.

1.Data on family background was not available for eleven individuals.
2.However, our corpus includes the names of two persons from an English-speaking background. These two name signs are initialized and both are signed at specific body locations which do not seem to bring any particular meaning to the sign. It seems that these are probably the arbitrary name signs in the sense of Supalla [1990, 1992].

Bibliography

Hedberg, T. [1989]. *Name signs in Swedish Sign Language*. Paper presented at The Deaf Way, Gallaudet University, Washington, DC.

— [1992]. Name signs in Swedish Sign Language: their formation and use, in: *Equality and Self-Reliance: Proceedings of the XI World Congress of the World Federation of the Deaf*.

Klima, E. and Bellugi, U. [1979]. *The Signs of Language*. Harvard University Press, Cambridge, Mass.

Meadow, K. [1977]. Name signs as identity symbols in the Deaf community. *Sign Language Studies* 16, pp. 237–246.

Mindess, A. [1990]. What name signs can tell us about Deaf culture. *Sign Language Studies* 66, pp. 1–24.

Supalla, S. [1990]. The arbitrary name sign system in American Sign Language. *Sign Language Studies* 67, pp. 99–126.

— [1992]. *The Book of Name Signs*. Dawn Sign Press, San Diego.

World Federation of the Deaf [1992]. *Equality and Self-Reliance: Proceedings of the XI World Congress of the World Federation of the Deaf*.

Yau, S and He, J. [1989]. How deaf children in a Chinese school get their name signs. *Sign Language Studies* 65, pp. 305–322.

Language contact phenomena in Deaf communities

CEIL LUCAS *

Sociolinguistic research on contact phenomena in Deaf communities has, to date, been shaped by at least four interrelated considerations: 1) the relationship between the spoken language of the majority of the community and the sign language of the community, particularly in educational settings, 2) limited knowledge of the linguistic structure of the sign language, 3) doubts as to the status of the sign language as a "real language", and 4) application of spoken language sociolinguistic models to sign language situations. In terms of the first consideration, the traditional insistence in deaf educational settings on the use of the spoken language of the community or the use of some combined form of signing and speaking, to the exclusion of sign language has contributed to the focus in sociolinguistic research on the interaction between spoken language and sign language. In American Sign Language, for example, while there are some studies on sociolinguistic variation within ASL, there are an equal number of studies on the diglossic nature of the Deaf community, on the so-called continuum of varieties between English and ASL and the outcome of contact between English and ASL traditionally labelled PSE (Pidgin Sign English). (See for example, Woodward, 1973; Woodward and Markowicz, 1975). There are very few studies, if any, that describe the result of contact between two sign languages. Part of this has been due to the second and third considerations— limited knowledge of the structure of the sign language and doubts as to its status as a "real language". In terms of the second consideration, it is difficult to describe sociolinguistic variation within a sign language or to see what the effects of contact are until we have a clear idea of the basic structure of the language. In fact, some early studies of variation in ASL described as variable structural features, such as negative incorporation and verb agreement features, which are not variable in a native signer's production. The third consideration-doubts as to status- is one that has hindered all areas of linguistic research on sign languages, not just sociolinguistic research. The fourth consideration- the application of spoken language sociolinguistic models to sign language situations-is one that often has had the effect of assigning labels to situations that, upon re-examination, do not exactly fit the label assigned. Such is the case with the use of the terms *diglossia*, *code-switching*, *bilingualism*, and *pidgin*, among others.

Based on these four considerations, it would seem that language contact phenomena in Deaf communities deserve some re-examination. In this paper, I will first present a model for approaching language contact phenomena, and I will then focus on one such phenomenon, contact signing. The model is presented in Figure 1.

Figure 1: Outcome of language contact in the Deaf community

Between 2 sign languages	Between a sign language and a spoken language	
Lexical borrowing	following spoken language	
Code-switching	criteria literally	unique phenomena
Foreigner talk	code-switching	fingerspelling
Interference	lexical borrowing	fingerspelling/ sign combination
Pigdins, creoles, and mixed systems		CODA-speak
		TTY Conversations
		mouthing
		code-switching
		contact signing

We see immediately that before individual phenomena can be discussed, a fundamental distinction must be made. The distinction is between a situation involving contact between two sign languages, and a situation involving a sign language and a spoken language. This distinction is necessary simply because of the difference in modality between sign languages and spoken languages. That is, the basic structural units are, of necessity, fundamentally very different: morphemes composed of sounds articulated in specific manners and places in the vocal tract, and morphemes composed of parts articulated by the hands, face, and body. This is not to say that spoken language morphemes never include the hands, face, or body, or conversely, that sign language morphemes never include verbal articulation. But the basic structure is different, so the kind of contact phenomena that result from the contact between two sign languages, both in a visual modality, differ from those that result from the contact between a spoken language and a sign language, one in the oral-aural modality and one in the visual-manual modality. Naturally, the situation is not entirely straightforward, as two sign languages may be in contact, both of which may incorporate outcomes of contact with their respective spoken languages which may then play a role in their own contact. For example, the Italian Sign Language (LIS) sign NEVER is a lexicalized fingerspelled sign related to the spoken Italian word mai. The handshape is i̠, representative of the last letter of the written Italian word. American ASL users in contact with LIS users may learn and use this sign and use it in conversation with ASL-LIS bilinguals. It is the result of spoken-sign contact and gets used in sign-sign contact situations.

First I will focus on the outcomes of contact between two sign languages. It is important to stress that what I am presenting is a model: while there are anecdotal examples of some of the phenomena I will mention, there is as yet limited empirical research, and as there is more research and as we learn more about deaf communities around the world, the model may change. For example, we are beginning to know more about communities such as the Yucatec Maya one in the Yucatan Peninsula, in which all members of the community, both hearing and deaf, sign (Johnson, 1991). This of course is reminiscent of the Martha's Vineyard community in the United States, and reports of other such communities are beginning to surface- for example, in Venezuela (Pietrosemoli, personal communication). Not only are these communities in which everyone signs, but in the Yucatec case, neither language involved is written. As Johnson observes (personal communication), the bulk of the language contact research concerns contact between languages at least one of which has a written form, and that is the case in the contact between ASL and English. It is not clear what the outcomes of language contact are, if any, in communities in which everyone signs and in which none of the languages in contact has a written form. However, based on this model, one outcome is *lexical borrowing*: sign languages borrow lexical items from each other. For example, in ASL, the older signs for many place names such as CHINA, JAPAN, SWEDEN, ITALY, and AFRICA have been replaced by the signs for those places used by signers in those places. Signers can also *code-switch*: a signer who knows two sign languages could conceivably be using one sign language and momentarily switch to the other sign language. Signers use *foreigner talk*: that is, a native signer of one sign language signing to another deaf person who is learning that sign language may alter the form of his signing- he may sign slower or larger or choose signs that he thinks may be more easily understood. Signers may also experience *interference*: a native signer of one sign language may be signing a second sign language and inadvertently incorporate elements of his native sign language in the second language. Finally, while there is no empirical research on it, it is conceivable that, given the right social conditions, the contact between two or more sign languages could give rise to pidgins, creoles, or mixed systems such as have been attested for spoken languages. The situation for the emergence of a pidgin might be as follows: two adult native signers of two different sign languages are in contact and they both want to learn a third sign language, for reasons of upward social mobility and enhancing their economic situation. Their contact with native users of the third sign language is limited so they end up teaching it to each other. Furthermore, their contact with their respective native languages is restricted if not discontinued altogether. These are the social conditions under which spoken language pidgins arise, and it is not impossible to imagine such a situation for sign languages.

I turn now to the contact between a spoken language and a sign language and again you can see a further distinction is necessary. I make a separation between outcomes described by following spoken language criteria literally and unique phenomena. By "following spoken language criteria literally", I mean, for example, that the person literally stops signing and starts speaking (or vice-versa) either across a sentence boundary or within it. There is alot of anecdotal evidence that both of these situations occur. For example, hearing bilinguals may produce ASL sentences or signs with each other (with no deaf people present) in the course of spoken English conversations I can easily imagine the following English sentence: "And when he told me about it, my mouth went like this: JAW-DROP-OPEN." Deaf and hearing bilinguals may speak English words or sentences with each other or with hearing bilinguals for example, during a conversation in a restaurant concerning how the bill was going to be paid, a deaf acquaintance switched from ASL to English, mouthed "Have cash", and then immediately went back to ASL. Likewise, examples of lexical borrowing that follow the criteria established for spoken language borrowing occur. One kind of lexical borrowing in spoken languages is called *loan translation*, in which the lexical items of one language are translated into another language and used with the same meaning examples include the Italian, French and Spanish words for the English word skyscraper: grattacielo, gratteciel, and rascacielos, respectively. There are numerous examples of this in ASL: the signs BOY^FRIEND, GIRL^FRIEND, HOME^WORK, and HOME^SICK are loan translations of English words. Loan translations also occur in English, when hearing bilinguals form spoken English morphemes from the mouth configuration that is part of an ASL sign. For example, the mouth configuration that is part of the classifier predicate meaning LARGE PILE OF PAPERS or THICK BOOK—a mouth configuration having an adverbial meaning of LARGE QUANTITY or THICK ENTITY—can be glossed as "cha", phonetically [ca]. Hearing bilingual students have been heard to say, in English, "I have cha homework."

I turn now to the unique phenomena that result from the contact between a spoken language and a sign language. One such phenomenon is *fingerspelling*. It can be said that were there no contact between the written form of the spoken language and the sign language, there would be no fingerspelling. But it is a unique phenomenon. It has been described as lexical borrowing by some researchers (Battison, 1978) but as a result of long discussions with Scott Liddell and Bob Johnson, I share their position that it is not best characterized as borrowing. Lexical borrowing typically means a relationship between the *phonologies* of two languages, be they spoken or signed, and I have already provided some examples of lexical borrowing between sign languages. But fingerspelling is not a relationship between two phonologies; it is a relationship between the *writing* system of a spoken language and the phonology of a sign language. The forms used belong to the phonology of the sign language. Hence, it is a unique event resulting from contact.

In addition, we see examples of sign-fingerspelling combinations, such as the ASL sign LIFE#STYLE, and we are becoming aware of the kind of fingerspelling produced by Deaf people in contact with other kinds of writing systems such as Arabic, Chinese, Japanese, Russian, and Hebrew. Another unique phenomenon is *mouthing*, distinct from speaking the spoken language. Davis (1989) presents a model for a continuum of mouthing, ranging from full mouthing of spoken words to lexicalized mouthing as in the ASL signs FINISH and HAVE, whose mouth configurations clearly derive from English but have become part of the ASL sign. Mouthing is distinct from the mouth configurations that accompany some ASL signs and have no connection to the spoken word, as in the ASL sign PAH or NOT-YET. Yet another unique phenomenon is what has been described as CODA-speak (Jacobs, 1992). CODA is the acronym often used in the United States to identify the hearing children of deaf adults, individuals who may have ASL as their native language. Anecdotal evidence indicates that CODA-speak consists of spoken English words produced with ASL syntactic structure, what might be called "spoken ASL". It has not yet been described, so we cannot say what its morphological and prosodic features might be but it probably also occurs with the hearing children of deaf people in other countries and is clearly a contact outcome unique to spoken language sign language bilinguals. Finally, signers may code-switch between ASL and one of the codes invented for manually representing English. I distinguish this from code-switching between two sign languages because the manual code is based on the structure of a spoken language.

I turn finally to a unique phenomenon to which Clayton Valli and I have devoted a fair amount of research time. It is what has been labelled Pidgin Sign English (PSE) in the United States. Time will only allow me to briefly summarize our project on contact signing but our findings have been and will be published. Figure 2 summarizes the project.

Figure 2: *Project summary*

Informants: 10 groups of 2, 2 groups of 3, total = 26 (12 White, 14 African American), in 5 situations. 14 hours of data judgement tape with 20 clips, 15 not ASL, 5 ASL and 30 judges.	
9 clips	agreement, not ASL
4	linguists and community disagree
1	Black and White disagree

Those of you who know our work will recall that we set up an interview situation designed to elicit contact signing; we interviewed 10 groups of two signers and 2 groups of 3, for a total of 26 informants (12 White and 14 African American); we then made a judgment tape from our data tapes consisting of 20 clips, 5 of which were ASL and 15 or which were not ASL; 30 judges all deaf, members of the Deaf community judged the clips and based on their judgments, we isolated 9 clips for which there was a high degree of agreement that they were not ASL, and 5 whose structure is not ASL but for which there was a lot of disagreement in the judgments. figure 3

Figure 3: Comparison of linguistic features among various systems

Features	Spoken English	ASL	Signed English	Contact Signing	English-based Spoken Language Pidgins
Lexical form	English	ASL	ASL, ASL-like signs, non-ASL spoken English	ASL and ASL-like signs, English whispering and mouthing, single spoken words	English, some substrate some idiosyncratic
Lexical function and meaning	English	ASL	English	ASL, idiosyncratic, English	Usually English, some idiosyncratic
Morphology	English	ASL	Reduced English and ASL, signed representation of bound morphemes	Reduced ASL and English, some signs for English morphemes, some ASL inflected verbs and nonmanual signals	Reduced English
Syntax	English	ASL	Reduced English	Reduced English, some idiosyncratic constructions, ASL use of space, eyegaze, pronouns, determiners, discourse markers	Basically SVO, reduced use of pronouns and prepositions embedding rare

Figure 3 provides a comparison of the features of different systems, including contact signing. We can see from this that contact signing differs from Signed English, ASL, and from spoken language pidgins. What I want to focus on is the evidence for contact signing as a third system which combines elements of English and ASL in a unique way. You will recall that there were 5 clips on the judgment tape which cannot be said to have ASL syntactic structure and which have many features of English such as embedded constructions with that and constructions with prepositions but which many judges consistently judged as ASL. Our question, of course, was why? Upon closer examination, we found that while these clips did indeed have many English features, they also shared several ASL syntactic features that may account for the judgment of these clips as ASL. These features include the establishment of a topic in space, the use of eye gaze to refer to the established topic, the use of body shifting both in conjunction with an established topic and for role shifting, and the use of ASL pronouns and determiners. In several instances, for example, the signer established two separate topics, one on the right and one on the left for example, mainstream programs and residential schools, African American signers and White signers and then consistently referred to those points by signing in the same place or directing eye gaze or body to those points. The structure of the sentences used to discuss those referents cannot be said to be ASL, as it has many English features. So, the occurrence of these ASL features probably explains the judgments of these clips as ASL, even though their overall structure is not ASL. The structure of all of the clips is unique in part because the ASL features frequently occur simultaneously with English mouthing, so that what we see is a kind of code-mixing that has not been described for spoken languages; it is also unique for the ASL and English features that do not occur: we do not see bound English morphemes such as third person singular -s, plural -s, possessive -s, past tense -ed, and we do not see ASL syntactic constructions such as topicalization and relativization. But it does seem to be a third system and not the predominantly English-based system we initially thought it was. Third systems have been described for spoken languages (see for example Romaine, 1989; Whinnom, 1971; Grosjean, 1992), but what we see seems to be a unique outcome of the contact between a spoken language and a sign language.

Footnotes

* Ceil Lucas: Department of Linguistics and Interpreting, Gallaudet University, Washington, D.C., USA.

Bibliography

Battison, R. [1978]. *Lexical Borrowing in American Sign Language.* Linstok Press, Silver Spring, MD.

Davis, J. [1989]. Distinguishing language contact phenomena in ASL interpretation, in: Lucas, C. (ed) *The Sociolinguistics of the Deaf Community,* pp. 85–102. Academic Press, San Diego.

Jacobs, S. [1992]. Coda talk column. *Coda Connection* 9:1 (February), pp. 1–3.

Johnson, R.E. [1991]. Sign language, culture and community in a traditional Yucatec Maya village. *Sign Language Studies* 73, pp. 461–478.

Romaine, S. [1989]. *Bilingualism.* Basil Blackwell, Oxford.

Whinnom, K. [1971]. Linguistic hybridization and the 'special case' of pidgins and creoles, in: Hymes, D. (ed) *Pidginization and Creolization of Language*. pp. 91–115. Cambridge University Press, Cambridge.

Woodward, J. [1973]. Some characteristics of Pidgin Sign English. *Sign Language Studies* 3, pp. 39–46.

Woodward, J. and Markowicz, H. [1975]. *Some Handy New Ideas On Pidgins and Creoles: Pidgin Sign Languages*. Paper presented at Conference on Pidgin and Creole Languages, Honolulu, Hawaii.

Sign language and Deaf interaction:
a preliminary study of sign talk in Northern Finland

PAUL MCILVENNY AND PIRKKO RAUDASKOSKI

Abstract

We will present the preliminary results of an attempt to analyse the talk activities of the Finnish deaf signing community from the perspective of conversation analysis (CA). The premise of this research is that one must not only study the structure of a language, but also how it is constituted, maintained and used in real, practical settings that the deaf must encounter and actively construct in their community.

We have developed a deeply empirical methodology which has evolved from our attempts to deal with the particular problems that arise when the procedures of collection, transcription and analysis are applied to sign talk. Video data has been collected from several natural settings involving native signers using Finnish Sign Language (FiSL). The study focuses particularly on a small deaf community in Northern Finland. After our initial survey it is becoming clear that deaf sign interaction has a complex and rich social organisation. Deaf people engage in diverse practical activities in and through which deaf life, language and culture is produced and reproduced. In this paper we will elaborate on the discovery of some of the distinctive features of the organisation of turns-at-talk in sign interaction. We can then begin to show how particular linguistic resources in FiSL are interactively deployed within the mutual production of senseful sign talk and thus are reproduced as stable structures.

The analyses will be illustrated with transcripts of fragments of natural sign talk activity and interaction recorded on video, and with provisional transcripts and pictures of that activity taken from the video data.

1 INTRODUCTION

The study of the organisation of conversation, discourse or language use in general is firmly based on the analysis of the speech and writing of hearing communities. In contrast, we will discuss the preliminary results of an attempt to analyse the talk and interaction of the Finnish deaf signing community[1] from the perspective of conversation analysis (CA). The premise of this research is that one must not only study the structure of the language, but also how it is constituted, maintained and used in real, practical settings that the deaf must encounter and actively construct in their community. The analyses will be illustrated with transcripts of fragments of natural sign language talk activity and interaction recorded on video, and with pictures of that activity taken from the video data.

2 WHAT IS CONVERSATION ANALYSIS?

Before discussing sign language talk, a brief introduction to the principles and practices of conversation analysis will follow so that the methods upon which we draw are clear. In conversation analysis (CA) it is claimed that conversation is a routine and complex accomplishment carried through by almost all members of society with great skill and transparent ease. The central goal of conversation analytic research is the description and explication of the competences that ordinary speakers use and rely on when participating in senseful conversation. Meaning is not just built into the codes of language as in structural accounts, nor is it to be found in the relation of cognitive representations to that which is represented. Meaning is constructed *in situ* by interactants who are "simultaneously engaged in fine-grained real time co-ordination of speaking turns tracked predominantly in terms of surface structural features and... organising their actions in terms of publicly accountable normative expectations bearing on the nature and design of their turns at talk. " (Heritage 1989, p. 26)

The early work in the 1960s has been taken up increasingly in Europe, especially in Britain, but the original pioneering work of Sacks has been generally unavailable except for the original published papers and a few monographs transcribed by Gail Jefferson. However, recently some of the transcribed lectures have been published, Harvey Sacks (1989), and all of them will be available later in full. Useful summaries of CA can be found in Levinson (1983), Atkinson & Heritage (1984), Heritage (1984, ch. 8), Button & Lee (1987), Psathas (1990) and Boden & Zimmerman (1991). The classic work, much referenced and misinterpreted, is Sacks *et al* (1978), which was first published in 1974.

In this approach the analysis of conversations is strongly 'data-driven'. The methodology avoids the use of interviewing techniques, the use of field notes or pre-coded schedules, the use of native intuitions to invent examples, and the use of experimental manipulation or directing behaviour which may restrict the range and authenticity of the activities which are elicited. Instead, the interest is in revealing the "organised procedures of talk as they are employed in real worldly contexts between persons in real relationships whose talk has a real consequentiality and accountability." (Heritage 1989)

Some record of the phenomena is essential in order to study it in detail. However, the record must be of the details that were meaningful for the participants, and constitutive of the activities under investigation. CA has shown that audio and video tapings are adequate for investigating spoken conversation on the telephone and face-to-face. A recording allows repeated viewing of the event and peer group ratification of a finding. Also, an impressionistic transcription system has evolved that is now quite complex (Psathas & Anderson 1990).

When we consider CA work, most of the foundational work on natural conversation has focused on British or American spoken culture. Work is in progress on Indo-European and Asian spoken languages and the Finnish spoken language has recently been subjected to analysis using these techniques by Hakulinen (1989) and others. But, CA methods have not so far been applied to sign conversation[2] and at first glance this does raise some distinctive problems because of the difference in modality as well as culture. If one attempts to equate speech and sign language then the techniques developed for collecting, rendering and analysing spoken talk may not be appropriate for sign or may be problematic in their routine application. These issues are discussed separately in McIlvenny (1991) and will not be mentioned further.

In contrast to the principles of conversation analysis, discourse analytic studies of sign language have been reported in Hall (1983), Wilbur (1983), Prinz & Prinz (1985), Roy (1989) and Nowell (1989). Also, an initial analysis of features of dyadic turn-taking in sign from the perspective of signal theory has been reported in Baker (1977) and this analysis forms the backbone of almost all of the later analyses of sign discourse. However, this work was based on the signal theory of turn-taking and the data was drawn from recordings of experimental dyadic conversations. Her paper does present some interesting observations of features of sign conversation, but here we present a competing theory of turn-taking based on analyses of natural multi-party conversations[3].

3 THE PRELIMINARY STUDY

The analyses presented here are based on video recordings made over a period of a few months in Oulu deaf club, which takes place once a week in the evening (see Kyle 1990 for a discussion of the central features of deaf community life in Britain). It is a regular time for deaf people in Oulu to congregate and chat, or attend a meeting or watch a talk given by an official from outside the community. A view of the deaf community main hall can be seen in Figure 1.

Figure 1: General view of the deaf club in Oulu

Some other data was gathered from the deaf youth club which meets once a week and from a meeting of deaf youth in Finland which takes place once a year. Two cameras were used to film most of these events and both researchers worked together to obtain complementary perspectives on the events if this was possible. However, none of the recordings were pre-planned or set-up; they were all recorded discretely as they evolved in situ without interference from the researchers. Initially our analyses were conducted with the aid of one hearing interpreter, who is a native signer born to deaf parents, but later we also worked with a deaf informant, Anne Hämäläinen, and a second hearing interpreter. In addition, the deaf informant worked in the filming team to obtain video data.

In the remainder of the paper we will discuss evidence for some initial hypotheses about the organisation[4] of talk and interaction in a deaf sign language community. First, the *distributed and local nature* of much sign talk activity is shown. The organisation of participation frameworks, group dynamics, applause and laughter is accomplished within the visual-spatial modality of sign. Second, examples of attention getting are presented in order to spotlight the *pervasive and explicit work of creating and maintaining mutual orientation and of reorganising participation frameworks*; also, an example is given in which the spatial orientation of participants is shown to be crucial for tracking the conversation. Third, we will look at turn transition, which is the space in which one signer stops and another signer gains the floor. The working conjecture is that in this sign language community signers in a group routinely orient to 'one signer - one floor - no gap' just as English conversationalists have been shown to do, but in turn transitions a *different systematics is locally operable than in Anglo-American spoken conversations* because of the visual-spatial modality. In addition it is shown that competitive turn transitions are themselves accomplished through an ongoing process of interaction between speaker(s) and recipient(s).

The transcribed examples are given in Appendix 1–3 and the transcription conventions can be found in Appendix 4. The notation system is still undergoing development because it is difficult to represent sign activity in a way that is amenable to interactional as well as linguistic analysis, given the lack of an established written form. It would be best to see the video in combination with the rendered materials presented here; instead, we have attempted to provide a visual snapshot of the most important details with a transcript for some of the examples.

3.1 Distributed activities: local access, reflection and cascades

We will claim in this section that many of the activities of the deaf community in gatherings are conducted through the *distributed* work of members of the group. It is essential to understand this before looking at turn transitions in talk. We will attempt to show that this property results in *cascades*, ie. activities that propagate or chain-react in transitions between one group focused activity and another. One clue to the distributed nature of much of group sign activity is that each member has only restricted and *local access* to the activities of all the other members. This may be the reason for the repeated *scanning* and side-to-side head movements that many hearing people tend to call 'distracted' or 'disinterested' when they first try to converse with deaf people. But these behaviours cannot obviate the *mutual-exclusivity* (or catch-22) of focal regions, ie. that focusing on one visual field automatically excludes another visual field because one cannot focus on both simultaneously. However, we claim here that the blind region[5] (normally about 170 degrees) for one person at any one moment is compensated for by the *reflection* in the activities of members who are visible to that person of activity in the blind region.

In Example 2 the propagation of a look through reflection is displayed. The three men A, B, and C are watching an interpreted lecture from the periphery of the group (in the middle of the long hall) when the lights at the back of the hall were switched off accidentally. In the deaf community, flashing the lights is a common signal for group attention because it is simultaneously visible by all. Maybe for this reason, B turns to *scan* the back of the hall; C then turns, followed by A after he happens to glance at C. At this moment (see Figure 2) the three men are thus attending to a potentially relevant activity behind them and their collective attentiveness is triggered in turn first by B and then C, such that through *reflection* A, B and C come to 'see together' what may be relevant behind them. This phenomenon occurs on many occasions in deaf gatherings and conversations (see Example 6). In this case, they find nothing to attend to and indulge in new scans.

Figure 2.

'What are you looking at?'

In Example 3, the deaf leader in Oulu (DL) has just apparently finished a topic in a closing piece at the end of a lecture by a guest. One section of the audience on the left begins to distribute leaflets and thus the audience as a focused group starts to dissolve. However, the deaf leader calls for attention again with a sweep of the arm during which he notices the distracted section to the left. He waves several times, first side-to-side then up-and-down, upon which other members of the group start waving and signing to the distracted parties, too. The *propagation* of attention getting works to the back of the room as different attentive members (marked A on Figure 3) work at different times on particular inattentive or otherwise engaged people who are only *locally accessible*, ie. those who are not-yet-attentive move into new positions which are differentially accessible to members of the attentive audience. Much *supportive and distributed work* is required to reorient the people in the room to focus on the deaf leader. He then signs that there is one more thing to inform them about thus orienting to the prior activity as a distraction to a not-yet-finished address which has one more item to complete before closure.

Figure 3.

'Hey, he hasn't finished yet!'

Atkinson (1984) has shown that applause and group appreciation displays are interesting phenomena in hearing communities, but in the deaf community sound is no carrier of meaning. We see in Example 4 evidence of an appropriate means of displaying appreciation - a two handed handwave with the hands high above the head - but we must ask how an audience pulls off such a display (see Figure 4). On the video it is noticeable that audience members as well as those on the 'stage' are monitoring closely the behaviour of others. But certain dynamics occur because of *local access* and *mutual-exclusivity*. The audience cannot necessarily see all the other members nor the appropriate behaviour at the same time, ie. those at the front cannot see those at the back without turning around, while those on the periphery are otherwise engaged and may not see the response begin out of their visual field. What is noticeable is that movement into applause is swift as the behaviour *cascades* through the audience, though those members on the periphery of the audience who are engaged in conversations or incipient talk are commonly late starters and late finishers. This demonstrates that the main audience must be attentive to each other and this group display is built quickly as a publicly visible phenomenon from the distributed work of its members.

Figure 4.

'On your marks, get set, ...'

Figure 5.

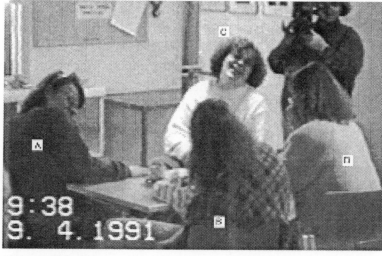

'Wasn't that funny... yes... yes'

For the same reasons above, it is also relevant to ask how signers engage in laughter activity - they do have a sense of humour - when, in contrast, hearing communities systematically orient to the sound of laughter (Jefferson 1985). Example 5 shows a group of four signers laughing at a miscalculation made by A which was pointed out by B. Note that three of the signers bend their bodies in the same direction (see Figure 5). Also, all signers displayed a teeth-smile and from the video it is apparent that all obtained mutual gaze with all the others except the pair B-D, though D did look to B twice. The mutual gazes were all accomplished in quick succession. More data is required to sort out whether these features are systematic phenomena in deaf laugh activity, and how prevalent they are in hearing communities, too.

3.2 Seeing and attending to conversations
3.2.1 Attention getting

Attention getting by means of hand and arm waves (*G) and body taps (*T) is a pervasive behaviour in sign talk and interaction that is often supported by third party members. In Example 6, attention getting behaviour is illustrated in the context of seeing another conversation. Displays are thus exposed on the video of appropriate times for interruption, viz. at possible transition relevance spaces indicated by a return to rest position, mutual eye gaze, etc.. C attempts to gain the attention of A, who is conversing with B, by waving her left hand up and down quickly (see Figure 6). She fails repeatedly as the conversation between A and B continues, though A is in a position to see C. Finally, just after she disattends their conversation for a moment she returns to find B and A looking away to the same neutral space (as in Example 2, B had looked first, then A tracked the look). She tracks the same space and returns her gaze to A as she begins to wave again. Unfortunately, A has just turned back to the front of the hall and thus is looking in the opposite direction. Her actions and that of A (and B) demonstrate that neither found talk relevant activity in the neutral space that they all scanned, but, during the scan, monitoring of each other was not possible because of *mutual exclusivity*. Thus *reflection* was both the resource for her gaining entry to a possible transition space, but also the undoing of a successful transition because A could not be monitored while monitoring the neutral space. Luckily B looks to C and C asks for him to contact A, whereupon he moves the chair in front of him to knock A's chair (third party messengers, vibration (*V) and air flow are other less common resources for attention getting). A turns around and C asks a question on a different topic from the conversation between A and B.

Figure 6.

'Can I say something')

Figure 7.

'Look at me, I'm talking to them'

Example 7 suggests that attention getting is not necessarily directed to one and the same recipient of the turn. Signer B waves repeatedly to C while C is currently signing with E in the context of the group. Upon potential gaze transition, B immediately turns to A (see Figure 7) and begins signing. This can be explained because signing is commonly directed to a recipient, who may change during the course of a turn, and this requires work to keep group attention. In this case, B must do explicit work to maintain a group focus (or the attentiveness of C in particular) as this is an endemic contingency in transitions. Not on this occasion, but often, the onset of the first sign during attention getting fails and attention getting is recycled along with the sign until mutual attention is achieved. We also have evidence that attention getting affects the form of sign onset in that dimensions of the sign are manipulated for interactional reasons, eg. the movement, arm orientation, or hand-to-hand relationship is reconfigured.

3.2.2 Not seeing conversations?

Figure 8.

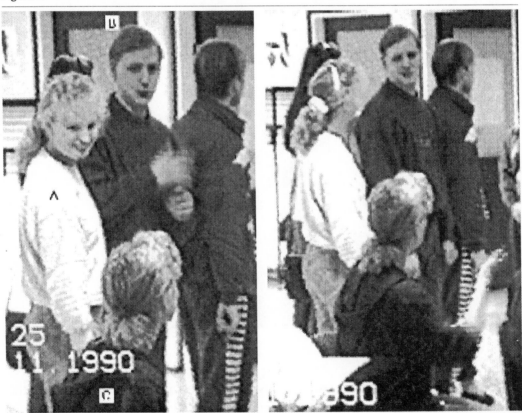

'If I look into your face can I see what they say?'

As participants have local access to the disparate activities of the group it is interesting to ask how signers monitor and take part in conversations in particular spatial configurations. In the next case (Example 8), the conversation is problematic for A because of the group's spatial configuration. Small talk results when participant C drops her orange and thus becomes accessible to A and B who are standing behind her. A initiates a conversation about the dirty orange, C responds and then B continues the conversation. At this point their participation is an *obtuse triangle* with A at the apex (almost piggy in the middle). A turns to look at B sign, but, at what seems like an appropriate transition relevance space, she returns her gaze to C at the moment B continues. C responds and A monitors, but A cannot see the three backchannels that B uses during C's signing (see Figure 8a). A returns gaze to B who glances at her; but meanwhile C begins signing again (see Figure 8b). B notices and shortly afterward A (through reflection) returns to look with expectancy at C, who has just finished and is now looking away. A appears to use the talk in progress and the gaze of the other participants to accomplish her 'seeing the conversation'. It has yet to be determined to what extent the participation space itself influences talk and turn-taking, particularly in the context of gatherings, both in deaf and hearing communities.

3.3 Turn transitions: onsets and glances

It is routinely evident in sign language talk that signers orient to a 'floor' on which signers take turns to sign and others as recipients attend to them. Sequential organisation is also apparent and it is unlikely to be affected much by the modality as it is a serial phenomenon. When turn transition has been accomplished and another signer has gained the floor then sequence time has been built. Cicourel has expressed doubt: "We do not know if the deaf are constrained by sequential ordering or chaining rules, because several signers can allow their signing to overlap continuously and several types of information can be communicated simultaneously which fall under the general notion of kinesic-visual communication."(1973, p. 168)

However, the observation that several signers can allow their signing to overlap *continuously* is just not true for FiSL talk - it just appears that way to the naive eye. In addition, it is dangerous to conflate sign languages with non-verbal gestures under the term kinesic-visual communication; the manual and non-manual features of deaf talk are major elements of a complex *natural language* with distinctive characteristics of its own.

Instead, let us consider turn transitions in multi-party sign talk. Unlike spoken talk, sign onsets are not always available to all participants and this is a fundamental feature of FiSL talk; thus just because two people start signing does not entail that they or any of the other participants will automatically see both or even one of these onsets. In effect we must challenge the assumption that self-selections by two or more participants will be received simultaneously by everyone, ie. it cannot be assumed as a matter of course that there is a single channel 'airspace' into which all contributions must be placed in competition with others.

In the turn-taking systematics of Sacks *et al.* (1978), self-selection is an option available in a TRP that is ordered after the first option, viz. current speaker selects next. The two options are given in full below: "a) If the turn-so-far is so constructed as to involve the use of 'current speaker selects next' technique, then the party so selected has rights, and is obliged, to take next turn to speak, and no others have such rights or obligations, transfer occurring at that place. b) If the turn-so-far is so constructed as not to involve the use of a 'current speaker selects next' technique, self selection for next speaker may, but need not, be instituted, with first starter acquiring rights to a turn, transfer occurring at that place." (p. 13)

The first option is definitely found in FiSL talk; it can be accomplished by a question, a shift in current speaker's gaze to a particular participant, etc.. However, a realisation of the second option in speech turn exchange is assumed to be simultaneously hearable by all and thus simultaneous overlaps, when two participants self-select in a TRP, are possible and orientable to by those involved moment by moment in a mutually addressable fashion. The assumption of mutual addressability is built into the rule set so to speak. But for sign talk this cannot be assumed. Because of the *distributed* nature of sign activities, the *mutual exclusivity of* gaze regions, and the *local access* of participants to the activities of the group, *self-selections can occur concurrently but without simultaneous visibility*; the construction of a mutually ratified 'floor' is an endemic problem in FiSL talk because of the modality, and consequently co-occurrence can be discovered later or remain unseen.

A second dimension of this section concerns the organisation of turn competition itself. It was a major result of the foundational work in CA that turns-at-talk were shown to be a locally managed, interactive accomplishment, ie. that speaker and recipient were mutually involved and that a speaker-centred analysis of utterances in isolation was missing something important. Later it was argued in Goodwin & Goodwin (1987) that "individual utterances and single turns at talk are themselves constituted through an ongoing process of interaction between speaker and recipient" (p. 3); that is, a speaker-centred analysis of turn construction itself is also inadequate. What we would also like to demonstrate is that a further step is required: we can no longer focus simply on a speaker-centred analysis of turn competition. Of course, CA has addressed the local management of resolution of overlap in TRPs but it is usually examined from the point of view of two speakers who find themselves competing for a turn-at-talk. For FiSL talk we will show that *competitive turn transitions are themselves accomplished through an ongoing process of interaction between speaker(s) and recipient(s)*.

In the following four examples we present some examples of how turn transitions are managed in FiSL within this distinctive modality. In Example 9 we see a special case in which a deaf-blind woman C, who became blind after acquiring sign language, interacts with two other deaf signers in the community. The asymmetry of participation is interesting - she can sign freely but obviously without being able to see her own signs or her participants', but only one person can sign to her at a time (A in Figure 9), except for simple touches to the body. Her hands (and head orientation) are the mechanism for turn taking—she can offer her hands to someone or they can grab them and start to sign-trace with them. It is *through her hands that talk is systematically accomplished*; however, this is a special case.

Figure 9.

'Take my hands and tell me about it'

In a similar scenario to that of a spoken conversation, Example 10 in Appendix 1 reports of a competitive onset that is resolved very quickly by one signer dropping out. Signer B finishes her turn (returns to rest position) and looks with a particular expression at D. C signs REALLY low on the table, self-selects by starting an attention getting table tap which is then followed by the sign SUNDAY, but mutual gaze is not been achieved. At this point several things happen in quick succession but without the global attention of all concerned, ie. locally managed through local access. D glances to C (a flick of the head) and in that glance finds C's hand moving to the table. Note that *glances* are restricted windows onto potentially relevant other-activity in which one must find evidence of a projected or expected activity, otherwise gaze returns or moves to another focal point/participant. D's gaze returns to B (Figure 10-1) and she begins signing FIRST to the same recipient. C concurrently finishes another attention wave and B begins to glance at C (tracking the just prior glance of C). However, C glances to D, maybe tracking the continued gaze, up until this moment and during her attention getting attempts, of B towards D. She then discovers a competitive onset by D (Figure 10-2). During this glance, B has glanced to C and thus finds her attending to D (Figure 10-2); B's gaze returns to D. Importantly, C upon finding a competitive onset returns gaze to B (Figure 10-3), the directed recipient of both signers, and recycles SUNDAY. But she is too late and finds B apparently still gazing at D. She drops the sign, returns to rest position and looks back to D (Figure 10-4), who is still signing. Thus the resolution is achieved through the *recipient's behaviour* in the context of finding the next signer, ie. the behaviour of C displays an orientation to recipient gaze in resolving competitive onsets. *Each participant is actively engaged—through scans, glances or noticings—in discovering sign activity, but in so doing they reorganise the possibilities for other signers and shift their own focal regions thus excluding attentiveness to other regions*, eg. if I turn my gaze (call this a focal region or a field of visual awareness) from one participant to another behind me I cannot then see the first.

Example 11 in Appendix 2 illustrates both the importance of gaze monitoring and the local and distributed nature of sign talk in transitions. One participant D, who is signing, reaches a transition relevance space. This is demonstrated in the immediate gaze shifts of B, A and C who reorient to a potential next signer. But the continued shifts of gaze suggest that a transition is not accomplished: B and A look to D again and C looks to the vicinity of her coffee cup. Here we have a *lapse* in the conversation (Figure 11-1). After a short period, A begins signing and B glances to A; as B's gaze settles on A, A's hand is falling low (Figure 11-2). Immediately, B returns gaze to D and starts an attention wave to D, having discovered no activity in the vicinity of D's apparent gaze (that is temporarily unmonitorable during B's glance). B does hesitate and double check halfway through the return of the gaze to D, but continues with the wave. However, A's signing continues, C notices B's attention waves, but, for B, D still does not attend to B. After a short period B returns to check what is attracting D's gaze and *discovers post-onset* a competitive sign activity. B monitors the signing while still waving, gets mutual gaze from A who returns to rest position, and nods (Figure 11-3) and returns to D. She discovers D is attending to her and immediately starts signing (Figure 11-4).

It will be interesting to study further how double onsets are resolved in different spatial configurations of multi-party talk and what consequences post-onset discoveries have for the organisation of talk. In two and three party talk, resolution must result in a group focus because signing normally requires a recipient and so in a triad the third participant cannot sign to either of the two otherwise occupied participants. In the next example this situation is illustrated. But in larger groups local activity in transitions could result in a temporary dissolution of a group focus.

We will consider next what happens when more than two participants self-select in multi-party talk. In Example 12 in Appendix 3, we have an instance of *tripartite directed self-selection* in which F is at the apex of an *obtuse triangle participation space*. After some turn exchanges W signs and returns to the rest position with F and M gazing at W and W gazing at M. In this transition relevance space, all three participants self-select but without all necessarily being immediately aware of the simultaneous onset. M signs a question to F (Figure 12-2), F turns from the W to M and signs to M (Figure 12-3), and W turns from M to F and waves and taps for attention (and discovers F signing in Figure 12-4). M resolves the triad of competitive onsets by shifting his gaze to F, to whom W is looking. It could be that M has already seen F signing or that he discovers that F is already signing in overlap; either way, by orienting to F at this moment a successful resolution is accomplished. F recycles CONFLICT upon M's gaze (Figure 12-5), M becomes a recipient and F continues signing having gained the floor. That F wants to sign to the triad is demonstrated when W looks away after failing to get F's attention: consequently, F taps while persevering with a one handed sign and recycles TWO-YEARS-AGO upon receipt of W's gaze once again (see the sequence of video pictures, Figures 12-6 to 12-8). Finally, F stops and W takes over the floor. An important finding here is that recipients' activities - the timing of glances, gaze transitions and mutual gaze - are systematically relevant to the resolution of speaker transition; it is not simply up to the competing signers to resolve a potentially troublesome overlap. It is not yet clear that the phenomenon of multiple directed onsets is a common occurrence.

4 CONCLUSION

The main hypothesis in this paper is that in turn transitions and group activities deaf signers display a heightened and distinctive use of visual space and the body in the accomplishment of these activities. The modality of sign language provides many materials out of which participants must construct their talk and their lives, and these constraints and resources clearly influence the organisation of the talk. However, it should not to be concluded that the talk of sign language communities is qualitatively different from all forms of spoken talk. One major reason why we should be cautious is that this research is based on a study of the Finnish Sign Language community and the findings compared in part to the work on European but particularly Anglo-American spoken language communities.

This is a preliminary study, but it has suggested that sign talk is worthy of analytic interest. It is of an intricate but locally managed complexity of the same order as that found in spoken talk. With much further work on the organisation and accomplishment of talk and interaction in a sign language community, access to the constitution of a sign language within its social context will become available. We may then hope to build a better understanding of both the structure and situated use of sign languages, in which both the analysis of linguistic structure and interactional function are firmly interleaved without the bias of a high status written form to influence the resulting theory and empirical observations.

Footnotes

* Paul McIlvenny and Pirkko Raudaskoski: Department of English, University of Oulu, PL III, SF-90571 Oulu, Finland. E-mail: ekl-pmi at finou.oulu.fi
† We would like to thank Anne Hämäläinen for her native insights into FiSL and for sharing tales of deaf life with us, Sirpa Suomela for her native insights and sign interpretation, Ulla Hiironen for sign interpretation, and the Deaf community in Finland for their kind assistance. The Department of English generously supplied technical facilities to support the study, Oulu University gave financial support for interpreter fees and The Finnish Academy gave financial support for travel expenses.

1. The sign language of the majority of deaf people in Finland is Finnish Sign Language, which we will abbreviate as FiSL for remainder of this paper. Linguistic studies of FiSL include Rissanen (1985) and Pimiä & Rissanen (1987). The only major sign language dictionary (glossary) in use is the Viittomakielen Kuvasanakirja (1973/77/88), although work is under way to produce a revised and computerised dictionary.

2. We should note at this point that we use the words 'talk', 'say', etc. to refer to the signing activities that deaf people engage in together because those are the terms that they themselves use to describe and refer to their own use of sign language. Unfortunately, some researchers are actively constructing an analytic discourse in which the deaf community do not talk. For example: "Conversation is not talk's sole form, but it does seem to be its most general one, composing many social scenes, leaking into others, and probably providing the source from which other forms of speech and writing derive. There is no doubt that some societies are more silent, some more terse, some more formal than others. Some communities - the deaf, for example - do not talk at all." (Moerman 1988, p. 3) But rather than reserve these terms for spoken language interaction, we will use them in the broad sense of language-rich interaction in practical everyday contexts. Why should the activities of deaf people be described in a different way? If deaf people do not converse, nor have a rich set of talk activities, then what do they do?

3. Some of our findings may seem familiar to sign language researchers, both deaf and hearing, and to deaf people who are not engaged in linguistic research. It is in the nature of our work - exposing and documenting the taken-for-granted world of everyday life - that once stated the results appear obvious and almost trivial. We hope you will appreciate this and look further into the explanatory power of the theory behind the results and of the methods that generated them.

4. The research reported here is a rather technical study concerned with the mechanics of sign exchange and deaf interaction. However, we prefer not to refer to findings as 'rules of behaviour' as Kyle (1990) has done, though we agree with his statement that "turn-taking is complex". Later studies will shift to the study of the organisation of talk in relation to the constitution of deaf life and culture.

5. Normal sighted people can notice things in their peripheral vision with a range of just over 90 degrees to the left and right when focusing straight ahead. However, peripheral movements or features are distinguished with much less clarity than when present in the focal region, cf. Swisher et al. (1989).

Bibliography

Atkinson, J. [1984]. *Our Masters' Voices: The Language and Body Language of Politics*. Methuen, London.

Atkinson, J. and Heritage, J. (eds) [1984]. *Structures of Social Action: Studies in Conversation Analysis*. Cambridge University Press, Cambridge.

Baker, C. [1977]. Regulators and turn-taking in American Sign Language discourse, in: Friedman, L. (ed) *On the Other Hand*. Academic Press, New York.

Boden, D. and Zimmerman, D. (eds) [1991]. *Talk and Social Structure*. Polity Press, Cambridge.

Button, G. and Lee, J. (eds) [1987]. *Talk and Social Organisation*. Multilingual Matters, Avon.

Cicourel, A.V. [1974]. *Cognitive Sociology*. Penguin, London.

Goodwin, C. and Goodwin, M. [1987]. Concurrent operations on talk: notes on the interactive organisation of assessments. *IPRA Papers in Pragmatics* 1:1, pp. 1–54.

Hakulinen, A. (ed) [1989]. *Kieli 4: Suomalaisen Keskustelun Keinoja I*. Yliopistopaino, Helsinki.

Hall, S. [1983]. Train—gone—sorry: the etiquette of social conversations in American Sign Language. *Sign Language Studies* 41, pp. 291–309.

Heritage, J. [1984]. *Garfinkel and Ethnomethodology*. Polity Press, Cambridge.

Heritage, J. [1989]. Current developments in conversation analysis, in: Roger, D. and Bull, P. (eds) *Conversation.*, pp. 21–47. Multilingual Matters, Clevedon.

Jefferson, G. [1985]. An exercise in the transcription of laughter, in: Dijk, T. van (ed) *Handbook of Discourse Analysis Vol 3*. Academic Press, London.

Kyle, J. [1990]. The Deaf community: custom, culture and tradition, in: Prillwitz, S. and Vollhaber, T. (eds) *Sign Language Research and Application*. Signum Press, Hamburg.

Levinson, S.C. [1983]. *Pragmatics*. Cambridge University Press, Cambridge.

McIlvenny, P. [1991]. Some thoughts on the study of sign language talk, in: Sajavaara, K. et al. (eds) *Communication and Discourse across Cultures and Languages*, pp. 187–202. AFinLA Yearbook 1991. Publications de L'Association Finlandaise de Linguistique Appliqueé, Jyväskylä University.

Moerman, M. [1988]. *Talking Culture: Ethnography and Conversation Analysis*. University of Philadelphia Press, Philadelphia.

Pimiä, P. and Rissanen, T. [1987]. *Kolme Kirjoitusta Viittomakielestä (Three Studies of Sign Language)* . Department of General Linguistics Pub. No. 17, University of Helsinki.

Prinz, P.M. and Prinz, E.A. [1985]. If only you could hear what I see: discourse development in sign language. *Discourse Processes* 8, pp. 1–19.

Psathas, G. (ed) [1990]. *Interaction Competence*. University of America Press, Washington, DC.

Psathas, G. and Anderson, T. [1990]. The 'practices' of transcription in conversation analysis. *Semiotica* 78:1/2, pp. 75–99.

Rissanen, T. [1985]. *Viittomakielen Perusrakenne (The Basic Structure of Sign Language)*. Department of General Linguistics Pub. No. 12, University of Helsinki.

Roy, C.B. [1989]. Features of discourse in an American Sign Language lecture, in: Lucas, C. (ed) *The Sociolinguistics of the Deaf Community*. Academic Press, New York.

Sacks, H. [1989]. Harvey Sacks: Lectures 1964-1965. Special Issue edited by G. Jefferson in *Human Studies* 12:3/4.

Sacks, H., Schegloff, E. and Jefferson, G. [1978]. A simplest systematics for the organisation of turn taking for conversation, in: Schenkein, J. (ed) *Studies in the Organisation of Conversational Interaction*, pp. 7–55. Academic Press, New York.

Stokoe, W.C. [1960]. Sign language structure: an outline of the visual communication system of the American deaf. *Studies in Linguistics Occasional Paper 8.* University of Buffalo.

Swisher, M.V., Christie, K. and Miller, S.L. [1989]. The Reception of Signs in Peripheral Vision. *Sign Language Studies* 63, pp. 99–125.

Viittomakielen Kuvasanakirja (Sign Language Picture Dictionary). [1973/1977/1988]. Edited by Lauri Paunu et al. Kuurojen Liito r.y., Helsinki.

Wilbur, R.B. [1983]. Discourse structure in American Sign Language conversations. *Discourse Processes* 6, pp. 225–241.

Appendix 1 : Example 10.

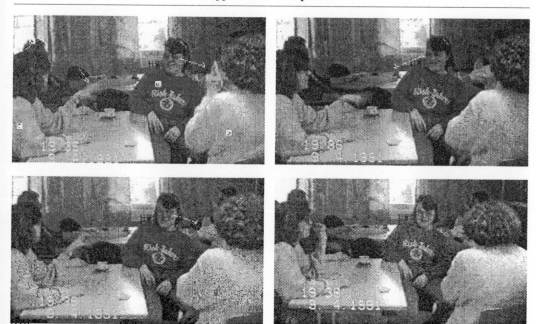

'Whose turn is it now?'

[3-19,2: pics 3–19,2 (a–f)]
Initial gaze: [a>?; b>d; c>b; d>b?]

B: couldn't give birth head first it was a difficult
        situation so it was born feet first and it went okay.

C: REALLY +
        oh really!

C: *G(V) SUNDAY   *G   +   SUNDAY ((rest))
        hey   on sunday-   hey   on sunday-
D: ⌊{hs}   ⌊(FIRST   )
                            (was it the first?)
Gaze: d>c=d>b
                          b>c=b>d
                             c>d=c>b   c>d
Pics: I   2   3   4

D: (FIRSTGIRL)
        the first was a girl
B: ⌊(   )
          (   )
Gaze: c>b

Appendix 2: Example 11.

'Why aren't you looking at me when I'm signing?'

[3–19: Pics 3–19 (a–j)]
Initial Gaze: [a<d; b>d; c>d; d>?]

```
D:        (               BOOK TEACH NOTHING)
          (               the book teaches nothing      )

Gaze: b>a                       b>ø=b>d
                  c>a                             c>ø
         a>b                    a>d
Pics:                                        1

A:        (      )        (     )
B:                        [*G   +   +   +      +               +
                                           {mth}
                          hey              yeah?     hey
Gaze:       b>a          (b>d)=b>d   b>a          b>d
                             c>d
                                        a>b
                                        d>b
Pics:                      2                    3
```

B: YOUNG-LAST BROTHER SECOND WAIT
   the youngest brother was waiting for the second baby.
Pics: 4

B: BORN BOY HAVE
   a boy was born.

Appendix 3: Example 12.

Escher loops

[3–13: Pics 3–13′ (a–r)]
Initial gaze: [f>w; w>m; m>w]

W: (   ) DEAF HOLIDAY   (*G) (ps-6) (HOTEL)   NO
       (   ) a deaf holiday thing   hey not that (hotel)
M: [ahh   [NO?
                     ahh   no?

W: DEAF HOLIDAY (ps-7)   {hn}
      a deaf holiday thing   yes
M: [I-SEE HOLIDAY I-SEE
                I see you mean a holiday thing

M: MEAN?
      what does it mean?
Gaze: f>m

W: (marketing) NOW
      marketing should start now
Gaze: f>w

M: MARKETING?
      what is marketing?

F: MARKETING +]
      marketing
W: [ASSOCIATION: *G + +
      the association, hey
Gaze: f>m   w>f   w>m
      m>f   f>w
                  m>w
Pics: 1

W: ASSOCIATION NEED SELF MARKETING NOW (ps-7) {so}
      the association needs self marketing now, so

M: WHAT MEAN MARKETING?
      what does marketing mean?
F: [MARKETING/CONFLICT
         there was a conflict
W: [*T   +
               hey
Gaze: f>m   w>f   m>f
Pics: 2   3   4

F: CONFLICT ONE- TWO-YEARS-AGO: *T: TWO-YEARS-AGO: *T:
      a conflict one- two years ago: hey two years ago hey
W: + +   +]
Gaze: f>ϕ   w>Ω   f>w   w>f
                          m>w
Pics: 5   6   7

F: TWO-YEARS-AGO CONFLICT   {bad}
      two years ago there was a conflict it was bad
W: [*T +
                      hey hey
Gaze: f>ϕ   f>w
                           m>w
Pics: 8

W: I (   ) BOARD

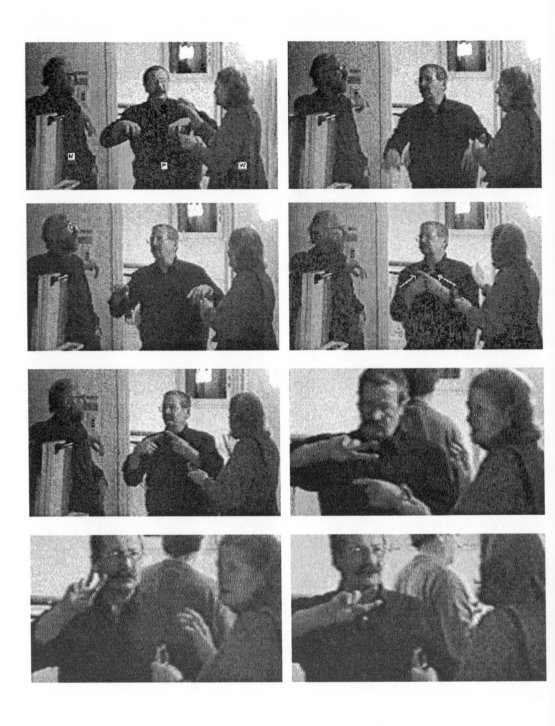

Appendix 4: Transcription conventions

To find out more about the transcription system used in conversation analysis for research on spoken conversation (which includes eye gaze and gesture) see Psathas & Anderson(1990) and the appendices in recent books on CA, such as Boden & Zimmerman (1991).

SMALL CAPITALS	Sign gloss (in English).
lowercase	Translation of sign(s) into English.
{lowercase}	Non-manual or mime translation.
SC/SC	One sign assimilates to the following sign.
*G	Attention gesture
*T	Attention tap (to the body)
*V	Attention through vibration
((comments))	Transcriber's comments.
{hs}	Head shake.
{hn}	Head nod.
{mth}	Special mouth shape.
( )	Unsure of sign activity.
(JFGH)	Unsure of sign.
?	Question indicated by sign or non-manual features.
(ps-n)	Point to signing space n: 5 2 6
	S is the signer. 3 4
	7 1 8
	S
[	Overlap onset, ie. simultaneous signing.
]	Overlap resolution.
+	Repetition of sign.
:	Prolongation of sign or part of sign (often with simultaneous gesture on the other hand or a non-manual component).
>	Gaze shift, eg. x>y means x shifted gaze to y.
Ω	Gaze outside group.
∅	Gaze to neutral space.
=	Glance, eg. x>y=x>z means x glances to y and then gazes at z.

The influence of television on the Deaf community in Britain [†]

BENCIE WOLL *

1 INTRODUCTION

The study reported here was designed with a number of aims:

to describe changes in British Sign Language as exemplified by changes in the signing used on *See Hear*, the first and longest-running television programme using BSL;

to explore changes in attitudes to varieties of signing since 1981;

to describe variation in signing and attitudes to that variation from a synchronic viewpoint by comparing signers on the programmes and viewers' attitudes to that signing;

to test the hypothesis that changes in signing reflected changing attitudes to BSL and loss of regional differences;

1.1 Research methodology

The methodology combined analyses of signing used by all deaf signers appearing on *See Hear*, analyses of the signing of the presenters on *See Hear* and interviews with a sample of deaf signers from different regions of Britain. Further details of project findings may be found in Woll, Sutton-Spence and Allsop 1990, Woll 1991, and Sutton-Spence & Woll 1991.

Although consisting of analyses of a range of different data, the study presents a unified whole in relation to variation, change, and attitudes to these processes. The research to be reported on here comprised a study of variation and change within BSL, focussing on lexical variation recorded on *See Hear*, and a study of comprehension of variant forms of BSL and attitudes to variation and change in the language.

Attitudes to variation and change were explored in individual interviews with members of the deaf community in different regions of Britain. Compared with research undertaken in 1980, in the Bristol area (Kyle & Allsop 1981), when deaf people claimed they had great difficulties in understanding other deaf people from geographically distant areas, subjects in this study rated most regional varieties as relatively easy to understand. A series of questions explored subjects' attitudes to the appropriate variety of signing for television. Interviewees overwhelmingly rejected the proposal that signing on television should be standardised toward English-like varieties. On the other hand, the majority felt that the variety of signing should be determined by the need to present some standard form of signing appropriate for television. It was strongly felt that the changes which had occurred in signing on television had improved it and made it easier to understand. There was a generally positive response to the introduction of new signs on television, particularly among younger subjects, who also reported that they changed their signing to incorporate new signs.

The relationship of television and the deaf community was explored in interviews with current and former presenters as well as with viewers. A picture has emerged of mutual influence, with the content of programmes changing over time as well, to reflect and influence changes in the deaf community.

Consistent changes were found over time in the signing found on television. Major changes included divergence between the forms of communication used by hearing and deaf people. While initially, both groups used sign with voice, deaf people moved towards the use of British Sign Language, and hearing people moved towards the use of English. These changes occurred both in the communication used by presenters and that used by other people appearing on *See Hear*, the earliest and longest-running television series for the deaf.

Changes found in the signing of deaf people included a decrease in the use of fingerspelling used to represent English words, and a standardisation of the lexicon in certain semantic fields. These changes were found by comparing programmes made between 1981 and 1989, and also by comparing signers of different ages and from different regions. These changes represent a general loss of regional variation in BSL. Folk beliefs about variation in fingerspelling were upheld, although patterns for lexical variation, for example, do not reflect either simple age or regional variation patterns.

2 BACKGROUND

At the time of the commencement of research into BSL, public settings for its use were very limited. As there was, and still is, no written form of the language, all publications for the Deaf community are in English. Schools for the deaf had not used BSL as a medium of instruction since the beginning of the century. Television programmes, such as *News Review*, targeted at deaf and hard-of-hearing audiences, used English subtitles. However, in 1981, following a programme on BSL, and pressure from Deaf people, the BBC began *See Hear*, the first magazine programme in Britain with content of specific Deaf interest, which used signing. Because of the lack of precedents in public contexts for signing, the programme has evolved in content and language variety used from the first series until the present day.

In parallel with the time in which the series has been on the BBC, there have been other initiatives relating to BSL. Signed English has been introduced in schools for the deaf; sign language interpreter training is now available, and the British Deaf

Association has launched a campaign to gain official governmental recognition of BSL as the language of the Deaf community. A number of public settings, such as political conferences, make BSL interpreters available; several national and local television programmes use interpreters and signing presenters; and BSL is now widely taught, including a BBC series for hearing people.

The rapid expansion of contexts for signing is likely to have affected BSL in two related ways: by exposing viewers to a much wider range of signers than they might have previously encountered, and by altering attitudes to the appropriateness of varieties of BSL for public use. This project has studied both changes in attitudes and changes in the language itself, using data from a variety of sources to explore these two areas.

3 LEXICAL VARIATION IN BSL
3.1 Methodology

A concordance program (Micro-concord 0.4) was applied to the transcripts of the subtitles from the 146 programmes in the first 8 series. This data base has been maintained and means that access to sign data via this concordance is available to other sign language researchers with access to a PC. Discs of the transcribed subtitles are held in the Centre for Deaf Studies. Thus, the location on any programme of all signs representing any English word can be identified together with the sentence in which the signs occur.

Each sign identified for the variation analysis was transcribed using SignWriting (Sutton 1991), a computer-based transcription system for sign language data, which enables coding of fine detail in the manual and non-manual components of a sign, together with an English translation. Individual components of a transcribed sign, such as handshape can be used to search the data base. The existing Signwriting system, originally developed for use with American Sign Language, was modified by the deaf research assistant on the team, working together with the American designer of Signwriting.

3.2 Lexical Variation

No comprehensive theory of lexical variation exists, because of the difficulty of collecting adequate relevant data and identifying the contributory factors. The extent of variation within the BSL lexicon may depend on socio-linguistic factors, such as age, region of origin or educational background. It may also vary with the semantic category of sign in question. Because of the absence of a standard form of BSL, the extent of language contact before television was limited to the distance travelled by individual signers, with inevitable divergence of regional dialects.

Lexical variation itself can be at different levels within BSL. Signs for the same concept may differ markedly in handshape, movement and place of articulation. Other variation may arise from choice of one-handed or two-handed versions of a sign or shift in place of articulation. It has also been recognised in the spoken language field that certain words are more prone to enter any dialect through electronic media than others. These words represent new concepts and as the concept is accepted, so is the word. Thus, these words are less likely to vary regionally, as they will have been introduced via a national medium. In BSL, this introduction is not so straightforward. Usually a new concept is introduced via English and there may be a period when fingerspelling and various signs are used around the country. One dominant sign may emerge after which its use on television will reinforce it nationally. Such signs are unlikely to show much regional variation but change over time as there is a struggle for one sign to become accepted. As well as technological fields where new inventions require new signs, signs which relate to new concepts arising from social and political change may also be subject to this process.

In this analysis of signs, 26 concepts were selected, with half chosen as likely to show considerable variation and half as likely to be fairly uniform throughout the corpus. For general analysis all signs similar at the level of visual metaphor were grouped together. In the section below, meanings are indicated by English words in quotes: "grassroots"; fingerspelled forms by lower-case letters separated by hyphens: -g-r-a-s-s-r-o-o-t-s; glosses of specific signs by small capitals: GRASSROOTS); descriptions of sign forms are given in square brackets [non-dominant hand, fingers extended and together, palm towards body; dominant hand in front, fingers extended and spread].

The number of variants (grouped as described above) recorded for each gloss ranged from one for "research" to 9 for "country" with an average of 4.70 variants per gloss. The following four factors contributed most to variation in these glosses: age, time (over the 8 series from 1981-1989), region, semantic field; although for each example, different factors predominated. Examples of these will be discussed below to illustrate the complexity of lexical variation in BSL.

3.3 Technology

Not all technological terms in our study were influenced by the time span of the series, and none showed any marked regional variation. The changes seen in these signs were linked to the length of time that the concept and hence the need for a sign existed. There was one basic sign "video" (although it was fingerspelled once in the first series) and it did not change [both hands in V handshape, palms down at waist height. The hands move in small circles in the horizontal plane.]. One sublexical shift seen in the presenters' signing of VIDEO was towards mirror symmetry in movement. The sign "vistel" (brand name of textphone) in contrast, changed greatly over time. The sign first glossed as "vistel" later generalised to both VISTEL and MINICOM (two competing brands of teletext device) [non-dominant hand with fingers extended and together, palm down; dominant hand above non-dominant hand, with little finger and thumb extended]. The sign clearly was highly unstable, with variant signs used by a single person on a single programme. Standardisation amongst programme presenters appeared by the fourth series, but there was no general agreement amongst others appearing on the programme until series 8.

In contrast, the sign "telephone" did not change over time. One sign was used by 83% of our population [hand at ear, little finger and thumb extended]. The major determining variable for this sign is age of signer. One elderly signer used the two-handed sign derived from a visual representation of an old phone with separate ear and mouthpieces, while another elderly signer used a one-handed variant which maintained the fist handshape at the ear. The relative stability of what may appear to be a visually inappropriate image in "telephone", in contrast with the rapid shifts in MINICOM, is probably due to the length of time in which telephones have existed.

3.4 Deaf Culture

The semantic field of Deaf political awareness might be expected to yield signs influenced by time, as many signs express concepts new to Deaf society. It is the case that all four of the glosses we chose did show effects of the progression of time. There are two patterns of progression in signs for new concepts. They may initially be fingerspelled (g-r-a-s-s-r-o-o-t-s- and c-u-l-t-u-r-e-) or there may be another sign with a similar meaning extended for use in this context (GROUP used for "community"; or REJECT or OPPRESS for "discrimination" in conjunction with the mouth pattern of the words "community" or "discrimination". Presenters, in interview, said that they had devised their own sign for "discrimination", which was used consistently by all presenters on the programme. It was not, however, adopted by members of the Deaf community. They showed a great range of signs for this, but even in later series often fingerspelled the English word. The use of the sign OPPRESS did, however, drop out, perhaps indicating that there was an awareness of the different meanings that were emerging. "Community" showed a similar pattern of change. Initially the most common signs used were those also glossed as "group" or "council". Later a sign emerged which was similar to another form of "group". Both signs began to decline in use as the sign adopted for "community" was introduced. This sign overlapped for some time with the sign then being used for "culture". As late as Series 8 (1989), presenters fingerspelled -c-o-m-m-u-n-i-t-y- when discussing the Community Charge (British local tax). Clearly the semantic domain of the sign COMMUNITY did not extend to this meaning of tax at that time, although by Series 9, COMMUNITY CHARGE was the form used. "Culture" (almost always in the context of "Deaf culture") began as fingerspelling. One presenter in an early programme accompanied the spoken word "culture" with the sign phrase WAY DEAF PEOPLE LIVE. The first sign to consistently be used for "culture" was also used for "community". By Series 8, both presenters and members of the community were using a third distinct sign COMMUNITY. One other term in this group was "grassroots" (often in the context of contrasting members of the general Deaf community ("grassroots deaf" with Deaf activists). This was also originally fingerspelled, but later was signed with a completely new sign GRASSROOTS.

In contrast with these signs, which related to Deaf society, but which were new coinages, the other signs investigated in this corpus had been in use in BSL for some time. One example will illustrate the features of this subgroup. "Deaf" appeared in more than one form in 15% of the signers producing it. Variant 1 consists of the index and middle fingers extended and together, contacting the ear, while in Variant 2, the same handshape contacts the ear and then the lips. Variant 2 is an older sign and carries the implication "deaf and dumb", while Variant 1 appears to be a more recent sign, which has lost the reference to "dumb". Many signers now prefer the first variant, but are still influenced by the older sign. For other signs, there is a semantic distinction between the two variants. Variant 2 is used to talk about someone who is committed to Deaf culture and the Deaf community ("strong Deaf"), and Variant 1 is used for other meanings. Presenters using simultaneous signing and speaking only used the first variant. The presenters in later series, who used signing without voice, used both forms of "deaf". The association between using voice while signing and using Variant 1 is also seen in other members of the Deaf community. Of those using Simultaneous signing and speaking or signing with some voice, only 11% used Variant 2, and 64% used Variant 1, while of those using Sign Only, 35% used Variant 2 and 52% used Variant 1.

3.5 Other semantic fields

The other semantic fields investigated represented a wide variety of meanings: employment, holidays, countries, etc. Again, an example will illustrate the range found. Within the "employment" heading, several signs had two main competing variants: one a "BSL-based" sign, and one derived from fingerspelling. There were no changes over time for these two variants, nor was one or other confined to signers of any age or region. However, there was a correlation between communication mode and choice of sign. This may relate to Battison's (1978) observation for ASL that initialisations are more likely to be made by those whose signing is influenced by English. "Job" had two main signs, one of which was a loan sign from fingerspelling. This was usually reduced to either -j- alone or -j-b-. The other sign for "job" was the sign WORK Of those using Simultaneous Communication, 75% used the initialised form of "job" and only 25% used WORK. Of those using signing without any voice, 36% used the initialisation and 64% used the sign for "work". Both these forms are clearly well established within the dialects of those who use them. In contrast, within the semantic field of holidays, region was the most important contributing variable.

Overall, the finding is of extensive variability, with only 4% of the signs investigated showing no variation at all. Different factors contribute in greater or lesser degree. The most important of these are semantic field, region, age of signer, and newness of concept. There is no evidence that, apart from signs representing new concepts, television has influenced signers to change their preferred lexical choice. These findings can be compared to the results of the interviews.

4 INTERVIEW DATA
4.1 Methodology

Two samples of Deaf people were interviewed. In all cases interviews were conducted by the deaf researcher, in BSL, and interviews were recorded on video for later analysis. Subjects for interview were mainly recruited through contacts with local deaf club chairpersons or directors, although advertisements were also placed on the national teletext magazines for deaf people: Earshot and No Need to Shout. Two interview schedules were used: the first contained questions about attitudes to linguistic change and variation in BSL; the second schedule tested respondents' abilities to comprehend signing from different regions and their own preferred lexical variants. The first sample consists of 79 Deaf people, who received both the attitudes and comprehension schedules, and a second group of 37 subjects, who received only the attitudes schedule. Interviews with the sample who received both schedules were conducted in Bristol, London, Manchester, Glasgow and Newcastle. Interviews with the sample who received only the attitudes schedule were conducted in Leeds/Bradford and Belfast. Fourteen percent were under 25; 45% were between 26 and 45; and 40% were over 45.

The three age groups reflect three different sorts of experience of signing and languages: the youngest are those likely to have been educated in Partially Hearing Units and therefore have had less experience of sign; the oldest are likely to be those with the most conservative ideas about language and variation, and use the most "old-fashioned" signing; while the middle group were expected to combined mature language skills with more open views about language.

All those interviewed were regular viewers of See Hear and other programmes for the deaf.

Interviewees were presented with a set of questions about how easy or difficult they find it to understand signers from different regions. The only regional variety of BSL which was widely thought to be difficult to understand was Northern Ireland (44%) with the next most difficult region Scotland (12%). These findings are in striking contrast to those obtained in an earlier study, before the broadcasting on sign language on television.

In the 1980 survey (Kyle & Allsop 1981), over 40% of members of the Deaf community in Bristol and surrounding areas had never met a Deaf person from farther than 125 miles away. Only around half of respondents said they could understand the signing of people from those areas most of the time, although this figure rose to over 80% for those who had actually met signers from these areas.

4.2 Observations about change in Sign

Sixty-eight percent of subjects thought that signing in general had changed in the past 10 years. Factors identified by respondents included the amount of mouth patterning (32%); the form of signs (32%); the amount of fingerspelling (42%); and the use of new signs (75%). Sixty-five percent also thought their own signing had changed over the past ten years.

Sixty-six percent thought that the young generally signed differently from older signers: 41% thought the young used mouth patterns more; 64% that the young used more new signs; 46% that the young generally articulate signs differently; 55% that the young fingerspell more. These responses are opposite to those we had predicted, and for the question about fingerspelling, the reverse of actual findings for the use of fingerspelling on television.

Younger signers were more likely to report enjoying seeing new signs on television (81% of those under 45, compared with 65% of those over 45), and thought themselves more likely to use new signs themselves (61% of the under-45s, compared with 34% of the over-45s). However, older signers claimed fewer difficulties in understanding regional differences than younger signers did.

5 LEXICAL VARIATION

Two sets of data were obtained in this part of the second schedule. For the first set, respondents were presented with a set of cards bearing the English glosses of the signs analysed for the lexical variation study. Signers were asked to give their sign for the gloss presented. For the second set, signers were presented with a sample of the sign variants obtained in the *See Hear* lexical variation analysis, and asked what meaning that sign had. Because of the large number of variants recorded from *See Hear*, each subject received a random sample of variants. In presentation, Sets 1 and 2 were separated by the attitudes schedule. The sample was divided into two age groups (<45 and >45) and for each gloss, answers were coded as falling into one of three groups for each gloss: a) incorrect response in Set 2 (i.e. an incorrect definition of the sign as it was used on *See Hear*); b) correct response in Set 2 with the same sign offered in Set 1; c) correct response in Set 2 but with a different sign offered in Set 1. Answers of the Group A form reveal comprehension difficulties; answers in Group

B represent signers whose preferred form for a gloss happened to be the same as the example presented; answers in Group C represent signers who could recognise forms they did not use themselves. Younger signers offered responses in Group C significantly more often than older signers (p<0.002). This finding therefore supports the claim by older signers to be able to understand regional variants. Respondents' own region of origin also contributed significantly to the ability to understand the variants in Set 2, with Scottish signers and signers from Newcastle significantly more likely to offer incorrect definitions than signers from London and Manchester (p<0.005).

6 SUMMARY

Compared with research undertaken in 1980, in the Bristol area, when deaf people claimed they had great difficulties in understanding other deaf people from geographically distant areas, subjects in this study rated most regional varieties as relatively easy to understand. This confirms the importance of television as a means not of standardising BSL, but of introducing signers to the possibility of understanding variants and of a greater awareness of BSL and its forms.

Footnotes

* Bencie Woll: Centre for Deaf Studies, University of Bristol
† The research for this chapter was supported by the Economic and Social Research Council, Grant No. R000 23 14 75000, "Variation and Recent Change in British Sign Language".

Bibliography

Battison, R. [1978]. *Lexical Borrowing in American Sign Language.* Linstok Press, Silver Spring, MD.

Kyle, J.G. and Allsop, L. [1981]. *Deaf People and the Community.* Final Report to the Nuffield Trust. University of Bristol, Bristol.

Sutton, V. [1991]. *SignWriter PC 4.0.* Deaf Action Committee for SignWriting, La Jolla, Ca., U.S.A.

Sutton-Spence, R., Woll, B. and Allsop, L. [1990]. Variation and recent change in fingerspelling in British Sign Language. *Language Variation and Change 2,* pp. 313–330.

Sutton-Spence, R. and Woll, B. [in press]. The status and functional role of fingerspelling in BSL, in: Marschark, M. and Clark, D. (eds) *Psychological Perspectives on Deafness.* Lawrence Erlbaum Associates, Hillsdale, NJ.

Woll, B. [1991]. *Recent Variation and Change in BSL.* Report to the Economic and Social Research Council. Centre for Deaf Studies, Bristol.

PART 3

Acquisition

Attentional strategies used by Deaf mothers [†]

BEPPIE VAN DEN BOGAERDE [*]

1 INTRODUCTION

In a longitudinal project on the interaction and communication in deaf families conducted at the University of Amsterdam, three deaf and three hearing children and their deaf mothers are being followed. The results presented in this paper form part of this longitudinal research project. From earlier studies within the project (Blankenstijn and v.d.Bogaerde 1989; Mills and Coerts 1989; Coerts, Mills and v.d.Bogaerde 1990; Mills and Coerts 1990; Mills and v.d. Bogaerde 1991; v.d.Bogaerde and Mills [in press]) we know that the deaf mothers in our project use two languages with their children: Dutch (NL) and Sign Language of the Netherlands (SLN) and a third mode of communication, simultaneous communication (SC)[1]. This happens both with the deaf and with the hearing children, although the proportions of use are different. This multilingual situation has not been so clearly described in other research, although other researchers report use of spoken language with deaf children (Kyle and Ackerman 1990).

It is obvious that for communication involving signs visual attention has to be given to the signer. In parent-child interaction therefore the child must pay visual attention to the signs of the mother. In this paper I would like to discuss the various ways in which the deaf mothers hold or gain the attention of their deaf and hearing children for their utterances together with the development of the attentional behaviour of the children.

Deaf children must pay visual attention to NL, SLN and SC utterances in order to receive the linguistic information since they must lip-read NL and SC utterances and see the signs of SLN or SC. Hearing children on the other hand need to pay visual attention only to the signs used in SLN. From an earlier study (v.d.Bogaerde and Mills in press) we know, that the spoken part and the signed part of a high proportion of the SC utterances that the deaf mothers offer to their children have the same semantic content. This means, that the hearing children do not have to pay visual attention to receive the content of the utterance, because they have access to the spoken part without looking at the mother.

In the literature it is stated that deaf mothers more or less 'train' their children to pay visual attention to their signing during the first years. This was put forward by Kyle et al. [1987] amongst others, who wrote that "learning to look [...] may be one of the key elements in early interaction in deaf families" [1987 p.226]. On the basis of this observation we can expect that, as children grow older, they gradually learn to check back with the mother for possible linguistic information. Mothers need then to attract their child's attention for communication less often in an explicit way. The children are therefore expected to show a development in their visual attention-giving behaviour over time. The following hypotheses can be formulated :

1. Deaf mothers need to attract their child's attention explicitly less often as the child grows older

2. The child looks up spontaneously more often as she/he grows older

3. The deaf children will show a different development in attentional behaviour from the hearing children

Before going on to the results of the study, further information on the subjects will be given and the methods for data collection outlined.

2 SUBJECTS

The mothers in this study are all prelingually deaf and use Sign Language of the Netherlands as their first language. There are three deaf children, Carla, Laura and Mark, and three hearing children, Jonas, Sander and Alex. Relevant information on each child and its family is given below:

Carla was diagnosed deaf at the age of 0;9[2]. Her mother was born deaf of hearing parents, with no known deaf relatives, and has used SLN since the age of 3;0 when she came into contact with other deaf children at the school for the deaf. Carla's father is deaf (cause unknown) and she has one older deaf brother.

Laura was born severely hearing impaired ($\geq$ 70 dB hearing loss in best ear) of a deaf mother and a hearing father, who is himself a hearing child of deaf parents and a native signer. Her mother has hearing parents and one deaf sister. Laura has one deaf twin brother and a hearing older brother.

Mark was born deaf ($\geq$ 90 dB hearing loss in best ear). He is the brother of Laura and Jonas.

Jonas is the hearing older brother of Mark and Laura.

Sander is the hearing child of deaf parents. Both his maternal and his paternal grandparents are deaf, as well as many uncles and aunts in his family. He has two older hearing brothers, who are twins.

Alex is also a hearing child of deaf parents. His mother became deaf after meningitis at the age of 2;6 and his father has a severe hearing loss. He has one older hearing sister and one older hearing brother. There are no other deaf members in his family.

Table 1 summarizes the information on the children participating in the study.

Table 1: Names of the children in the longitudinal study, their hearing status and their age at the start of the study

Name of child	Hearing Status	Age at start of study
Carla	loss: ≥ 90 dB	1;6
Laura	loss: ≥ 70 dB	0;11
Mark	loss: ≥ 90 dB	0;11
Jonas	hearing	0;11
Sander	hearing	0;4
Alex	hearing	0;7

3 PROCEDURE AND ANALYSIS

The six children and their mothers have been filmed [3] monthly at home in a freeplay situation, with a free choice of toys and books. No specific instructions were given to the mothers. For the analysis for this paper, two videorecordings were chosen of each mother-child dyad, when the child was 0;11 and 1;11, to show development over one year. For Carla there is only data available for the 1;11 session, so that it will not be possible to consider development in her case. Carla's data at the age of 1;11 were included in order to be able to compare the deaf twins with another deaf child at this age.

Analysis of the interaction between mother and child began 5 minutes after starting the tape. 10 minutes of each videosample have been transcribed. All utterances of the mother were transcribed, as well as her non-verbal behaviour, that is all gestures and acts that could be considered an attentional strategy, like moving a toy or tapping the child. For the child, all attentional shifts to the mother were registered.

3.1 Attentional strategies of the mothers

To find out whether the mothers need to attract their (deaf or hearing) child's attention explicitly less often as the child grows older (hypothesis 1), each first utterance within a turn of the deaf mothers was coded for an attentional strategy.

Two non-explicit attentional strategies could be identified:

Strategy A: the mother does not actively try to gain the child's attention before an utterance is produced. The mother starts signing and/or talking after the child has looked up at her.

Strategy B consists of those utterances where the mother starts signing and/or talking when the child is not looking at her, assuming that the child will look up.

Two explicit attentional strategies are:

Strategy C, where the mother assumes responsibility for the visibility of her signing in an explicit way. For instance, the child may be looking at a picture of a horse and the mother makes the sign HORSE near the picture, within the visual field of the child, thus dislocating the sign.

Strategy D: before signing and/or talking the mother tries to attract the child's visual attention by moving an object, by calling the child's name, by tapping the child or waving an arm or hand in the child's visual field (for a more detailed description of the attentional strategies see Appendix 1).

The categorisation of the attentional strategies used by the deaf mothers is summarized as follows:

Attentional strategies used by the deaf mothers:

Non-explicit	A: mother signs and/or talks after child looks up
	B: mother starts signing and/or talking when child is not looking
Explicit	C: mother dislocates signs
	D: mother actively attracts child's attention

The next step in the analysis of the attentional strategies used by the mothers was to compare the use of a non-explicit strategy (A and B) to the use of an explicit strategy (C and D) in the two sessions. If hypothesis 1 is correct, an increase in categories A and B compared to categories C and D should be seen in the session when the children are aged 1;11.

3.2 Attentional behaviour of the deaf and hearing children.

To see whether the children show a development in attentional behaviour (hypothesis 2) the attentional shift from not-looking to looking at the mother was coded. Three different categories of attentional shift were used.

When the child looks up at the mother without being prompted in any way, this is coded as a spontaneous look (category 1). If the mother starts signing and/or talking while the child is not looking at her, the positive reaction of the child (measured in a shift in eye-gaze direction) is categorized as (2). When the mother explicitly tries to draw the child's attention (as in strategy D of the attentional strategies) and the child looks up at her, this attentional behaviour was coded as (3). It is expected that all children show a significant change in their attentional behaviour, that is that category (1) will increase over time and also in proportion to (2) and (3). Below the categories of the children's attentional shifts are summarized.

Attentional shifts of the children:

1. child looks up spontaneously at mother
2. child looks up after mother starts signing and/or talking
3. child looks up after attention has been explicitly drawn by mother

These three categories are clearly related to the strategies coded for the deaf mothers. It is obvious that strategy C (mother dislocates signs) does not require an attentional shift of the children and therefore there are only three categories for the attentional behaviour of the children. It is clear that the child can look spontaneously at the mother without this necessarily being followed by communication. It is also clear that the mothers can use attentional strategies B (start to sign/talk) and D (move object/tap/wave/call-name) without them being successful. These cases will not be discussed here.

3.3 Different development of deaf and hearing children

The third analysis concerns a comparison of the development of the attentional shift of the deaf and the hearing children.

The number of spontaneous looks of the deaf children is compared to the number of spontaneous looks of the hearing children for the two sessions. It is predicted that the deaf children will look up spontaneously more often. Furthermore, the number of positive reactions of the children to non-explicit strategy B (mother starts signing/talking) and to explicit strategy D (object/tap/wave/name-calling) are also compared. The deaf children are expected to show a larger increase in reaction to these strategies than the hearing children. This is expected because the hearing children have access to all spoken utterances without having to look at their mother, while the deaf children have no access to any of their mother's utterances, whether signed or spoken, unless they pay visual attention.

4 RESULTS
4.1 Attentional strategies used by the mothers

For the attentional strategies used by the deaf mothers it was predicted, that as the children grow older, the mothers would need to attract their attention explicitly less often (hypothesis 1). Table 2 shows the frequencies of the different strategies used by the deaf mothers[4] at the two ages of the children.

Table 2: Frequencies of attentional strategies A, B, C and D used by the deaf mothers (n=5) at ages 0;11 and 1;11 of the children (n=5)

Strategies used by Deaf mothers	Age of the children	
	0;11	1;11
A	37	109
B	139	165
C	39	76
D	51	59

To see if the mothers indeed used the explicit strategies less as the children grew older, the use of strategies A and B was compared to the use of strategies C and D. In

Table 3 the number of non-explicit and explicit strategies used by all mothers are given for the compared recordings. To test for statistical significance the Chi-square test was used (Everitt 1986).

Table 3: Number of non-explicit strategies and explicit strategies by the deaf mothers (n=5) with the children (n=5), at ages 0;11 and 1;11

Age of the children	Non-explicit A and B	Explicit C and D
0;11	176	90
1;11	274	135

Although there is an increase in the mothers' use of the non-explicit strategies A and B, this change was not significantly different from the increase in use of strategies C and D, the explicit strategies ($p \leq 0.001$; df=1; χ^2=0.049). This means that over one year, there is no significant difference in the level of explicitness in how the deaf mothers attract their child's attention. Therefore hypothesis 1 is not supported.

However, if strategy A is taken alone and compared to strategies B, C and D (see Table 4), we do find a significant change in the use of this strategy over time ($p \leq 0.001$; df=1; χ^2 =15.44)

Table 4: Use of strategy A compared to use of strategies B, C and D by the deaf mothers (n=5) at age 0;11 and 1;11 of the children (n=5)

Age of the children	Strategy A	Strategy B C D
0;11	37	229
1;11	109	300

A significant increase in strategy A implies a significant increase in spontaneous looking from the child. This analysis is presented in the following section.

4.2 Spontaneous visual attention of the deaf and hearing children

The number of spontaneous looks of the deaf and hearing children (category 1) were compared to the number of looks in response to strategy B (mother starts signing/talking) and strategy D (tap etc.) (categories 2 and 3). There was a significant change in the attentional behaviour of the children ($p \leq 0.005$; df=1; χ^2=7.879): the increase in spontaneous looks is significantly larger than the increase in responsive looks (see Table 5).

Table 5: Number of spontaneous looks of all children (n=5) compared to the number of looks responsive to strategies B and D used by the deaf mothers (n=5), at ages 0;11 and 1;11.

Age of the children	Spontaneous looks (1)	Responsive looks (2 and 3)
0;11	67	91
1;11	157	115

It can be concluded that the children check back with their mother more often when they are 1;11 than they do at the age of 0;11. Hypothesis 2 can be accepted. This is true for the children as a group.

On inspection of the individual scores[4] all children show an increase in the number of spontaneous looks taken over a period of 10 minutes. But the score of Sander (hearing) contributes most to the significant increase in the number of spontaneous looks compared to responsive looks.

4.3 Different development of deaf and hearing children

It was predicted that the deaf children will show a different development in their attentional behaviour compared to the hearing children.

4.3.1 Development of spontaneous looks of deaf children and of hearing children

Because the deaf children are dependent on visual information, it was predicted that the increase in spontaneous looks from 0;11 to 1;11 will be larger for the deaf children than for the hearing children.

Table 6: Number of spontaneous looks of deaf children(n=2) compared to number of spontaneous looks of hearing children (n=3).

Age of the children	Deaf children	Hearing children
0;11	29	38
1;11	84	73

The number of spontaneous looks at the mother increased between 0;11 and 1;11 for all children[5]. But there is no significant difference in this increase between the deaf children and the hearing children as groups ($p \leq 0.001$; df=1; $\chi^2=1.95$). However, the score of Sander is different from the other two hearing children, Jonas and Alex. Actually, Sander's development in visual attention giving resembles that of the twins, and at age 1;11 also that of Carla. If we exclude Sander from the group of hearing children in the statistical analysis, there is a significant difference between the deaf and hearing children in spontaneous visual behaviour ($p \leq 0.01$ df=1 $\chi^2=8.05$).

4.3.2 Response to strategy B

The prediction is that the deaf children will look more often when their mother starts signing and/or talking (strategy B) than the hearing children. In order to examine this, the positive and negative reactions were compared. By a negative reaction 'no observable reaction by the child' is meant. The data were classified in 2x2 and 2x2x2 tables to test for statistical significance by means of the Chi-square test (Everitt 1986). The frequencies of the children's responses to strategy B are presented in Table 7.

Table 7: Number of positive and negative reactions to strategy B by the deaf (n=2) and hearing children (n=3).

Age of the children	Deaf children		Hearing children	
	positive	negative	positive	negative
0;11	13	14	42	70
1;11	19	7	47	92

At both time points the hearing children react significantly less to strategy B than the deaf children (proportionally), but in fact the difference is highly significant at age 1;11 ($p \leq 0.001$; df=1; $\chi^2=14.607$). At this age, the hearing children show a significant increase in their ignoring (or at least not looking up at) their mother's starting to sign/talk ($p \leq 0.005$; df=1; $\chi^2=8.87$). The reaction of the children seems to be closely related to their hearing status and age ($p \leq 0.01$; df=3; $\chi^2=11.345$).

It is clear that the mothers use strategy B with the hearing children far more often than with the deaf children at both ages. But the deaf children respond positively more frequently to this strategy than the hearing children.

4.3.3 Response to strategy D

Just as for strategy B, it was expected that the deaf children would respond differently to their mother's actively trying to gain their attention (strategy D) than the hearing children. The 2x2x2 Chi-square test was used to test for statistical significance. The frequencies are presented in Table 8.

Table 8: Number of positive and negative reactions to strategy D by the deaf (n=2) and hearing children (n=3)

Age of the children	Deaf children		Hearing children	
	positive	negative	positive	negative
0;11	9	6	27	9
1;11	34	6	14	5

A significant difference is found between the deaf and the hearing children over time in their reactions to the use of strategy D by the deaf mothers ($p \leq 0.001$; df=4; $\chi^2=19.772$). The deaf children show an increase in the number of positive responses at age 1;11 whereas the hearing children show a decrease. There is a difference in the direction of development for the two groups of children over this age range. It is perhaps worth noting here that the mother of the deaf twins uses one sub-category of strategy D, that is attracting her children's attention by means of tapping or touching them, more often than the mothers of the hearing children if they are compared at age 1;11. The data from the mother of the other deaf child, Carla, also support this finding.

5 DISCUSSION

It can be concluded against expectation that there is no change in the attentional behaviour of the deaf mothers with respect to explicitness of attention getting. However, the deaf mothers do show a significant increase in communication after the child looks up spontaneously.

Correspondingly, all children show an increase in spontaneous looks over time.

There is no difference between the deaf and hearing children as groups in the development of spontaneous looks at their mother. However, one hearing child, Sander, showed a development similar to the deaf twins. If his data are excluded from the analysis, there is a difference between the deaf and the hearing children as groups in the development of spontaneous looks at their mother: the deaf children look more frequently.

A difference is found between the groups of children in their reactions to their mother's actively attracting their attention (strategy D) over time.

The deaf children show an increase in the number of positive responses, whereas the hearing children show a decrease at the age of 1;11. With the deaf children this strategy is used more frequently over time, and with the hearing children less frequently.

The deaf children are also more responsive to the mother's beginning to sign and/ or talk (strategy B), while the hearing children are significantly less responsive to this strategy. This is true despite the fact that the mothers use strategy B more often with the hearing children than with the deaf children.

A brief look at the language input the children receive seems to be in order. In Table 9 the percentages of the NL, SLN and SC utterances offered to the children are presented.

Table 9: Language input (%) offered to the deaf (n=2) and hearing children (n=3) by the deaf mothers (n=5) at ages 0;11 and 1;11.

Children	Language input	Age of the children	
		0;11	1;11
Deaf children	NL	3	4
	SLN	30	40
	SC	65	55
Hearing children	NL	60	25
	SLN	2	5
	SC	35	70

NL is Dutch, SLN is Sign Language of the Netherlands, SC is Simultaneous Communication.

The NL utterances addressed to the hearing children are all uttered with voice, as are all SC utterances. To the deaf children, it is irrelevant whether the NL or SC utterances are uttered with or without voice; what counts for them is that 95% of all utterances contain signs. So the hearing children consistently receive a large amount of input in which there is a spoken part (NL and SC), whereas the deaf children consistently receive a large amount of input in which signing is used (SLN and SC). In terms of receiving communication, the SLN utterances require the hearing children to give visual attention and these constitute only 5 % of the total language input at the age of 1;11.

So the visual attention giving behaviour of the children appears to be influenced by their hearing status and by the language input. A more detailed analysis at a later date will indicate the exact role of each of these factors, i.e. whether the specific language form of an utterance, that is the choice of Dutch, Sign Language of the Netherlands or Simultaneous Communication has an effect on the attentional behaviour of the children.

Footnotes

* Beppie van den Bogaerde: General Linguistics, University of Amsterdam, Spuistraat 210, 1012 VT Amsterdam, The Netherlands.
Tel.: +31-20-525-3853/3835. Fax: +31-20-525-3052. Email: beppie@alf.let.uva.nl
† I would like to thank Claudia Blankenstijn, Heleen Bos and Jane Coerts for their useful comments on earlier draftes of this paper, and give special thanks to Anne Mills for her help in preparing the final version. Also thanks to Rob Schoonen for his advice on the statistics. They are of course not responsible for my errors.

1. Simultaneous Communication has been defined in several ways in the literature on sign linguistics. The following definition is used in this study: all utterances in which non-obligatory spoken or mouthed components are produced together with signs. (see also Coerts, 1992; Schermer 1990; Pimiä 1990).
2. 0;9 means 0 years and 9 months.
3. The filming was done using a Panasonic Camcorder M7 CCD with a JVC monitor. The tapes were transcribed using a JVC monitor (TM 150 PSN) and a Panasonic (AG-6200) videorecorder.
4. Please note that for all data that are given and for all statistical analyses, the data of Carla and her mother are not included.
5. The individual scores of the number of spontaneous and responsive looks of the children are given in Appendix 2.

Bibliography

Barnes, S., Gutfreund, M., Satterley, D. and Wells, G. [1983]. Characteristics of adults' speech which predict children's language development. *Journal of Child Language* 10, pp. 65–84.

Blankenstijn, C. and Bogaerde van den, B. [1989]. *Hand in Hand. Tweetalige Aspecten in het Taalaanbod van Drie Dove Moeders aan hun Horende Kinderen*. Master thesis, Institute for General Linguistics, University of Amsterdam, Amsterdam.

Bogaerde van den, B. and Mills, A. [in press]. Word order in language input to children: SLN or Dutch. *Working papers of ISLA*.

Bruner, J. [1974]. The ontogenesis of speech acts. *Journal of Child Language* 2, pp. 1–19.

Coerts, J. [1992]. *Nonmanual Grammatical Markers: An Analysis of Interrogatives, Negations and Topicalisations in SLN*. Doctoral Dissertation. Drukkerij UvA, Amsterdam.

Coerts, J., Mills, A. and Bogaerde van den, B. [1990]. *Language Input, Interaction and the Acquisition of Sign Language of the Netherlands*. Paper related to poster presentation at the 4th European Conference of Developmental Psychology. Stirling, Scotland, August 1990.

Ebbinghaus, H. and Hessmann, J. [1990]. German words in German Sign Language, in: Prillwitz, S. and Vollhaber, T. (eds) *Current Trends in European Sign Language Research*. Signum Press, Hamburg.

Everitt, B.S. [1986]. *The Analysis of Contingency Tables*. Chapman and Hall, London.

Gregory, S. [1985]. *Deaf Infants and Their Mothers: The Development of Their Communication Skills*. Paper presented to the International Congress on Education of the Deaf. Manchester, England.

Harris, M., Clibbens, J., Chasin, J. and Tibbitts, R. [1989]. The social context of early sign language development. *First Language* 9, pp. 81–97.

Harris, M., Clibbens, J., Tibbitts, R. and Chasin, J. [1987]. Communication between deaf mothers and their deaf infants, in: Griffiths, P., Mills, A. and Local, J. (eds) *Proceedings of the Child Language Seminar*. University of York, York.

Kyle, J. and Ackerman, J. [1990]. Signing for infants: Deaf mothers using BSL, in: Edmondson, W.H. and Karlsson, F. (eds) *SLR '87: Papers from the Fourth International Symposium on Sign Language Research*. Signum Press, Hamburg.

Kyle, J.G., Ackerman, J. and Woll, B. [1987]. Early mother-infant interaction: language and pre-language in deaf families, in: Griffiths, P., Mills, A. and Local, J. (eds) *Proceedings of the Child Language Seminar*. University of York, York.

Maestas y Moores, L. [1980]. Early linguistic environment: interactions of deaf parents with their infants. *Sign Language Studies* 26, pp. 1–13.

Mills, A. and Bogaerde van den, B. [1991]. *Input and Interaction in Deaf Families*. Paper presented at the 16th Boston Conference on Language Acquisition, October 1991.

Mills, A. and Coerts, J. [1989]. *Uit de Eerste Hand*. Onderzoeksverslag van de werkgroep 'Adults' input to children learning sign'. Institute for General Linguistics, University of Amterdam.

— [1990]. Functions and forms of bilingual input: children learning a sign language as one of their first languages, in: Prillwitz, S. and Vollhaber, T. (eds) *Current Trends in European Sign Language Research*. Signum Press, Hamburg.

Mohay, H., Luttrell, R. and Milton, L. [1991]. *How Much, How Often and in What Form Should Linguistic Input Be Given to Deaf Infants?* Paper presented at the Australia and New Zealand Conference for Educators of the Deaf, Surfers Paradise, Queensland. Unpublished manuscript.

Pimiä, P. [1990]. Semantic features of some mouth patterns in Finnish Sign Language, in: Prillwitz, S. and Vollhaber, T. (eds) *Current Trends in European Sign Language Research*. Signum Press, Hamburg.

Schermer, T.M. [1990]. *In Search of a Language: Influences from Spoken Dutch on Sign Language of the Netherlands*. Doctoral Dissertation, University of Amsterdam. Eburon Publishers, Delft.

Swisher, M.V. [1986]. *Conversational Interaction between Deaf Children and Their Hearing Mothers: The Role of Visual Attention*. Paper presented at the Conference on Theoretical Issues in Sign Language Research. Rochester, NY.

Appendix 1

Attentional strategies used by deaf mothers (DM)

A	signs made in normal location
Anl	all spoken utterances produced after child looks up at DM
A1	second/more utterance in turn of DM in SLN or SC
A2	second/more utterance in turn of DM in NL
B1	mother starts SLN or SC utterance
B2	mother starts NL utterance
C1	sign(s) made on child
C2	sign(s) made in signing space of child
C3	sign(s) made in visual field of child
D1	1 DM moves object
	2 DM makes sound with object
	3 DM moves and makes sound with object
D2	1 DM adjusts position of child
	2 DM taps/touches child
D3	1 DM uses voice (calls name)
	2 DM waves
	3 DM makes noise/vibration

n.b.: For the purpose of this paper, all sub-categories are taken together.

Attentional behaviour of the children
1.   spontaneous look at deaf mother
2.   mother signs and child responds (+) or not (-)
     mother talks/uses SC and child responds (+) or not (-)
3.   D1.1   DM moves object and child responds (+) or not (-)
     D1.2   DM makes sound with object and child responds (+) or not (-)
     D1.3   DM makes sound + moves object and child responds (+) or not (-)
     D2.1   DM moves child and child responds (+) or not (-)
     D2.2   DM taps/touches child and child responds (+) or not (-)
     D3.1   DM calls name or shouts and child responds (+) or not (-)
     D3.2   DM waves and child responds (+) or not (-)
     D3.3   DM makes noise (+) vibration and child responds (+) or not (-)

Appendix 2

(see paragraph 4.2)
Spontaneous looks (1) versus looks responsive to strategy B (2) and D (3): individual scores of all children (data of Carla are not in statistical analysis). The Chi-square test (Everitt 1986) is used for the analysis:

	0;11		1;11		
	(1)	(2,3)	(1)	(2,3)	
(Carla	-	-	45	46)	
Laura	15	17	32	25	$(p \leq 0.001\ df=1\ X^2=0.606)$
Mark	14	5	52	28	$(p \leq 0.001\ df=1\ X^2=1.047)$
Jonas	19	14	20	17	$(p \leq 0.001\ df=1\ X^2=0.88)$
Sander	9	27	40	18	$(p \leq 0.001\ df=1\ X^2=17.2)$
Alex	10	28	13	27	$(p \leq 0.001\ df=1\ X^2=0.35)$

(see paragraph 4.3.1)
Individual scores of all children for spontaneous looks at ages 0;11 and 1;11. The Chi-square test (Everitt 1986) is used for the analysis:

	0;11	1;11	
Laura:	15	32	$(p \leq 0.001\ df=1\ X^2=6.14)$
Mark	14	52	$(p \leq 0.001\ df=1\ X^2=14.61)$
Jonas	19	20	$(p \leq 0.001\ df=1\ X^2=0.026)$
Sander	9	40	$(p \leq 0.001\ df=1\ X^2=19.612)$
Alex	10	13	$(p \leq 0.001\ df=1\ X^2=0.392)$

Early sign combinations of deaf children in Sign Language of The Netherlands †

JANE COERTS AND ANNE MILLS *

1 INTRODUCTION

In the early combinations of words or signs in children one can see the beginning of syntax. These utterances are the reflection of syntactic knowledge and thus of crucial interest to research in language acquisition. In particular they are relevant to the discussion on questions of innate knowledge versus general learning strategies.

Recent work on early syntax has concentrated on questions of determining the knowledge that is innate in the child. For example, questions have been addressed such as whether functional categories are available from the beginning and if so, which functional categories. In order to explain the acquisition of language features which are clearly specific and not universal, such as verb placement, the model of parameter setting derived from a generative syntactic model has been proposed (Hyams 1986). In this model children are faced with a limited number of choices which will specify the particular language the child will learn. An idea related to this is that before children make a choice on the basis of the evidence in their language, they have an unmarked form or default setting of the parameter (Hyams 1986), although this proposal is not undisputed (Lebeaux, 1987).

Much work has been done recently in the parameter framework, particularly in relationship to the expression of arguments and word order and agreement. These are some of the questions to be addressed here using the data from children learning Sign Language of the Netherlands (SLN).

On the basis of general acquisition principles as proposed by Hyams (1986) it is assumed that children will allow null arguments in subject position, since this is the default setting for this so-called 'pro-drop' parameter. That is, children will drop subjects in their earliest utterances whether or not the language they are learning is a language that allows this. If children are learning a language such as English which does not allow null subjects, then they will have to re-set the parameter in Hyams' terms and this resetting will have to be triggered. A child learning Italian will not have to re-set the parameter since Italian is a pro-drop language.

It is reported that subjects are dropped in the early child utterances in all the languages that have been investigated from a parameter perspective (e.g. Italian, English: Hyams 1986; Japanese: Mazuka et al. 1986; Hebrew: Berman 1990; French, German: Weissenborn 1992; ASL: Lillo-Martin 1992). In the course of development children learn to produce subjects in those languages that require them. It is assumed within a parametric framework that for these languages the parameter is reset on the basis of syntactic evidence from the language of the environment.

Other explanations have been proposed for children omitting subjects; these proposals involve pragmatic principles such as redundancy of information or processing problems such as constraints on the length of the verb phrase. Hyams & Wexler (1991) discuss these alternative proposals and reject them since the alternative explanations do not account for the fact that subjects are omitted more often compared to other constituents such as objects. We will return to this point later.

SLN appears to be a pro-drop language, that is the adult language allows null subjects although the quantity of and constraints on the dropping of subjects are not clear (Bos 1988, 1992; Coerts 1992).[1]

The prediction from a default parametric model is that children learning SLN will drop subjects from the beginning on the basis of the default setting and continue to do so, since no resetting is necessary. According to Hyams (1992) there should be an asymmetry between the quantity of subjects dropped and objects dropped. This prediction will be tested here, comparing the ommission of subjects with that of objects.

Order of constituents is also a language-specific feature which the child needs to set as a parameter, in particular with regard to verb-position. SLN appears to be a language with verb-final or SOV order, assuming the results of Coerts (1992, this volume) are representative. As she points out, her results are based on elicited signing and need to be confirmed from the study of spontaneous signing. In SLN orders other than SOV occur but it is not clear at this point what the conditions are that allow other orders and which orders in SLN are strictly ungrammatical. Some of the variations from SOV order appear to be in association with the type of semantic arguments present in the sentence.

Clearly children have to learn these regularities of order. Again within a parametric framework it is assumed that they quickly set the parameter for the basic order and later learn the movement rules necessary for the other possible orders (Clahsen & Muysken 1986; Weissenborn 1990).

It is impossible to strictly test these claims with regard to SLN until the description of the adult language is more complete. In particular the grammatical constraints in SLN need to be clear. We will work however here on the assumption that SLN is an SOV language. For SLN therefore children should learn to place the subject in initial position and verb in final position quickly. In adult SLN locative phrases appear to occur in first position as the result of a movement rule. Children should acquire this rule later, implying that locative phrases will not be in first position in early utterances.

In summary the following predictions were examined using the data from two children up to age 2;6.

Children will:

a) produce a large number of utterances with null subjects

b) where subjects are realized, rapidly produce them in first position

c) rapidly locate verbs in final position

d) later locate locative phrases in first position

2 DATA AND ANALYSIS

The spontaneous language from monthly recordings from two deaf children learning SLN was analyzed. These two children form part of the longitudinal acquisition data-base which is being built up in Amsterdam. In the data-base we have data from six children learning SLN in the family setting (see van den Bogaerde this volume).

The two children selected are the twins, Laura and Mark, who have been recorded since they were 11 months old. Both children were born with a severe hearing loss. Mark has a loss of more than 90dB, Laura a loss of 70dB in her best ear. She has a hearing aid but does not wear it in recording sessions and infrequently in general.

Their mother is deaf and their father is a hearing child of deaf parents and fluent in SLN. They have a hearing brother who is bilingual.

The data to be analyzed for this paper are taken from the monthly recordings between ages 1;4 and 2;6. Our interest was in the earliest sign combinations and this determined the beginning point of our analysis. Each recording was minimally 20 minutes long and made in a free play situation, the child playing alone with the mother.

All sign combinations from these recordings were analyzed together with one sign utterances which consisted of just a verb. These utterances were categorized with respect to the presence or absence of the subject. The subjects were categorized as lexical pronouns or lexical noun phrases. All utterances containing a transitive verb[2] were examined for the presence or absence of the object.

The order of arguments was listed for each clause; a distinction was made between declaratives and questions. (Questions will not be explored further here). In particular the position of the subjects and locative phrases in declaratives were noted.

A decision was taken to eliminate those utterances with a labelling function from the analysis since it is impossible to distinguish between the use of an INDEX as a referring pronoun and the use of an INDEX to indicate location. In the context of looking at a book where there is a picture of a cat, the child's utterance (Example 1) is ambiguous.

Example 1.

INDEX$_{book}$ CAT

The index may be indicating the location of a cat which would mean that the utterance should be translated as "there is a cat". On the other hand the index might be referring to the object 'cat' which would lead to the translation "that is a cat". The syntactic status of the index depends on the interpretation. [3] This lack of clarity would make it difficult to examine the predictions relating to the position of these two different constituents.

The position of the verb in declaratives was categorized as initial, medial and final. The categorization for medial position was only possible where there were more than two constituents in the clause. This may mean that the category verb-final is overrepresented. In two sign utterances, as in two word utterances, it is impossible to make a valid distinction between these two positions, as other researchers have reported for the acquisition of spoken languages.

3 RESULTS
3.1 General linguistic development

We will first give a general picture of the increase in complexity of the children's language over the period studied. For both children the number of sign combinations increased steadily until 2;6.

Laura produced her first combination of signs at age 1;10 and the majority of her utterances were combinations at age 2;4. Mark is somewhat in advance of his sister: his first combination was found at age 1;4 and the majority were combinations by 2;1. The number of combinations produced in the analyzed 20 minutes of the last recording (age 2;6) was 52 for Laura and 106 for Mark. Mark produces more multi-combinations than Laura and is in general more communicative.

Table 1: *The development of general complexity in the two children, Laura and Mark, until age 2;6*

	Laura	Mark
first combination	1;10	1;4
majority of utterances combinations	2;4	2;1
frequency at 2;6	52	106

The majority of clauses consist of an INDEX plus one or more lexical signs. Clauses containing just lexical signs increase proportionately but remain in the minority. The indexes the children use in these early combinations all refer to present referents; the use of an index to refer to an abstract location has not occurred by 2;6.

3.2 Missing subjects

We will first consider the prediction that a large number of subjects will be missing since the form of all early grammars should allow this. Because SLN appears to license null arguments in subject position, children should continue to drop subjects.

Firstly we considered all utterances which were combinations of signs for the presence of a subject irrespective of the presence of a verb. This analysis showed that for both children 20% of subjects are missing from the beginning and that this proportion does not change over time—that is until our analysis stopped at 2;6. Utterances such as Examples 2 and 3 are illustrative of the language production from both children.

Example 2.

INDEX$_I$ CLEVER
'I am clever.'

Example 3.

INDEX$_{doll}$ SLEEP
'the doll must go to sleep.'

Previous analyses of missing subjects, however, usually consider only those utterances containing a verb and many exclude the verb 'to be' or equivalents. We therefore carried out a second analysis in which all utterances containing a verb [4] were counted and then further categorized into utterances with a missing subject, or utterances containing a pronominal subject (INDEX) or lexical subject. The utterances could consist of a verb only or a verb in combination with one or more other signs. It must be pointed out here that for both children less than half the sign combinations taken over all recordings contained a verb: Laura 38% and Mark 47% (see discussion below).

The results of this analysis are presented in Table 2. We set out the utterances consisting of a verb only in a separate column since we consider it important to make the distinction between missing subjects in single word utterances and in combinations. We give the figures for two periods: up to age 2;0 and 2;0 - 2;6. A division was made at age 2;0 since from this age combinations are clearly evident in the production of both children (see Table 1).

Table 2: Numbers (and percentages) of missing subjects in Laura and Mark in the periods to 2;0 and 2;0-2;6.

Age	verb only		verb + X total utt		verb + X no subject		verb + X % no subj	
	L	M	L	M	L	M	L	M
→2;0	21	21	1	11	0	5	(0%)	45
→2;6	49	34	46	95	18	30	39%	32%

These results indicate that the early period up to 2;0 is problematic for the analysis since both children are producing predominantly verb-only utterances compared to the verb combinations. The percentage of missing subjects in the verb combinations cannot reliably be calculated since the figures are so small. If the verb-only utterances, which necessarily have a missing subject, are included, then the percentage of missing subjects increases for the period up to 2;0 for Linda to 95% and for Mark to 81%, for the period from 2;0 to 2;6 for Linda to 50% and for Mark to 60%. This seems an inflated percentage which is not indicative of missing subjects but rather of the constraint of producing one-sign utterances. Both children prior to 2;0 have a predominance of one-sign utterances (see Table 1). In previous studies the children studied were older and so it can be assumed that they were definitely not still in the one-word stage. In Hyams' analysis of the data from Brown's children learning English (Hyams & Wexler 1991), for example, Adam has 55% missing subjects at around two and a half years and this declines to 29% around three years. For Eve the rate of missing subjects is 39% which drops to 15%.

Hyams and Wexler interpret this drop as evidence for the re-setting of the pro-drop parameter. This variation between children raises the general question of how large the rate of missing subjects must be for there to be plausible interpretation that the omission of subjects is syntactic. Hyams (1992:265) argues that frequency is not important but that the two significant aspects for interpretation is the change over time (for children acquiring a non-pro-drop language) and the asymmetry of missing subjects compared to missing objects. SLN is a language which allows missing subjects, therefore change over time is not relevant. It is not evident to what extent null subjects are possible in the adult language and therefore it cannot be assessed to what extent the children are close to the adult norm. In these two children there is no evident development from 2;0 to 2;6 if the six recordings after age 2;0 presented in Table 2 are considered individually: the level stays around 30%.

The subject/object asymmetry is predicted for all languages and therefore relevant for SLN. Hyams (1992:262-3) argues that there will always be a subject/object asymmetry in the child's use of null arguments since, according to the analysis which she adopts, null objects are dependent on the presence of variables in the child's grammar. Early child grammars are assumed to always be without variables;

variables will appear on the basis of maturation. Little *pro* is assumed to be present from the beginning. On the basis of this grammatical analysis and acquisition assumptions, null objects will always be later than null subjects in those languages which allow them. Hyams cites evidence from Japanese (Mazuka et al. 1986) that this is the case. SLN allows null objects (Bos 1988 & 1992), as does Japanese, and this assymetry should also occur.

From the utterances considered for the analysis of missing subjects (that is verb-only and verb in combination) a null object was determined when the verb was transitive and an object could be expected from the context. [5] Table 3 presents the results of this analysis.

Table 3: *Numbers (and percentages) of missing objects in Laura and Mark in the periods to 2;0 and 2;0-2;6*

Age	verb only total utt.		trans. verb no object		trans. verb no object		verb + X	
	L	M	L	M	L	M	L	M
→2;0	2	5	0	0	0	0	–	–
→2;6	11	8	15	38	6	16	40%	42%

As with the null subject analysis if the percentage of null objects is calculated including the verb-only utterances then the percentage for Laura in the period from 2;0 to 2;6 is 65% and for Mark 52%. The same objections to this percentage calculation apply as in the null subject analysis, that is the percentage would seem to be inflated, particularly for Linda because of her larger number of one sign utterances in relation to her generally slower language development.

A comparison of Tables 2 and 3 does not reveal a clear asymmetry between null subjects and null objects. Whichever percentages are compared, there are equal or even larger amounts of null objects compared to null subjects. The predicted dominance of null subjects is not evident.

This quantitative result would seem to challenge Hyams' grammatical account of missing subjects since her account predicts the subject/object asymmetry for every language. The higher percentage of object drop in SLN cannot easily be explained in terms of processing principles (Hyams & Wexler 1991). It would seem to reflect a language-specific feature and suggests that children can acquire a grammar with variables early.

It is also striking from our data that the children acquire a lexical pronoun with the form INDEX early: both children produce roughly equal numbers of full lexical and lexical pronoun subjects from the beginning. According to the Avoid Pronoun Principle of Hymas (1986:96) children produce very few pronouns in early productions whatever type of language they are learning. For the pro-drop language,

Italian, Hyams suggests that the use of lexical pronouns is rare. In the English data Hyams presents from Adam (1992:256) it appears that the use of lexical pronoun subjects is low in the first recordings at age 2;7 compared to the amount of full lexical subjects [6] but increases. In our data, the form INDEX is comparatively frequent from the beginning but it is used far more often for subjects than for objects: approximately three times as often. This suggests that the acquisition of INDEX should be seen as linked to the syntactic function of subject: it has to be acquired as little pro. If a total explanation of the early acquisition of the form INDEX were to lie in the fact that it ressembles a deictic gesture, then it should be used equally for subjects and objects, which is not the case. Redundancy as a pragmatic explanation might account for the smaller number of lexical pronouns INDEX for objects since objects are more often new information in the utterance. On the other hand redundancy does not explain the equal use of null subjects and null objects.

3.3 Position of subject

On the basis of adult sign order it was predicted that children would quickly learn to position the subject in first position in declarative clauses, in those utterances where they produce the subject.

The analysis showed that for both children the majority of subjects do occur in first position, whether the first subject is an index as in Example 2 or a lexical subject as in Example 4.

Example 4.

MARK TURN-OVER
'I (Mark) have turned (the pieces) over.'

But the percentage is higher for Laura than for Mark: 77% vs. 58%. There is no difference in these percentages whether all utterances are considered or only those containing a verb. Neither is there a clear shift in the proportion of utterances with subject in first position over time. We considered whether Mark's lower percentage might be attributable to his having learned to position locative phrases in first position. This was however not the case. Laura clearly places locative phrases after the subject (24 of 27 cases) as Example 5 shows.

Example 5.

BIKE RED OUTSIDE
'the red bike is outside.'

Mark has a tendency to do this but it is less strong. He produces more multi-sign combinations and in general his order is more varied.

3.4 Verb position

It was predicted that the verb would quickly be produced in final position. As remarked above, for both children less than half the sign combinations contained a verb: Laura 38% and Mark 47%. From the analysis of the language input to the children at age 1;11 (van den Bogaerde & Mills 1992) we observed that the mother of the twins, just as the other mothers in the project, produces the majority of utterances with no verb—as high as 70%. These utterances are mostly non-verbal predicate constructions. If the frequency of verb use and variation of the types of verb in the input is a predictor of verb frequency in children (Gillis & Verlinden 1988:28) then this would account for the low frequency found in the children.

The results of the analysis of position of the verb is set out in Table 4. The positions are defined as initial, final and medial but as was pointed out above, in clauses containing two constituents it is impossible to find medial position. It was decided to count the verb in a two constituent utterance as being in final position but this may bias the results.

Table 4: The position of the verb in Laura and Mark in the periods to 2;0 and 2;0-2;6.

Age	tot. utt. verb + X		V initial		V medial		V final	
L	M	L	M	L	M	L	M&P	
→2;0	I	II	0	5	0	0	I	6
			0 %	45%	0%	0%	100%	55%
→2;6	46	95	16	29	4	13	26	53
			35%	31%	8%	14%	57%	56%

The two children show a trend in the direction of the adult language, that is positioning the verb in final position. The strongest evidence for verb in final position are utterances with more than 2 constituents but of the verb-final utterances only 3 and 19 utterances for Linda and Mark respectively were of that length. Of the verb-initial utterances a considerable proportion had null subjects (9 utterances for both Linda and Mark) which might suggest that the verb would otherwise have been in second position.

An analysis of verb position in the input at age 1;11 (van den Bogaerde & Mills 1992) showed that the verb was approximately 50% of the time in final position in the adult utterances. For the children it must therefore be difficult to perceive the regularity which does exist in adult-adult sign: the same mother produces the verb in final position more than 90% of the time in adult-adult sign, just as other adult signers of SLN. It is another question why this regularity is not so strongly present in adult-child interaction.

4 RESULTS

The results with regard to the various predictions are varied. The predictions on constituent order were partly confirmed. The verb was more often in final position than not but this was only a tendency. The children did show a tendency to place subject in first position, although there was individual variation here.

When interpreting the data for the analysis of order of constituents it appeared that language input is clearly relevant. The children appear to be getting a blurred picture of the regularities, at least on the basis of our analysis of input at 1;11, than they would if exposed to the adult-adult form of SLN. We need to go much further with the analysis of variation in adult language since it has clear implications for learnability accounts of acquisition.

The data from missing subjects indicate that the grammatical account of Hyams is problematic. On the basis of her arguments there should exist a subject/object asymmetry with fewer null objects than null subjects in all early child grammars whatever the form of the adult grammar. In our data we found proportionally at least as many null objects as null subjects. If it is correct that children need to have access to variables in order to produce null objects, then it would appear that they have access to them very early in SLN acquisition.

Adone (1992) reports similar results in the acquisition of Mauritian Creole which also allows object drop in the adult form.

There is no a priori reason to think that this may be a characteristic of sign languages in general: the data from ASL (Lillo-Martin 1992) are not clear on whether such an subject/object asymmetry exists but certainly the children have null objects as well as null subjects.

The whole discussion of null arguments is fraught with the problem of frequency. Hyams (1992:265) writes that she doubts whether: "...a Null-subject parameter account (however formulated) of null subjects in child language is weakened or falsified by the fact that children vary in the frequency with which they use null subjects."

Other authors *however are* concerned with the difference in frequencies (see Weissenborn 1992 for a comparison of German and French) and draw different conclusions for a parametric model. It is not clear from any paper what change in frequencies constitute a 'change over time' relevant in the interpretation of the acquisition data of non-null subject languages: for example the German child of Weissenborn shifts from around 80% to around 20% whereas the French child shifts from 30% to 6%. For null subject languages this change over time is not crucial to the interpretation but it is not clear what constitutes a target level of null subjects and whether this is relevant.

Frequency is a problem too in the interpretation of 'a clear subject/object asymmetry'. As Lillo-Martin (1992) points out, the Japanese children studied by

Mazuka et al. (1986) have 17% null objects compared to 8% in the English children analyzed by Hyams (1992), both have an asymmetrical pattern in which null subjects dominate but can the 17% null objects be treated as evidence that the children acquire a grammar with variables later? The evidence presented here is not difficult to interpret since there is no asymmetry. We are also sure that we have representative data from the beginning of acquisition.

On the basis of the absence of asymmmetry we must conclude that a no-variable grammar is not necessarily acquired later but that the rate of acquisition is dependent on the language the child is exposed to. All our analyses also indicated that it is essential to consider the language input to the child, not just the adult form of the grammar, in order to be aware of the regularities the child is exposed to.

Footnotes

---

† This work was partly carried out while the second author was at the Netherlands Institute for Advanced Science as part of the Language Acquisition group,1991; we are grateful for the support of the Institute and colleagues from the group. Further we wish to express our gratitude to the Faculty of Arts, University of Amsterdam for their financial support of this project. Thanks also go to Hans den Besten, Beppie van den Bogaerde, Heleen Bos, Adrienne Bruyn and Maaike Verrips for their useful criticism of earlier versions of this paper.
* Jane Coerts and Anne Mills: General Linguistics, University of Amsterdam, Spuistraat 210, 1012 VT Amsterdam, The Netherlands.
Tel.: +31-20-525-3853/3835. Fax: +31-20-525-3052. Email: aemills@alf.let.uva.nl, or: jane@alf.let.uva.nl

1. It is possible that SLN is not a pro-drop language like Italian but a topic-drop language like Chinese (Huang 1984). This rests on a division of languages into sentence-oriented and discourse oriented, which we will not pursue here.
2. The classification of SLN verbs for transitivity is currently an object of research (Bos, forthcoming). For this analysis we partly based the classification on our knowledge of SLN but also drew on the Dutch verb system. Later results on the SLN verb system could mean that these data have to be re-analysed.
3. We will not enter here on a discussion of a point as a representational gesture (non-linguistic) as opposed to a symbolic gesture (linguistic). The utterances we have given a labelling function fall under the category which are seen as frequently having a non-linguistic function (Volterra, pers.comm.). These are excluded from analysis and therefore will not blur the results.
4. SLN like most sign languages investigated does not have a copula; the figures can therefore realistically be compared to the counts of other researchers in which utterances containing the verb 'to be' are usually omitted.

5. We are aware that we do not have a full enough description of SLN to be able to be able to determine transitivity in every case (see note 2).

6. The exact figures are not given in Hyams (1992) but from the figures given here and elsewhere it can be calculated that Adam's use of lexical pronouns was at least four times smaller than his use of NP lexical subjects.

Bibliography

Adone, D. [1992]. *Empty Categories in Mauritian Creole Child and Adult Grammar*. Paper to the Dept. of General Linguistics, University of Amsterdam, June 1992.

Berman, R. [1990]. On acquiring an (S)VO language: subjectless sentences in children's Hebrew. *Linguistics* 28, pp. 1135–1166.

Bogaerde, B. van den and Mills, A.E. [in press]. Word order in input to children: data from SLN, in: *ISLA Working Papers* .

Bos, H. [1994]. An auxiliary verb in Sign Language of the Netherlands (this volume).

Bos, H., Alons, L., Emmerik, W. et al. [1988]. *Persoons- en Locatiemarkering.:Een Onderzoek naar Acht Directionele Werkwoorden in de Nederlandse Gebarentaal*. Verslag van de Onderzoeksgroep 'Gebarentaal'. Institute for General Linguistics, University of Amsterdam.

Clahsen, H. and Muysken, P. [1986]. The availability of universal grammar to adult and child learners: a study of the acquisition of German word order. *Second Language Research* 2, pp. 93–119.

Coerts, J. [1994]. Constituent order in Sign Language of the Netherlands and the functions of pre-posed elements. (this volume).

— [in press]. Constituent order in Sign Language of the Netherlands, in: *ISLA Working Papers* .

Gillis, S. and Verlinden, A. [1988]. Nouns and verbs in early lexical development: effects of input frequency? *Antwerp Papers in Linguistics* 54, University of Antwerp.

Huang, J. [1984]. On the distribution and reference of empty pronouns. *Linguistic Inquiry* 15, pp. 531-574.

Hyams, N.M. [1986]. *Language Acquisition and the Theory of Parameters*. D. Reidel Publishing Company, Dordrecht.

— [1992]. A reanalysis of null subjects in child language, in: Weissenborn, J., Goodluck, H. and Roeper, T. (eds) *Theoretical Issues in Language Acquisition: Continuity and Change in Development*, pp. 249–268. Lawrence Erlbaum Associates, Hillsdale, NJ.

Hyams, N.M. and Wexler, K. [1991]. *On the Grammatical Basis of Null Subjects in Child Language*. Paper to NIAS, Wassenaar, March 1991.

Lebeaux, D. [1987]. Comments on Hyams, in: Roeper, T. and Williams, E. (eds) *Parameter Setting*, pp. 23–40. D. Reidel Publishing Company, Dordrecht.

Lillo-Martin, D. [1992]. Comments on Hyams and Weissenborn: on licensing and identification, in: Weissenborn, J., Goodluck, H. and Roeper, T. (eds) *Theoretical Issues in Language Acquisition: Continuity and Change in Development*, pp. 301–308. Lawrence Erlbaum Associates, Hillsdale, NJ.

Mazuka, R., Lust, B., Wakayama, T. and Snyder, W. [1986]. Distinguishing effects of parameters in early syntax acquisition: a cross-linguistic study of Japanese and English. *Papers and Reports on Child Language Development*. Stanford University, pp. 73–82.

Weissenborn, J. [1990]. Functional categories and verb movement: the acquisition of German syntax reconsidered, in: Rothweiler, M. (ed) *Spracherwerb und Grammatik: Linguistische Untersuchungen zum Erwerb von Syntax und Morphologie. Linguistische Berichte: Sonderheft 3*.

— [1992]. Null subjects in early grammars: implications for parameter-setting theories, in: Weissenborn, J., Goodluck, H. and Roeper, T. (eds) *Theoretical Issues in Language Acquisition: Continuity and Change in Development*, pp. 269–300. Lawrence Erlbaum Associates, Hillsdale, NJ.

School Sign Language of the Netherlands: the language of Dutch non-native signing deaf children.

HARRY KNOORS *

1 INTRODUCTION

The vast majority of deaf children have hearing parents who cannot sign at the moment that the deafness of their child is detected. In contrast with many deaf children of deaf parents, deaf children of hearing parents (DCHP) learn to sign later in life. In the Netherlands, as in many other countries, most of these non-native signing deaf children are brought up and educated in an environment in which the communication is supposed to take place through Sign Supported Speech. The philosophy of Total Communication (TC), prevalent in contemporary deaf education, resulted in a monolingual educational policy. The Sign Supported Dutch (SSD) used in the Netherlands consists of signs taken from the language of the deaf community, Sign Language of the Netherlands (SLN), and combined in a simultaneous way of communication, thus more or less adequately agreeing with the grammatical rules of Dutch (Harder & Knoors, 1987).

For some time educators of deaf children believed that the linguistic environment which surrounds DCHP is rather simple. Dutch would be the predominant language in this environment, be it in spoken and signed or in written form. Language acquisition by these deaf children could be viewed as a monolingual process in which Dutch in some form was both the input and the output. What we in fact have begun to realise is that quite the contrary is the case: the situation in which DCHP have to acquire language is far from simple (Bochner & Albertini, 1988; Loncke, Hoiting, Knoors & Moerman, 1988).

2 THE LINGUISTIC ENVIRONMENT OF NON-NATIVE SIGNING DEAF CHILDREN

There are several factors which make the linguistic environment of DCHP extremely complex. Although education is intended to be monolingual, in reality the linguistic environment is characterised by two languages, Dutch and Sign Language of the Netherlands. Access to both languages is restricted. Dutch is mainly represented in SSD. In this rather loose sign system there is no one-to-one match between morphemes of Dutch and signs. Rather the signs are intended to reproduce the semantic content of the utterance. With respect to the grammatical structure of these utterances, this means that through the sign component children receive information about the word order, but almost none about the morphological properties of Dutch. This information has to be acquired through speechreading, a task which is very difficult for deaf children. Differences in speechreading proficiency cause perceptual variability. Productive variability stems from the fact that production of utterances through simultaneous communication by parents or teachers turns out to be a complex and difficult task (Marmor & Petitto, 1979; Swisher, 1984; Strong & Charlson, 1987). There is a great deal of inter- and intra-individual variation, not only caused by a differing amount of practice, but also by fundamental problems like cognitive overload and asynchronality.

In some studies into the use of signs by DCHP, researchers claim the linguistic environment of these children to be a monolingual one (eg. Livingston, 1983). It is easy to see that this presupposition is not correct. At the school for the deaf, DCHP come into contact with other deaf children, and, in the Netherlands infrequently, with deaf adults. The school for the deaf is the first place where DCHP have the opportunity to socialise in the Deaf community; most often in an indirect way, not resulting from educational policy, the sign language and culture of this community are being transmitted (Johnson & Erting, 1989). More often than not, SLN comes to DCHP in indirect ways, through communication with older pupils who in many cases themselves are non-native signers. Variability in transmission of SLN is created by factors such as the availability of native signers and the proficiency in SLN by non-native signing older pupils.

So in conclusion we see that DCHP in the Netherlands are in a situation in which the highly mixed language input on the one hand consists of a variable, inconsistently used sign system SSD and, on the other hand, of varieties of sign language, SLN. The exact input and intake can differ considerably between children, dependent on the communicative competence of parents and teachers, age of onset of sign communication, degree of speechreading proficiency and age of onset, frequency and intensity of contact with users of SLN.

In fact DCHP find themselves in a rather bizarre language contact situation. In normal cases of language contact, several languages are present and accessible (Appel & Muysken, 1987). Although for DCHP a sign language is an accessible one, it is virtually never available in the primary linguistic input. Most DCHP come during the first ten or so years of their lives only in contact with hybridical fragments of SLN, transmitted in a rather indirect way. The second language which is at stake, Dutch, is dominant in education, but relatively inaccessible. The situation is made even more complicated by educators, who deliberately have mixed both languages to a certain extent in creating sign systems like SSD.

Livingston (1983) has claimed that American DCHP in a similar situation acquire ASL without any linguistic input. In her own words: " This study has revealed that the subjects across a ten year age range have acquired greater facility in the use of grammatical ASL processes than in those of Signed English and that ASL processes appear earlier than do their Signed English equivalents—even though all signing to the subjects is in Signed English and not ASL." (Livingston, 1983, 282)

This conclusion is very remarkable, not only for the (in my view untenable) presupposition that ASL was not at all available to the DCHP, but also because of the claim that it was ASL which was acquired. The situation in which these first generation signers find themselves is multilingual, complex, inconsistent and variable. It is the kind of situation which gives rise to creolisation (Mühlhäusler, 1986). It is therefore my expectation that Dutch DCHP will acquire a sign language as their first language, but that this sign language will differ considerably from the SLN of native signers.

3 RESEARCH GOAL AND HYPOTHESES

The goal of the research reported here was to test the hypothesis that the sign language of DCHP would differ from the SLN of native signers, against Livingstons conclusion. It was decided to focus on the use of spatial grammar in mutual communication of non-native and native signers. Spatial grammar is viewed upon as an intricate system of reference, created by refering to arbitrary loci in the signing space (Klima & Bellugi, 1979; Wilbur, 1987; Petitto & Bellugi, 1988; for SLN: Schermer, Fortgens, Harder & De Nobel, 1991). Spatial grammar consists of three subsystems. Through localisation referents are associated with arbitrary loci. Pointing after signing a referent is one of the mechanisms to realise localisation.

The second subsystem is verb agreement. In sign languages, at least two major classes of verbs can be identified, invariant and variant verbs (Padden, 1983; Wilbur, 1987; Bos, 1990). This last class consists of verbs of which the movement can be manipulated to agree with a locus, which stands for a referent. The locus-referent relationship has been established by localisation. Some variant verbs can agree with two loci, others only with one. Dependent on semantic features of the verb, the direction of movement and the order of incorporated loci, the referents associated with these loci function grammaticaly as the subject, object, or locative in an utterance. Further subdivision of these variant verbs is possible using formal or functional criteria, but was not done in this research project.

Anaphoric reference by overt pronouns is the third subcomponent. By pointing or looking in the direction of loci, previously associated with referents (Baker & Cokely, 1980), anaphoric reference is realised.

In the research project, all three subsystems were taken into account. The following hypotheses were tested:
1. Compared to native signers, DCHP will use spatial grammatical structures less frequently.
2. DCHP will produce fewer correct spatial structures than native signers.
More specifically I expected DCHP to use less clauses with localisation. The same

expectation holds for the use of verb agreement with arbitrary loci. These loci are associated with referents which are physically not present, and the same pattern would have to occur with respect to anaphoric reference to referents associated with arbitrary loci.

I would also expect DCHP to use verb agreement more often in cases where localisation did not take place and where consequently, in some cases at least, reference is unclear because the referent cannot be deduced from the conversational context. I thought it equally probable that DCHP will use anaphoric reference in the same incorrect way.

The third hypothesis that was tested is:

3. There are qualitative differences between the use of spatial grammar by DCHP and by native signers. These differences are reflected in the integration of subcomponents, in the integration with other sign language mechanisms and in the use of idiosyncratic structures.

Integration of subcomponents of spatial grammar is a rather late step in the course of normal sign language acquisition by deaf children with deaf parents (Bellugi, Lillo-Martin, O'Grady & VanHoek, 1990). There are some indications that DCHP have severe difficulties with this kind of integration (Loncke, Quertinmont & Ferreyra, 1990; Loncke, 1990). Use of idiosyncratic structures by DCHP in a monolingual TC-environment was reported by Supalla (1986).

4 METHOD

The study involves seventeen pupils of the Rudolf Mees Institute. This is a day school for deaf children in Rotterdam, part of the Royal Amman Foundation in the same city. All seventeen pupils took part in a more comprehensive research project that started in 1987 (see Knoors, 1992). These pupils were divided in three age groups. Six were eight years old, six were eleven years old and five were fourteen years old. All pupils involved have hearing parents who speak Dutch with their child and who support their speech more or less adequately with signs. All these DCHP are prelingually deaf, have normal intelligence and no additional handicaps.

Of course I would have liked to compare the signing of DCHP with that of equally aged DCDP, but this was not possible since at the time of the study almost none DCDP were available in the Rotterdam area. Therefore the decision was made to contrast the signed utterances of the oldest pupils, the adolescents of fourteen years of age, with utterances, signed by three adult native signers, thus assuming that language proficiency of adolescents and adults in normal situations can be regarded as predominantly equal in grammatical aspects. All three native signers selected had deaf parents, one had deaf grandparents too.

The sign language productions of the DCHP and the native signers were elicited by asking them to retell eight short stories to a peer or, in case of the native signers, to a deaf adult. Each of these eight stories consists of a small number of drawings without text. The DCHP first had to describe every picture to a deaf research assistant. If these descriptions were correct, they were asked to tell the whole story to a peer. The sign productions were videotaped, transcribed and analysed for instances of spatial grammatical devices. The idea and procedure was taken from a publication by Lillo-Martin, Bellugi, Struxness & O'Grady (1985).

5 QUANTITATIVE RESULTS

A quantitative analyses was undertaken in order to test the first two hypotheses. The differences in mean frequencies between the three groups DCHP were tested for statistical significance with SPSS-X. The non-parametric Kruskal-Wallis test for one way analyses of variance was used. Differences in mean frequencies between the DCHP and the native signers were not tested for statistical significance because of the very small number of native signers. The frequencies have been calculated over the total amount of clauses used by each individual to retell all eight stories.

Table 1: Frequency of occurence of subcomponents of spatial grammar: means and standard deviations by group.

	I	II	III	IV
Localisation	7.56	12.86	13.66*	21.86
	(4.31)	(5.22)	(3.73)	(4.91)
Verb agreement,	21.45	27.62	30.48	40.29
arbitrairy loci	(9.94)	(11.25)	(10.21)	(5.93)
Verb agreement	6.73	5.92	2.83*	0.30
without localisation	(3.84)	(6.43)	(2.14)	(0.52)
Verb agreement,	3.82	1.97	0.18‡	0.00
reference unclear	(4.36)	(2.49)	(0.40)	(0.00)
Anaphoric reference,	5.70	17.83	12.90†	24.78
overt pronouns	(2.23)	(9.41)	(4.13)	(1.95)
Anaphoric reference	4.06	6.48	2.58	0.00
without localisation	(2.40)	(4.64)	(1.66)	(0.00)
Anaphoric reference,	1.68	2.10	0.59	0.00
reference unclear	(1.41)	(3.29)	(0.73)	(0.00)

* p<0.001   I: eight year olds
† p<0.01   II: eleven year olds
‡ p<0.05   III: fourteen year olds
            IV: adults

The results as presented in the table indicate that with increasing age DCHP use localisation and anaphoric reference more frequently. The difference in frequency of localisation occurs most prominently between the two younger groups, whereas the pattern with respect to anaphoric reference is much less straightforward. The relatively high frequency of occurence of this subcomponent in the sign productions of the eleven year olds is due to two pupils who use this mechanism disproportianally often. The differences in the use of verb agreement do not reach statistical significance, but the pattern is in line with the results on localisation: the older the group, the more frequent the usage.

In general older DCHP tend to make more correct use of verb agreement and anaphoric reference, although with respect to this last group of structures the effects are not significant. It seems on the whole that anaphoric reference is the more difficult subcomponent to master if we look at the proportion between mean frequency of occurence and mean frequency of incorrect usage. Analysis of individual results shows that in some cases a DCHP uses a subcomponent of the spatial grammar as frequently as native signers do. There were no cases however, in which the connected use of all three subcomponents could match the frequency of use by native signers. In general, all quantitative results point at huge variance within groups of DCHP. The sign language use of the groups of DCHP is less homogeneous, compared to the group of native signers.

In relation to the first two hypotheses the results point out that these hypotheses cannot be rejected, since the frequency of occurence of localisation, verb agreement and anaphoric reference with arbitrary loci in the sign productions of the native signers, exceeds the use of these subcomponents of spatial grammar by DCHP. Incorrect usage of these structures is almost non-existent in the group of native signers, whereas the siging of the non-native signers shows evidence of incomplete mastery. Analysis of individual results however, makes it clear that the first hypothesis is in need of reformulation in order to account for all the individual patterns of use of the signing space. The following, rephrased hypothesis is suggested:

Compared to native signers' sign productions, the sign productions of DCHP show evidence of a less frequent use of connected spatial grammatical structures, compared to native signers. This unconnectedness is reflected in the relatively infrequent occurence of at least one subcomponent of spatial grammar.

6 QUALITATIVE RESULTS

In our analyses we found remarkable qualitative differences between the signing of DCHP and the SLN of the native signers. The following example will illustrate some of these differences. The story is about two boys who fight with each other. A girl passes by, looks at them and shows her disapproval. The boys are ashamed.

One of the native signers signs:

Example 1.

(gaze: 3b;   manner:intense)
TWO BOYS   SHOUT-AT-EACH OTHER /

(manner:calm)
INDEX3a GIRL 3a[I-CL]-MOVE3b /

(gaze: 3b)
TWO SHOUT-AT-EACH OTHER /

(role:girl; gaze: 3a)
        "surprise"   /

(role:girl; gaze:3b)
INDEX3a GIRL IDISAPPROVE3b /

(role:boys; gaze:3a)
        ASHAMED /

The same story in the version of one of the oldest DCHP:

Example 2.

TWO BOYS FIGHT/

BUT 3aICOME SKINNY GIRL /

3aI[I-CL]-MOVE3bI /

(role: girl; gaze:3a2)
LOOK-AT TWO QUARREL /

(role: girl; gaze 3a2)
[V-CL]-LOCATED-AT3bI /

(role:girl; gaze:3a2)
LOOK-AT3a2 /

(role:boys; gaze:3b2*)
TWO BOYS   "frightened"   /

The native signer localises the two boys immediately at locus 3b. The DCHP starts his story without localisation. Only in the fourth utterance we find rather indirect localisation of the boys. In the fifth one, the DCHP has already taken role for the girl, but while taking role he localises the boys once again by using a classifier verb (By the way, in this context an incorrect one according to the rules of SLN). This second localisation may reflect uncertainty about the effectiveness of the earlier localisation.

In the last utterance he changes role, but the accompanying gaze direction is incorrect. The girl is not located at locus 3b2, but at locus 3b1, as follows from the use of the verb MOVE in the third utterance. In contrast with the DCHP, the native signer is very consistent in the use of role, combined with the use of loci. This example thus indicates that in the signing of older DCHP there is already some integration of spatial subcomponents as well as of these components with role taking and classifier use. These integrative processes however are not always handled in correct ways.

All the stories that we analysed show the same characteristics. The main difference between the use of spatial grammar by the DCHP, even the oldest ones, and the native signers is related to the integration of subcomponents and the integration with other sign language mechanisms. Compared to DCHP the native signers localise more systematically. The localisations of DCHP are more of an incidental nature (see also Knoors, 1990). In many cases they are just localisations, not used for grammatical purposes at all. The native signers almost never localise just for the sake of localisation. Loci are integrated in the processes of verb agreement and use of overt anaphoric pronouns. In effect this means that where native signers really create a flexible frame of reference, DCHP do not succeed in this task, at least not before the age of fourteen.

Another example of the high degree of integration native signers achieve in their SLN productions, is the adjustment of Size and Shape Specifiers (SASS), used to refer to objects, according to the physical characteristics of the person who handles the object. If a signer signs about a squirrel eating a nut, the SASS which is used to refer to the object 'nut', will differ from the one that is used in telling a story about an adult human being eating the same kind of nuts. This kind of integration was never found in the sign productions of DCHP.

Idiosyncratic structures in the sign productions of DCHP were found only very infrequently. One of the few examples is localisation by fingerspelling the first letter of the name of a referent at a certain locus, a mechanism not found in SLN. Since the distance between SSD and SLN is less than the one between ASL and American sign systems, this may well explain the discrepancy of my data with the results of Suppala's study (Supalla, 1986).

Related to the third hypothesis the results of the qualitative analyses points out that for Dutch DCHP this hypothesis cannot be rejected, except for the use of idiosyncratic structures.

7 DISCUSSION AND CONCLUSIONS

Both the quantitative and the qualitative research outcomes indicate that DCHP in a monolingual TC-environment in which SLN-input is minimal and incidental, use spatial grammatical structures typical of sign languages like SLN more often with increasing age. These findings are not tied to this specific elicitation task, but are confirmed for spontaneous language use as well (Knoors, 1989; 1992). In this respect, the results for these Dutch DCHP are in line with previous research into the sign language use of DCHP in other countries (Livingston, 1983; Loncke, 1990). The huge individual differences with respect to both the occurence of spatial grammatical subcomponents and the correctness of use seem to be a reflection of the variability of the input.

Variability is a key issue in the language acquisition process of DCHP, as was shown also for American DCHP (Gee & Goodhart, 1985; Bochner & Albertini, 1988).

Stating that DCHP in similar linguistic environments acquire a full-fledged sign language, as Livingston (1983) has done, is not in line with our data. The differences between the sign language productions of DCHP and native signers are remarkable. Their nature is both quantitative and qualitative. It is equally clear however that the mutual communication between DCHP does not take place in SSD. More usefull and in line with the data is the conception of the language used in mutual communication of DCHP as a separate though related sign language variety: School Sign Language of the Netherlands (SSLN).

The emergence of this SSLN seems to result partly from an internally driven restructuring of the SSD-input in the direction of perceptual and productive capabilities. External norms do influence the resultant language, but often in individually varying ways, dependent on the processibility and availability of languages. One of the main reasons DCHP do not prefer SSD in their mutual communication seems to be the fact that this sign system does not satisfy certain demands on language: clear expression of grammatical functions, perceptible in ongoing time and easily comprehensible and producible (Slobin, 1975). In all cases DCHP capitalise intensively on the relatively few instances of rather hybrid sign language structures in the input.

Despite the fact that what the task DCHP achieve in their sign language acquisition is considerable, there are two points about this acquisition under atypical conditions which are troublesome.

The first point is the huge variation in the structure of sign language productions of DCHP, which indicates that to some extent each DCHP applies his/her own grammatical rules. My own observations make me think that in some instances this may lead to misunderstandings between DCHP in daily communication, but even more so in tasks which are more challenging and require more cognitive energy: tasks related to the acquisition of cognitive-academic language proficiency. In the literature incidentally similar observations have been reported (Edmondson, 1981; Preisler, 1983).

The second point is that the level of grammatical complexity in School Sign Language of the Netherlands is lower than in SLN.

Looking at language acquisition of these DCHP is in fact looking at the acquisition of two languages, Dutch and SLN, without acquiring full proficiency in one of them. It is doubtfull wether non-native signers later in life ever will be able to catch up with native signers with respect to the morphosyntactic complexity of their sign language productions (Newport, 1984). Be that as it may, as Cummins (1976, 1984) would put it, many DCHP remain well into their adolescence 'semilinguals', with all its negative effects on the cognitive development of these children.

Therefore, the results of the research reported in this article stress once again the importance of introducing sign language in the education of deaf children and thus the importance of bilingual/bicultural education. Only this educational concept seems to entail the promise of avoiding the two troublesome points mentioned above, as well as to offer deaf children a chance to acquire all sorts of information through accessible language input.

Footnotes

* Harry Knoors: Royal Amman Foundation, Rotterdam, The Netherlands.

Bibliography

Appel, R. and Muysken, P. [1987]. *Language Contact and Bilingualism*. Edward Arnold, London.

Baker C. and Cokely, D. [1980]. *American Sign Language: A Teacher's Resource Text on Grammar and Culture.* T.J. Publishers, Silver Spring, MD.

Bellugi, U., Lillo-Martin, D., O'Grady, L. and Van Hoek, K. [1990]. The development of spatialized syntactic mechanisms in American Sign Language, in: Edmondson, W.H. and Karlsson, F. (eds) *SLR'87: Papers from the Fourth International Symposium on Sign Language Research*, pp. 16–25. Signum Press, Hamburg.

Bochner, J.H. and Albertini, J.A. [1988]. Language varieties in the deaf population and their acquisition by children and adults, in: Strong, M. (ed). *Language Learning and Deafness*, pp. 3–48. Cambridge University Press, Cambridge.

Bos. H. [1990]. Person and location marking in Sign Language of the Netherlands: some implications of a spatially expressed syntactic system, in: Prillwitz, S. and Vollhaber, T. (eds) *Current Trends in European Sign Language Research.*, pp. 231—246. Signum Press, Hamburg.

Cummins, J. [1976]. The influence of bilingualism on cognitive growth: a synthesis of research findings and explanatory hypotheses. *Working Papers on Bilingualism 19*, pp. 121–129.

—[1984]. *Bilingualism and Special Education: Issues in Assessment and Pedagogy.* Multilingual Matters, Clevedon.

Edmondson, W. [1981]. Sign language in an unfavourable setting: a perspective, in: Woll, B., Kyle, J.G. and Deuchar, M. (eds) *Perspectives on British Sign Language and Deafness*, pp. 204–217. Croom Helm, London.

Gee, J.P. and Goodhart, W. [1985]. Nativization, linguistic theory, and deaf language acquisition. *Sign Language Studies 49*, pp. 291–342.

Harder, R. and Knoors, H. [1987]. Consolidation of method or future changes? Use of signs in the education of the deaf in the Netherlands, in: J. Kyle (ed) *Sign and School: Using Signs in Deaf Children's Development*, pp. 109–119. Multilingual Matters, Clevedon.

Johnson, R.E. and Erting, C. [1989]. Ethnicity and socialization in a classroom for deaf children, in: Lucas, C. (ed) *The Sociolinguistics of the Deaf Community*, pp. 41–84. Academic Press, San Diego.

Klima, E. and Bellugi, U. [1979]. *The Signs of Language*. Harvard University Press, Cambridge, Mass.

Knoors, H. [1989]. Verwerving van congruentie in Nederlandse Gebarentaal door dove kinderen zonder primair gebarentaalaanbod (Acquisition of verb agreement in Sign Language of the Netherlands by deaf children without primary sign language input), in: Hagen, A.P.M. van and Knoors, H. (eds) *Onderwijs aan Doven*, pp. 29–42. Swets and Zeitlinger, Lisse.

— [1990]. De gebaarruimte benoemen: benoeming van abstracte punten door late gebarentaalverwervers. (Localisation: nominal establishment by late learners of sign language). *Van Horen Zeggen* 30: 4, pp. 156–163.

— [1992]. *Exploratie van de Gebarenruimte: Een Onderzoek naar de Verwerving van Ruimtelijke Morfosyntactische Gebarentaalstructuren door Dove Kinderen met Horende Ouders (Exploration of the Signing space: A Study into the Acquisition of Spatial Morphosyntactic Sign Language Structures by Deaf Children with Hearing Parents)*. Eburon Publishers, Delft.

Lillo-Martin, D., Bellugi, U., Struxness, L. and O'Grady, M. [1985]. The acquisition of spatially organized syntax. *Papers and Reports on Child Language Development* 24, pp. 70–77, Department of Linguistics, Stanford University.

Livingston, S. [1983]. Levels of development in the language of deaf children: ASL grammatical processes, Signed English structures, semantic features. *Sign Language Studies* 40, pp. 193–284.

Loncke, F. [1990]. *Modaliteitsinvloed op Taalstructuur en Taalverwerving in Gebarencommunicatie. (Influence of Modality on Language Structure and Language Acquisition in Sign Communication)* Ph.D. Dissertation, Vrije Universiteit, Brussels.

Loncke, F., Hoiting, N., Knoors, H. and Moerman, D. [1988]. Native and non-native language acquisition: the case of signing deaf children, in: Besien, F. van (ed) *First Language Acquisition*. ABLA-papers 13. Gent-Antwerpen.

Loncke, F., Quertinmont, S. and Ferreyra, P. [1990]. Deaf children in schools: more or less native signers? in: Prillwitz, S. and Vollhaber, T. (eds) *Current Trends in European Sign Language Research*, pp. 163–178. Signum Press, Hamburg

Marmor, G.S. and Petitto, L. [1979]. Simultaneous communication in the classroom: how well is English grammar represented? *Sign Language Studies* 23, pp. 99–136.

Mühlhäusler, P. [1986]. *Pidgin and Creole Linguistics*. Basil Blackwell, Oxford.

Newport, E. [1984]. Constraints on learning: studies in the acquisition of American Sign Language. *Papers and Reports on Child Language Development* 23, pp. 1–22. Department of Linguistics, Stanford University.

Padden, C. [1983]. *Interaction of Morphology and Syntax in American Sign Language.* Ph.D. Dissertation, University of California, San Diego.

Petitto, L.A. and Bellugi, U. [1988]. Spatial cognition and brain organization: clues from the acquisition of a language in space, in: Stiles-Davis, J., Kritchevsky, M. and Bellugi, U. (eds) *Spatial Cognition: Brain Bases and Development*, pp. 299–326. Lawrence Erlbaum, Hillsdale, NJ.

Preisler, G. [1983]. *Deaf Children in Communication: A Study of Communicative Strategies Used By Deaf Children in Social Interactions.* Trydells Tryckeri, Laholm.

Schermer, G.M., Fortgens, C., Harder, R. and Nobel, E. de (eds) [1991]. *De Nederlandse Gebarentaal. (Sign Language of the Netherlands).* Van Tricht, Twello.

Slobin, D.I. [1975]. The more it changes... on understanding language by watching it move through time. *Papers and Reports on Child Language Development* 10, pp. 1–30. Department of Linguistics, Stanford University.

Strong, M. and Charlson, E.S. [1987]. Teachers' strategies for using simultaneous communication. *Teaching English to Deaf and Second-Language Students* 4:1, pp. 21–24.

Supalla, S. [1986]. *Manually Coded English: An Understanding of Modality's Role in Signed Language Development.* Paper presented at the Theoretical Issues in Sign Language Research Conference, Rochester, 13–16 June 1986.

Swisher, M.V. [1984]. Signed input of hearing mothers to deaf children. *Language Learning* 34:2, pp. 69–85.

Wilbur, R. [1987]. *American Sign Language: Linguistic and Applied Dimensions.* Second edition. College-Hill Press, Boston.

The development of symbolic play and language in profoundly deaf children

ALVARO MARCHESI, MARIAN VALMASEDA, PILAR ALONSO
AND GEMA PANIAGUA

1 INTRODUCTION

Theories on intelligence by Piaget (1946) and by Werner and Kaplan (1963) maintained that the development of play and language reflect the ability of the child to employ symbols. Both theories, which assume that underlying changes in the cognitive structure are reflected in all dimensions of behaviour, like those others which support more limited structural effects (Bates et al 1979, Fisher 1980), state that there must be a close relationship between language and symbolic play. In symbolic play, the child uses gestures, sounds and objects to represent or "symbolize" other events and objects. In language, sound and words carry out this function.

During the last 10 years, a number of studies have been conducted which have revealed strong correlation between symbolic play and language during the first stages of language acquisition, both for normal and mentally retarded children.

Lowe and Costello (1976) discovered partial correlations, having controlled the effect of age, of approximately 0,30 between symbolic play and two measurements of language, the M.L.U. and a linguistic comprehension test. Bates et al (1979) found great similarity in levels and sequences of development between both areas, plus high correlation in frequency and speed and a considerable superposition in the referential content. Fein (1978) demonstrated that symbolic play was closely linked to the production of language and comprehension, something which does not happen with other types of play. Finally, studies with mentally retarded children (Jeffree and McConkey 1976) found positive correlations between symbolic play and language.

Research carried out by McCune-Nicholich (1981, 1982, 1984) put forward structural comparison between the different levels of play and language. The results obtained indicated that the beginnings of the first words were closely linked with the actual behaviour of the level of auto-symbolic play and that the increase in vocabulary was parallel to the expansion of symbolism shown on the level of the symbolic decentralised games. After play, the first symbolic combinations are produced as well as the first simple verbal combinations. These verbal combinations imply routines learnt and sequences of two words, in which each word produces its own direct relationship with the non-linguistic answer. Subsequent linguistic combinations are hierarchical, in a more organized structure, which fit into sequences of planned games, where a previous intention exists.

Other studies (Bretherton and Bates 1984, Shore et al 1990) have revealed that one should also bear in mind the differences between the language and the symbolic game. Language is expressed without perceptive support and a conventional structure. Moreover, there is strong social pressure for its use. Play, on the contrary, finds perceptive support in the objects, its structure depends on individual wishes and it is more voluntary and optional in nature.

Correlation between the development of language and symbolic play has been found in hearing children who have acquired oral language, but profoundly deaf children have hardly been considered.

Numerous studies have been made on acquisition and development of sign language, of manual communication systems and oral language in profoundly deaf children (see Marchesi, 1986 for a revision of these studies). Hardly any research has been conducted into the development of symbolic play, and it is therefore impossible to confirm the combined evolution of language and symbolic play in profoundly deaf children. However, the specific characteristics of these children and their different possibilities of communication—sign, oral or bi-modal—could become an important field of study which, on the one hand, would generate knowledge about the symbolic evolution of deaf children and on the other, present new data to confirm whether the established model about correlation between the language and symbolic game was a fact.

1 RESEARCH OBJECTIVES

One of the research objectives was to confirm the hypothesis of the correlation between certain levels of linguistic development and certain levels of symbolic play in profoundly deaf children who acquire different linguistic systems.

The said correlation was established in the following manner:

Age	Language	Symbolic game
13 months	First signs or words	Symbolic actions referred to passive or active agent.
20 months	First syntax of two signs or words	Logical sequence of actions.
28-30 months	First syntax of three signs or words	Logical sequence in which various agents interact or planning of isolated action or a sequence of actions.

Long term follow-up of the evolution of play and language in profoundly deaf children will facilitate confirmation of this hypothesis and could contribute new facts to the problems of the relationship between language and thought.

2 DIMENSIONS OF PLAY AND LANGUAGE STUDIED

Four different dimensions for the study of symbolic play were distinguished:

1. Decentralization: the child was progressively more capable of carrying out symbolic actions, assimilating the point of view of others. Four levels were taken into consideration:
1.1 Self-referring symbolic actions.
1.2 Symbolic actions referring to a passive agent.
1.3 Symbolic actions referring to an active agent.
1.4 Interaction between several agents.
2. Identity: the child is capable of giving the dolls a role and making them do the right actions of the appointed character. Levels distinguished were the following:
2.1 The child identifies the characters but then does not make them act.
2.2 The actions the child undertakes are those which define the doll's identity.
2.3 There is identification with the doll and it also carries out the actions in accordance with its role.
3. Substitution: the child is capable of using objects with a specific function for another, different function. The levels established were the following:
3.1 Use of realistic objects.
3.2 Substitution of an ambiguous object.
3.3 Substitution of various ambiguous objects in a game sequence.
3.4 Substitution of a realistic object for another function, different from the one it has.
3.5 Open substitution.
4. Integration of actions. This dimension refers to the growing ability of the child to integrate his/her actions into sequences. The levels were the following:
4.1 Isolated individual actions.
4.2 Repetition of action with different agents.
4.3 Sequence of two actions.
4.4 Logical sequence of more than two actions.
4.5 Logical sequence in which several agents interact.
5. Planning: the child previously plans the game. Levels were the following:
5.1 Absence of planning.
5.2 Planning of an isolated action.
5.3 Planning of an action integrated into a game sequence.
5.4 Planning of several actions.
5.5 Planning of a whole game sequence.

The communicative and linguistic productions of the children were studied, taking into consideration the following dimensions:

1.   Level of symbolism and linguistic combinations. The following were distinguished:
   • Natural gestures.
   • Deictic gestures
   • Vocalizations.
   • Gestures, words or signs of a symbolic nature.
   • Combinations of deictic gestures with symbolic productions.
   • Combinations of two or more symbolic productions.
2.   Mode of expression. The linguistic productions were also analysed, according to the mode - oral or gesture-sign - used, as well as the possible combination of both.
3.   Communicative function. The different communicative expressions were analysed in accordance with the communicative interaction transmitted. The following functions were distinguished:
   • Regulators: General attention, Petition of action and Petition of object.
   • Declaratives: General, Identification of object or person, Description of events, Information about internal aspects, Attribution of characteristics to objects or people, Explanations.
   • Questions
   • Expressive
   • Imitation
   • Self-regulators
4.   Children studied.

   Research was finally carried out with 12 children in four separate groups. Four children who began the study did not continue with it long enough and they have therefore not been included in the data analysis.
• Deaf children of deaf parents who used sign language: 3.
• Deaf children of hearing parents who used bi-modal communication: 6.
• Deaf children with hearing parents who only used oral language: 1.
• Hearing children: 2.

   The distribution of children in these four groups, initially correct, should be expressed in greater detail to gain a better idea of the communicative reality of these children. Not all deaf parents used sign language with their children from the beginning. In one case, they initially adopted the decision to exclusively use oral language, although later they changed ideas. Parents who used the bimodal communication did not maintain this position throughout the time period either. Some decided to abandon the use of signs and concentrate exclusively on oral communication. Only the group of deaf children with exclusively oral communication and the group of hearing children were constant throughout.

   The follow-up of development of these children mostly began before they were two, although in the case of three of them the study began when they were two. The range of ages at the beginning of follow-up oscillated between 12 months and 26 months. Only those profoundly deaf children with losses higher than 90 dB in both ears, and who had no other detected associated deficiencies, were chosen.

3 METHODOLOGY

The research on symbolic play began at 12 months and continued throughout the follow-up of the child. From 12 to 24 months an evaluation took place once a month; from that age, every two months, approximately. Different materials were offered to the children in order to evaluate their behaviour when playing, for each of the established dimensions.

One of the main characteristics of these materials is that they cover different grades of realism: from very realistic groups of toys (dolls, small animals, miniature foods, etc.) to the absolute abstract (pieces of wood, plastic, etc), using intermediate combinations of realistic and abstract materials as well. Another characteristic is that some of them encourage the realization of action sequences, facilitating the observation of the child's ability to integrate during play. The special material data collected was combined with data taken from stimulation sessions, where symbolic play was frequently a means of interchange and communication at these ages.

Video recordings were made of the communicative and linguistic development of the children. These video recordings were made on a monthly basis when the children were less than 24 months old and twice-monthly when they are older. It was not always possible to maintain this rhythm, owing to external circumstances such as sickness, holidays, etc.

Recordings were taken in situations of play, reading stories and when direct interaction took place with the mother or another member of the family. Situations varied according to the child's age and characteristics. The most frequent context in which the taping sessions were conduced was rehabilitation or educational, either in working sessions with the child in the speech therapy unit of the Children's hospital or the Kindergarten.

The duration of these sessions was thirty minutes, with subsequent analysis of the five minutes when the child's communication was at its richest.

4 RESULTS AND CONCLUSIONS

Facts obtained during research were very numerous and it is not the objective of this article to present them all. It would be a difficult task to achieve, given the limitations of existing space. What will be presented and discussed here will be the most relevant findings relating to the hypothesis of the correlation between the development of language and the development of symbolic play mentioned at the beginning of this article. This hypothesis has only considered some of the facts obtained about the evolution of language and play. In the case of language, the combinations of words or signs. In the case of play, several levels of each one of the dimensions studied. Posterior analysis of this correlation should be made, when other linguistic elements, such as the development of the communicative functions, are included or when all dimensions of symbolic play are simultaneously considered.

Before presenting the findings relating to the hypothesis formulated, some of the most important tendencies found in the evolution of language and symbolic play in deaf children will be noted. Deaf children whose parents normally use sign language evolved in a similar way to hearing children, although there was greater variety of commitment on the part of the parents to use it. When hearing parents confidently and assuredly use bimodal communication with deaf children, the evolution of their language is similar to the group of deaf children with deaf parents. The development of the language is much slower when the parents only use oral language with deaf children.

Very few differences were found in the development of symbolic play between the different groups of children in comparison to those existing in the development of language. They do not appear in the dimensions of decentralization, substitution and integration. This indicates that the deaf child is capable of expressing his/her symbolic ability in situations of play, : 1. the symbols are more individual and less conventional. 2. the presence of objects aids expression in play, although he/she does not manage to do so in the linguistic area, aided by two of the characteristics of play.

The most serious differences between deaf and hearing children are to be found in identity, at the beginning of role play and in planning of the game rules. These differences become apparent as the game develops and it can thus be said that in the first stages of symbolic play development, whatever the linguistic level of the child is, there were no notable differences between the children studied. Several reasons to explain the differences found have been previously mentioned. The dimension of identity supposes, on a more developed level, not only appointing a role to dolls but also that the child himself assumes a specific role in relation to that played by the doll. There are also differences in play language between children who express their individual capacity to use language to give life and identity to the different characters in the game. Children who have had greater opportunities for adapting a linguistic code demonstrated greater expressive richness in those levels close to the game of roles. There is therefore a stage when, from thirty months onwards, language and communicative interchange are more relevant to childrens' games.

Differences are finally to be found in planning. This is not a specific activity of the symbolic game, but more a previous requirement which helps organization and affords more relevance to the game. There are also clear differences to be found here between the groups of children with better language skills and those with a poorer linguistic level. Language plays a more direct part here, and the differences found are easily explained. Language plays an important role at this age for organizing thought and guiding and controlling behaviour. The absence of language limits children's possibilities for doing these things. Those groups of children with the greatest difficulties of obtaining linguistic codes clearly lacked game planning activities.

Having expressed these general tendencies, specific data relating to each of the children will follow, to prove the link between the development of the game and the language. (Table 1)

Table 1: Data of the children studied related with the different dimensions.

Sonia (sign language)

Months	Lang.	Dec.	Ident.	Subst.	Integ.	Plan.
24	S	1.3	-	3.4	4.5	-
-	S+S	-	-	-	-	-
-	S+S+S	-	-	-	-	-
29	-	1.3	2.2	4.6	5.4	-
-	-	1.4	2.3	-	-	-

Juan (Sign language)

Months	Lang	Dec.	Ident.	Subst.	Integ.	Plan.
18	-	1.2	-	3.1	4.2	-
24	S	1.3	2.3	3.4	4.3	-
-	-	-	2.3	3.5	4.3	-
26	S+S	-	-	-	-	-
36	S+S+S	-	-	-	-	-
39	-	1.4	-	-	4.7	-

Irene (Sign language)

Months	Lang.	Dec.	Ident.	Subst.	Integ.	Plan.
18	-	1.2	-	3.2	-	-
21	S	-	-	3.4	4.6	5.2
28	-	1.3	2.2	3.4	4.6	5.4
-	-	-	2.2	-	-	-
32	S+S	1.4	-	3.5	-	-
-	S+S+S	-	-	-	-	-

Lucia (Oral language)

Months	Lang.	Dec.	Ident.	Subst.	Integ.	Plan.
25	-	1.2	-	-	4.5	-
29	V	1.3	-	3.5	4.6	-

Months	Lang.	Dec.	Ident.	Subst.	Integ.	Plan.
37	-	1.4	2.2	-	4.7	-
45	V+V	-	2.2	-	-	5.2
-	V+V+V+	-	-	-	-	-

Lucas (Bidmodal system)

Months	Lang.	Dec.	Ident.	Subst.	Integ.	Plan.
20	-	1.2	-	3.2	4.5	-
23	S	-	-	-	-	-
25	-	1.3	-	-	-	-
29	S+S	-	-	-	4.6	-
32	-	-	-	-	3.3	5.2

Sara (Bimodal system)

Months	Lang.	Dec.	Ident.	Subst.	Integ.	Plan.
13	-	1.2	-	-	4.2	-
17	S	-	-	-	4.3	-
21	-	-	-	3.5	4.5	-
25	S+S	-	-	-	4.6	5.3
-	S+S+S	-	-	-	-	-

David (Bimodal system)

Months	Lang.	Dec.	Ident.	Subst.	Integ.	Plan.
14	S	1.2	-	-	4.2	-
18-19	S+S	1.3	-	-	3.2	4.3, 5.2
22	S+S+S	-	-	-	-	-
25	-	1.4	2.3	3.3	4.5	-

Pedro (Bimodal system)

Months	Lang.	Dec.	Ident.	Subst.	Integ.	Plan.
19	S	1.2	-	-	-	-
21	-	-	-	3.4	4.6	-
25	S+S	1.4	2.3	-	-	-
-	S+S	-	-	-	-	-
31	-	-	-	4.7	5.3	-

Elvira (Bimodal system)

Months	Lang.	Dec.	Ident.	Subst.	Integ.	Plan.
16-17	S	1.3	-	3.2	4.5	-
21	-	-	-	3.3	-	5.2
28	-	-	-	3.4	4.6	-
32	-	1.4	2.3	-	4.6	5.3

Alvaro (Bimodal system)

Months	Lang.	Dec.	Ident.	Subst.	Integ.	Plan.
26	-	1.3	-	3.3	4.5	-
35	S	-	-	3.5	4.6	5.4

| 37 | S+S | 1.4 | 2.2 | - | 4.6 | - |
| - | S+S+S | - | 2.2 | - | - | - |

Luis (Hearing)

Months	Lang.	Dec.	Ident.	Subst.	Integ.	Plan.
13	V	-	-	-	4.2	-
15	-	1.2	-	-	4.3	-
19-20	V+V	-	-	-	4.5	-
22	V+V+V	-	-	3.2	-	-
24	-	1.3	-	3.4	-	-
29+30	-	1.4	2.3	3.5	4.6	5.4

Maria (Hearing)

Months	Lang.	Dec.	Ident.	Subst.	Integ.	Plan.
14	V	1.2	-	-	4.2	-
20	V+V	-	-	-	4.5	-
22	V+V+V	1.3	2.3	3.2	-	5.2
34	-	1.3	2.3	-	4.6	5.4

(Lang.= Language; S= one sign; S+S= two signs; S+S+S= three signs; Dec.= decentralization; Ident.= identity; Subst.= substitution; Integ.= integration; Plan.= planification.
The figures correspond with the levels of each dimensions shown above.

The hearing children data revealed a wide structural coherence, which confirmed the initial hypothesis. The first words and the first syntax of two words appeared at the predicted time and with the predicted play behaviour. The correlation was less clear for three-word combinations. Our data is doubtlessly too specific, for the first syntax of words, and it would therefore be possible to seek the relationship in subsequent months, when combinations were more extensive and consolidated. Both Luis and María had levels of integration at 29-30 months, with this arrangement (sequence of various logical actions) and expected planning.

However, the data of deaf children bears no correlation between development of play and language. The development of play, in its dimensions of decentralisation, substitution and integration, is similar to that of hearing children. However, its linguistic development is, on average, more backward. Therefore, in the majority of deaf children studies, evolution of symbolic play came before that of language, and it was not possible to find the expected correlation. This general confirmation can be further specified, since there are significant differences to be found among the deaf children themselves in development of both dimensions. In some deaf children correlation was discovered more clearly. This was the case of children with better linguistic development, whose results are logically closer to hearing children.

How can all these results be interpreted and what do they contribute to the debate about the relationships between the cognitive-symbolic development and the language? Data obtained would support the presence of a basic symbolic capacity which would allow for various tasks to be carried out. The execution of these tasks, symbolic play or language, would also depend on other factors, which would become apparent through different styles of expression or action in the children. In the linguistic dimension three main factors should be borne in mind: the existence of an accessible linguistic code for the children, the communicative style used by the parents and the actual communicative variations of each individual child. The latter should be emphasized since up until now it has hardly been taken into consideration. The differences found do not only depend on the first two factors.

Children also adopt specific forms of communication, not strictly dependent upon their capacity of linguistic expression. There are children who like to communicate with adults to a greater or lesser extent. There are children who prefer individual activity with objects than communicative exchange. The case of Juan, a child of deaf parents, is paradigmatic. He scarcely expresses himself, scarcely interacts with adults—his conduct derives from the overly strict style of the adults—but he demonstrates an enormous richness in play. His development in symbolic play is surprising for its richness. On the contrary, his linguistic expression is very poor. What was not possible to divine was whether linguistic competence existed, which was not yet obvious in the ages of the children studied.

In symbolic play the style of play developed by the children would have to be considered, possibly linked to motivational or personal characteristics. In the game rules studied we found a more realistic style as well as another more imaginative one. Perhaps there are other more specific aspects which influence the game activities of the children and which make it possible to explain progress or advances of children in some dimensions. For example, there are children who prefer playing with adults and interacting in play with them, whilst there are other children who prefer to play on their own. There are more impulsive children who enjoy playing with the first toys they see and others who prefer more relaxed, more organized , and to a certain extent, premeditated games. These styles of play, which are also an expression of incipient styles of behaviour or personality are greatly important in symbolic games developed by the children. Research about symbolic development should also consider the communicative and expressive styles of each individual child.

Footnotes

---

* Alvaro Marchesi, Marian Valmaseda, Pilar Alonso and Gema Paniagua: Centro Nacional de Recursos para la Educacion Especial. General Oraa 55, 28006 Madrid, Spain.

Bibliography

Bates, E., Begnini, L., Bretherton, I., Camaioni, L. and Volterra, V. [1979]. *The Emergence of Symbols: Cognition and Communication in Infancy*. Academic Press, New York.

Bretherton, I. and Bates, E. [1984]. The development from 10 to 28 months: differential stability of language and symbolic play, in: Enide, R.N. and Harmon, R.J. (eds) *Continuities and Discontinuities in Development*. Plenum, New York.

Fein, G.A. [1978]. Play revisited, in: Lamb, M. (ed): *Social and Personality Development*. Holt, Renehart and Winston, New York.

Fisher, K. [1980]. A theory of cognitive development: the control and construction of hierarchies of skills. *Psychological Review* 87, pp. 477–531.

Jeffrey, D. and McConkey, R. [1976]. An observation scheme for recording children's imaginative doll play. *Journal of Child Psychology and Psychiatry* 17, pp. 189–197.

Lowe, M. and Costello, A. [1976]. *A Manual for Symbolic Play Test*. NFER, London.

McCune-Nicholich, L. [1981]. Toward symbolic functioning: structure of early pretend games and potential parallels with language. *Child Development* 52, pp. 785–797.

— [1982]. Combinatorial competency in play and language, in: Pepler, D.J. and Rubin, K.H. (eds) *The Play of Children: Current Theory and Research*. Karger, Basel.

McCune-Nicholich, L. and Fenson, L. [1984]. Methodological issues in studying early pretend play, in: Yawkey, T.D. and Pellegrini, A.D. (eds) *Child's Play: Development and Applied*. Lawrence Erlbaum, Hillsdale, NJ.

Piaget, J. [1946]. *La Formation du Symbole Chez L'Enfant*. Delachaux and Niestlé, Neuchatel.

Shore, C., Bates, E., Bretherton, I., Beeghly, M. and O'Connell, B. [1990]. Vocal and gestural symbols: similarities and differences from 13 to 28 Months, in: Volterra, V. and Erting, C.J. (eds) *From Gesture to Language in Hearing and Deaf Children*. Springer-Verlag, New York.

Werner, H. and Kaplan, B. [1963]. *Symbol Formation*. Wiley, New York.

Sign articulation of a deaf boy
at the age of 2–3 years, 6 years and 8 years

RITVA TAKKINEN *

Abstract

This paper presents an analysis of the sign language used by a young, deaf Finnish boy. Handforms, articulation movements, place of articulation and hand orientation are discussed with specific reference to Finnish sign language. The subject is a deaf boy whose parents are also deaf. The Finnish sign language is the boy's native language.

A longitudinal study of the boy's sign articulation was carried out at three stages. The first stage covers the age between 2 years 3 months and 3 years 4 months, the second stage the age of 5 years 9 months, and the final set of data was gathered when the boy was 7 years 10 months old.

At the age of 2-3 years, most of the variation occurred in the articulation movements and the handforms. In the places of articulation and the orientation of the hand, there were less variation. The articulation movements were somewhat clumsy, and poorly co-ordinated. The independent control of the fingers, the lack of visual feedback, the careless, loose articulation and the presence of movement in the sign produced difficulties in the handforms. At the age of 5 years 9 months, the amount of variation in the articulation movements and the handforms had remarkably diminished. In the two-handed signs there were variations both in handforms and in the articulation movements. At the age of 7 years 10 months, there was almost equal amount (only a few) variations in each of the four parameters. Peter's signing was similar to the adult's way of signing with regard to the mastering of the cheremes.

1 STUDY

In this study I discuss the sign articulation of a deaf boy born to deaf parents. His native language is sign language (Finnish sign language). The subject, I will call him Peter, is a normally developed boy. I carried out a longitudinal study on the development of his sign articulation. The first set of data was gathered between the age of 2 years 3 months and 3 years 4 months, the second period of study was at the age of 5 years 9 months, and the third period at 7 years and 10 months.

During the first period I met Peter about twice a month, 19 times in all. Eleven of them were recorded in written transcription and eight were videotaped. Most of the data was gathered at Peter's home, when he was playing and reading books with his mother and sister. The last four sessions were videotaped at the nursery school in a small group of signing children. The deaf teacher supervised this group during three sessions. At the age of two, Peter did not sign very much, but when he was three years old, he signed considerably more.

At the age of 5 years and 9 months, the data was gathered at the nursery school, and at the age of 7 years and 10 months, at home, twice at each age. I videotaped at the nursery school and at home during the narration of books and sessions, when Peter was talking to the deaf assistant teacher (at the nursery school) and to his mother (at home) about his hobbies, the school etc.

I analysed how the cheremes - handforms, articulation movements, places of articulation and orientation of the hand were realized in the signing of a small child.

2 RESULTS

2.1 Handforms

At the age of 2-3 years, 22 handforms were substituted by some other hand form. At the age of about 6 years, there were variations in eight signs, and at the age of 8 years, in four signs. The total of variations was reduced with age, as expected.

At the age of 2-3 years, the most common substitute was the handform ⅸ. It was used as a substitute for the handforms A (e.g. in the signs MOTHER, BOY) S (BROKEN), B (e.g. CAT, MIRROR) 5 (ELK), ö (VIOLIN), o (BINOCULARS) and C (DRINK). The substitution was due to imprecise, loose articulation. The other reason for the variation was the difficulty in controlling the fingers independently. In this case, the handform ⅸ substituted the handforms v̆ (SIT), ḽ (THROAT), bo (DRAW) and 3 (COCK).

Peter often used the handform G as a substitute for those handforms which were difficult to form. These were I (DUMMY), 8 (JESUS), Y (COW), bo (WASP), B (SKY), 5 (SMOKE) and T-finger alphabet. The handform A replaced the handforms G (GUN), F (DRINK-COFFEE), ʏ (AEROPLANE), 3 (INJECTION) and c (GIRAFFE). Simplification was also evident in these replacements.

The handform B replaced the handforms H (EGG, BUTTER) c (DRINK), ⅸ (GRANDMA) and 6 (BUS). The handforms H (CRAYFISH) and v (HEN) were simplified through the handform 5, and the handform B (e.g. SCHOOL, BLACK) changed to 5 because of imprecise articulation.

At the age of 2-3 years, Peter generally signed imprecisely, and he often signed the two-handed signs with one hand.

At the age of 5 years 9 months, the most common handform substitutes were again the handform ⅸ (which replaced the handforms A, B and c), the handform G (replacing the handforms A and 8) and the handform A, which replaced the handforms L and 3.

The variation was partly occasional, depending on the situation or context. For instance, Peter once signed FATHER with G-handform (it should be A-handform), because of the following sign which was signed with G-handform (the sign for his sister's name). This was an example of assimilation where the preceding handform was changed because of the handform of the following sign.

The second reason for variation was imprecise articulation. For example MOTHER was signed with a loose hand (handform 5̈) instead of a fist (handform A).

The third reason for a change seemed to be a difficulty in controlling the fingers independently. One example of this difficulty was the sign JESUS which is signed with 8-handform (the middle finger touching the palm of the other hand). Peter signed it with G-handform touching the palm.

At the age of 7 years 10 months only four handforms were changed. The reasons for substitutions were the imprecise articulation which seems to be Peter's personal way of signing, and the simplification of the handforms. Examples of imprecise articulation are the signs FATHER and BOY which are usually signed with A-handform (a fist), but which Peter signed with 5̈-handform (a loose hand).

The substitutes Peter used were still the handforms 5̈, G and B. The substitutes were the same from the age of 2 to 8. These handforms belong to the basic handforms of the Finnish sign language (Rissanen, 1985), and they are the earliest handforms acquired by children (see Boyes-Braem, 1973, Mc Intire, 1977).

2.2 Articulation movements

In articulation movements, I analysed the direction and the manner of the movement, the interaction of the hands and contacts of the dominant hand. At the age of 2-3 years the total of variations in the four studied parameters was highest in the articulation movements.

The most common variation in the direction of the movement was signing to the opposite direction, e.g. in the signs CAT and BED, the direction changed away from the signer, although it should be towards the signer. In the sign BLUE the direction from the contralateral to the ipsilateral side changed to the direction from the ipsilateral to the contralateral side. According to Loncke (1984), the natural way of the linear, horizontal movement is from the contralateral to the ipsilateral side.

In some signs, the movement from or to the signer changed to side-to-side-movement (GRANDFATHER), or to up-and-down-movement (SKIS).

As far as the manner of the movement is concerned, the circular movements caused difficulties. On the vertical plane, they changed to linear up-and-down-movement (e.g. in the sign SIGN), and on the horizontal plane to linear side-to-side-movement (e.g. in the signs SWIM and PORRIDGE).

Peter had difficulties in micro-movements (movements of the fingers and the wrist) and macro-movements (movements beginning from the upper arm or the forearm). For instance in the sign FISH, the macro-movement changed to the micro-movement of the fingers, or in the sign TEXT-TELEPHONE, the micro-movement changed to macro-movement from the forearm.

Bending of the wrist did not always succeed, e.g. in the sign POUR, Peter substituted linear movement for bending, and in the sign AMBULANCE, he did not bent the wrist at all.

Most difficulties occurred in the opening and closing movements of the hand. For example in the sign FLOWER, the hand should open, but it had already been open from the beginning. In the sign SHEEP, the fingers usually close, but in Peter's signing they were closed all the time.

Most variations in the interaction of the hands occurred between coping and alternating movement. For instance in the signs COOK and SCALES, there should be alternating movement, but Peter signed with coping movement, and in the sign SKATE only the strong hand moved. The interaction of the hands demands motor co-ordination, and therefore it is difficult for the children.

As far as the contact of the articulating hand with the other hand or the body is concerned, occasionally there was no contact, e.g. in the sign BOAT, the hands did not touch. In some signs contact did not occur at all either in the beginning or at the end, e.g. in the signs MOTHER and FATHER.

In the two-handed signs, the movement was often vague or it did not occur at all. Generally, the movements were clumsy and poorly co-ordinated. Most of the variation occurred in the two-hand-signs.

At the age of 5 years 9 months most of the variation still occurred in the two-handed signs. In the manner of the movement some micro- and macro-movements were difficult. For example in the sign SPIDER, the micro-movement, wiggling of the fingers, was absent, and only the linear macro-movement upwards appeared. The circular movement still caused some difficulties, and Peter changed it to linear side-to-side-movement (PORRIDGE).

In the interaction of the hands there was some variation. For example in the sign EGG (2-H-D = two-hand-sign with different handforms and only the strong hand moving) the weak hand copied the movement of the strong hand. In the signs SCALES and OVERTURN (2-H-S = two-hand sign with a similar handform and movement in both hands) the weak hand did not move at all.

As far as the direction of the movement and the contact of the hands or the hand and the body is concerned, very little variation was observed. However, there was other kind of variation where the movement was vague, and as if unfinished. In the sign HOUSE, which has two parts, the movement was also imprecise. The signs CRAYFISH and BURN include both micro- and macro-movement, and they are therefore difficult for a child to sign. In these signs the movement was quite ambiguous but the context helped in decoding the meaning.

At the age of 7 years 10 months there was very little variation in the movements. The variation could mainly be seen in the manner of movement. For instance in the sign smoke, the circular movement was not used, and in the sign AUTUMN, the wiggling of the fingers was not evident either.

At the age of 8 years the combinations of micro- and macro-movements still caused some difficulties in signing. When teaching hearing adults how to sign I have noticed similar difficulties in these types of signs, and especially in two-handed signs.

2.3 Place of articulation

During the first period, I observed neutralization in the place of articulation. Some signs which are usually signed on the area of the head moved to the neutral area, e.g. the signs BOY and CRY. The sign DOCTOR is usually signed on the chest, but Peter signed it in the neutral area. One reason for the neutralization might have been Peter's imprecise articulation. However, in adults' signing there is also a tendency to neutralize signs which are signed on the head area and on the body, especially in discourse (Rissanen, 1985).

Some signs moved from the middle parts of the face to one side, e.g. in the sign APPLE, which is usually signed near the mouth, moved further on the cheek. Some signs moved downwards on the face, e.g. the sign RED moved from the lip to the chin. This kind of variation is also usual in adults' signing.

At the age of 6 years and 8 years, I observed very similar variation as at the age of 2-3 years. The neutralization and the transition from the middle parts of the face or the body to the side were evident features in Peter's signing during the whole period of observation. At the age of 2-3 years there was considerably less variation in the places of articulation than in the handforms and in the articulation movements. The variations in the place of articulation had not reduced very much. This illustrates the fact that the place of articulation is not difficult for a child to acquire, and he/she learns it early (see Kantor 1980). The place of articulation, however, is a flexible parameter; it allows much idiolectic variation and variation due to the signing situation and style.

2.4 Orientation of the hand

Orientation of the hand is closely connected to the handform. At the age of 2-3 years, the variation in orientation often simplified the articulation of the sign, e.g. in the sign OLD, where the orientation forward from the signer was changed to the orientation to the left. In the sign BABY, the orientation upwards changed to the orientation towards the signer. Occasionally, the orientation was changed by imprecise articulation, e.g. in the sign MIRROR, where the orientation towards the signer changed to the orientation to the left.

At the age of 6 years and 8 years, the variation in the orientation of the hand had reduced more than the variation in the place of articulation. During the first period there were equally many of both. The reason for the variation was to some extent the simplification of the articulation, e.g. in the sign EGG, where the hands are usually orientated opposite each other in up-and-down- direction, Peter's hands were orientated in side-to-side-direction. In the sign SPRING, the hands are orientated upwards, Peter's hand were orientated towards ego.

Another reason for the variation was Peter's imprecise articulation, e.g. in the sign READY, which he signed very quickly, and the orientation changed from the direction towards ego to the direction downwards. Some signs with a difficult handform and a difficult articulation movement caused some variations in orientation, e.g. in the sign SKIP.

3 SUMMARY

Table 1 shows the amount of variation in different cheremes at each age (in other words, in how many separate signs there were variations). One can expect a developmental direction: the variations diminished with age, and the "child language" changed to more "adult like" language with its idiolectic features. It would be interesting to compare Peter's signing with the signing of other deaf children at the same age.

Table 1: The amount of variation in different cheremes

	2-3 years	6 years	8 years
Handforms	57	13	7
Movements	80	17	6
Place	19	9	10
Orientation	19	5	5

At the age of 2-3 years, most variation in sign articulation, compared with the adult's way of signing, occurred in the articulation movements and the handforms. In the place of articulation and in the hand orientation there were fewer variations. The articulation movements were somewhat clumsy and poorly co-ordinated. The independent control of the fingers, the lack of visual feedback, the careless, loose articulation and the presence of movement in the sign produced difficulties in the handforms (see also Boyes-Braem 1973, Mc Intire 1977, Carter 1980).

At the age of 5 years 9 months, most variation occurred in the articulation movements, and secondly in handforms, thirdly in the places of articulation, and the least amount of variation was found in the orientation of the hand. The total amount of variation in the articulation movements and the handforms was remarkably lower than at the age of 2-3 years. The years up to 5-6 years represent important and intense time in the development of the phonological system and the child's output of the sign language. There was variation in the two-handed signs both in the handforms and in the articulation movements. The left hand was weaker. The circular movement and the bending of the wrist sometimes changed to an easier, linear movement.

There occurred an interesting type of variation which I call "playing with cheremes". Hearing children play with phonemes, creating variations which do not belong to the normal phoneme system of their language. This kind of play with phonemes occurred e.g. in the sign giraffe where Peter continued the articulation movement ("the neck of the giraffe") as far up as his hand could reach. Another example was the sign priest where Peter continued the movement to his stomach, although it is signed on the upper part of the chest.

At the age of 7 years 10 months, there was not much difference in the total of changes in each parameter. The data includes a few simplifications of handforms and articulation movements. In the place of articulation some places became neutralized and some moved downward. In the longitudinal development of the sign articulation one can see some idiolectic features (e.g. the lax way of articulation), which remained through the whole period of study.

Footnotes

---

* Ritva Takkinen: Department of Phonetics, University of Helsinki, Finland.

Bibliography

Boyes-Braem, P. [1973]. *Acquisition of the Handshape in American Sign Language: A Preliminary Analysis.* Unpublished paper. Centre for Sign Language Research, Basel.

Carter, M. [1981]. *The Acquisition of British Sign Language (BSL): A First Analysis.* Unpublished paper. Centre for Deaf Studies, University of Bristol.

Kantor, R. [1980]. The acquisition of classifiers in American Sign Language. *Sign Language Studies* 28, pp. 193–208.

Loncke, F. [1984]. On the interface between sign phonology and kinesiology, in: Loncke, F., Boyes-Braem, P. and Lebrun, Y. (eds) *Recent Research on European Sign Languages*, pp. 129–137. Swets and Zeitlinger BV, Lisse.

McIntire, M. [1977]. The Acquisition of American Sign Language Hand Configurations. *Sign Language Studies* 16, pp. 247–266.

Rissanen, T. [1985]. *Viittomakielen perusrakenne.* Helsingin yliopisto, Yleisen kielitieteen laitos.

Takkinen, R. [1988]. *Kereemipoikkeavuudet Kuuron Lapsen Viittomakielessä 2v 3kk–3v 4kk Iässä. Tapaustutkimus. Pro Gradu-Tutkielma.* Helsingin yliopisto, Fonetiikan laitos.

Appendix 1: Description of the signs

AEROPLANE	ʸ hand moving in the neutral area imitating a flying aeroplane
AMBULANCE	˝5-hand (knuckles orientated upwards) turning inwards from the wrist in the neutral area
APPLE	˝5-hand (the palm faced to the cheek) beside the mouth turning inwards from the wrist
AUTUMN	5-hand (dominant) the fingers wiggling and the palm contacting the thumb of the A-hand (non-dominant)
BABY	B-handform in both hands (the palms orientated upwards); the hands one on the other in front of the signer
BED	B-handform in both hands with palms facing each other in the neutral area moving at the same time to the signer
BINOCULARS	o-handform in both hands in front of the eyes
BLACK	B-hand (the palm facing to the signer) on the eye
BLUE	B-hand (with the palm orientated from the signer) moving in the neutral area from middle to the ipsilateral side
BOAT	B-handform in both hands (the palms facing each other) with the contact of fingertips moving forward in the neutral area
BOY	A-hand (a fist) on the temple as if lifting the cap
BROKEN	s-handform in both hands beside each other (the palms orientated down) the hands turning down from the wrist
BURN	˝5-hand in both hands the palms orientated upwards moving simultaneously with circular movement
BUS	ɓ-handforms in both hands (the palms faced to each other) moving forward in the neutral area
BUTTER	H-hand (dominant) moving on the non-dominant hand (B-hand) to the signer as if spreading the butter on the bread
CAT	B-hand moving on the back of the hand towards the signer as if stroking the cat
COCK	3-hand (the palm faced to the contralateral side) the thumb contacting the top of the head
COOK	G-handform in both hands (the knuckles orientated upwards) moving alternately up and down in the neutral area
COW	Y-hand (the palm faced to the contralateral side) the thumb contacting the temple
CRAYFISH	v-handform in both hands (the palms facing each other) closing to H-hand, both hands moving simultaneously to the signer
CRY	G-handform in both hands with palms facing to the signer moving alternately downwards on the cheeks

DUMMY	ı-hand (the palm faced to the signer) on the mouth
DOCTOR	н-handform in both hands with palms orientated to the signer; the non-dominant hand on the chest, the fingers of the dominant hand tapping on the fingers of the non-dominant hand
DRAW	bo-hand (the palm faced from the signer) making circling movement in the neutral area
DRINK	c-hand making drinking movement in front of the mouth
DRINK-COFFEE	F-hand making drinking movement
EGG	н-hand (dominant) touching repeatedly the fingertips of the o-hand (non-dominant) in the neutral area
ELK	5-handform in both hands (the palm faced from the signer) the thumbs contacting the temples
FATHER	A-hand (a fist with the palm faced to the contralateral side) contacting first the forehead and moving then to the chin
FISH	в-hand (the palm faced to the contralateral side) moving forward in the neutral area including the repeated wiggling with the wrist
FLOWER	o-hand (the palm orientated upwards) opening to 5-hand in the neutral area
GIRAFFE	c-hand with the palm faced to the signer moving up in front of the throat
GRANDFATHER	A-hand moving to the signer in the neutral area as if having a cane in the hand
GRANDMA	5̈-hand; the fingertips contacting the cheek two times
GUN	ɢ-hand in the neutral area moving as firing the gun
HEN	v-hand (the palm orientated to the contralateral side) contacting the nose
HOUSE	в-handform in both hands moving in the neutral area as if depicting a house
INJECTION	3-hand closing (fingers together) on the upper arm
JESUS	8-hand with palms facing each other - the middle finger touching the palm of the other hand, both hands doing the same after each other
MIRROR	в-hand in front of the face (the palm orientated to the signer) turning to-and-fro from the forearm
MOTHER	A-hand (a fist with the palm facing to the signer) contacting first the breast and then moving to the chin
OLD	ƀ-hand with the palm facing from the signer beside the cheek closing to o-hand

OVERTURN	5̈-hand in both hands facing each other moving simultaneously as if overturning an bowl
PORRIDGE	A-hand making circular movement in the neutral area on the horizontal plane as if stirring the porridge
POUR	L-hand with the palm facing to the signer bending to the contralateral side in the neutral area
READY	B-handform in both hands (the palms orientated to the signer) almost one on the other in front of the signer; the dominant hand bending downwards from the wrist
RED	G-hand on the lower lip moving forth and back
SCALES	B-handform in both hands (the palms orientated upwards) moving alternately up and down in the neutral area
SCHOOL	B-handform in both hands (the palms orientated to the signer) moving simultaneously to each other two times in the neutral area
SHEEP	v-hand with the palm faced down closing to H-hand (several times) on the forearm of the non-dominant hand
SIGN	5-handform in both hands faced each others making alternating circular movement on the vertical plane in the neutral area
SIT	the fingers of v̈-hand (dominant) on the fingers of the H-hand (non-dominant) (the fingers describe the sitting)
SKATE	B-handform in both hands faced each other moving forth and back in the neutral area
SKIP	A-handform in both hands moving as if circling the rope
SKIS	ẞ̈-handform in both hands (the palms orientated upwards) moving alternately towards the signer
SKY	B-hand (the palm orientated down) moving from the contralateral side to ipsilateral side in the neutral area
SMOKE	5̈-hand (the palm faced downwards) moving upwards with circular movement in the neutral area
SPIDER	5̈-handform in both hands with palms faced downwards thumbs contacting - the hands moving simultaneously upwards with wiggling fingers
SPRING	ẞ̇-handform in both hands (the palms faced each other) closing to o-hand
SWIM	B-handform in both hands faced downwards making simultaneous circular movement on the horizontal plane in the neutral area
THROAT	L̈-hand (the palm faced to the signer) moving down in front of the throat

TEXT-TELEPHONE ꕕ-handform in both hands fingers wiggling in the neutral area
as if typing

VIOLIN ŏ-hand (dominant) and c-hand (non-dominant)
depicting the playing of violin

WASP bo-hand contacting the cheek

Notation symbols: *Durham TS sansserif* by Ernst Thoutenhoofd. © 1989 Deaf Studies Research Unit.

PART 4

Dictionaries

Pragmatics and productivity

MARY BRENNAN *

1 INTRODUCTION

This discussion focuses on the nature of the productive lexicon in British Sign Language (BSL) and the extent to which information on productive forms can or should be included within a BSL dictionary. It also seeks to develop some strands of the relationship between the nature of BSL discourse and the particular types of vocabulary items exploited. It will be suggested that although certain kinds of vocabulary usage can be predicted from the pragmatics of the dicourse involved, a full and elaborated set of relationships is not available at the present time; nevertheless there are relationships which can be made explicit.

Let us begin then with some central claims around which the rest of this paper will focus.

• A crucial distinction can be drawn between the productive lexicon and the frozen or established lexicon in BSL, as in other (possibly all) sign languages (see McDonald 1982, Supalla 1982, Brennan 1990).

• The use of different types of lexical resource is partly governed by pragmatic/discourse requirements.

• To date, relatively little attention has been paid to the productive lexicon within sign language dictionaries or other collections of lexical resources (eg computer, video and text listings of signs).

• Productive forms should be included in dictonaries and should be the proper concern of lexicographers.

2 THE FROZEN/PRODUCTIVE DISTINCTION

The suggestion that a distinction can be drawn between the frozen forms of a sign language and the productive lexical forms is stressed and exemplified in the work of several sign linguists, including McDonald, 1982; Supalla, 1978, 1980, 1982, 1986, and Brennan, 1990a, Brennan, 1990b and Brennan et al, 1993). At its simplest, the distinction separates out two specific groups of signs:

• those that are fully established and therefore, almost by definition, are capable of being stored separately as individual items of the specific sign language lexicon: the frozen forms;

• those that are created as required by the signer from a set of component parts (morphemes); these component parts can be put together in different ways at different times to suit the needs of the discourse: the productive forms.

The former have been described as 'off the shelf' items, already made up and ready to use, while the latter have been described as making up a kind of DIY ('Do it yourself') lexicon, where the signer can select the most appropriate set of forms and assemble them as required: a kind of linguistic 'pick 'n' mix" (see Brennan, 1990 and Brennan et al, 1993). It is suggested here that virtually all kinds of sign discourse are likely to include both types of lexical choice, although certain kinds of discourse lend themselves more to the use of productive forms. Generally there has been an assumption, that these are the types of discourse in which the signer is expected to use more linguistic resourcefulness or creativity, eg in the telling of stories, in telling jokes, in playing with the language for various types of effect and so on. Before examining the discourse implications, let us explore this basic distinction a little further.

2.1 Classifiers

McDonald's 1982 thesis provides an excellent starting point for any discussion of the productive lexicon, since she describes a large set of examples of the component parts of such forms. Her focus is on what might be called 'classifier predicates'. Similarly the work by Supalla (listed above) and Newport and Supalla (1980) focuses on classifier forms, particularly verbs of motion and location. Classifiers have been widely discussed in the sign language literature (cf above references). They can be seen as linguistic indicators of classification. Thus in BSL and ASL, specific handshapes may function as markers of the particular class to which a given entity belongs. Typical classes include such categories as those listed in Figure 1; related handshapes which serve as markers of this class membership are also listed.

Figure 1: Examples of classifications marked by handshape classifiers in BSL.

B   G   V   A   Ĝ

- the class of vehicles   B
- the class of persons   G
- the class of two-legged beings V
- the class of long thin things   G
- the classs of flat entities   B
- the class of round entities   A
- the class of objects which may be held within a closed fist   A
- the class of objects which may be held within the finger and thumb   Ĝ
- the class of objects which may be held between flat hands   B B

It is worth stressing that there is not necessarily a one-to-one relationship between classification and handshape. Thus round items in BSL may be marked by the A, O, F and V handshapes, as in Figure 2:

Figure 2: Classifiers for round objects in BSL.

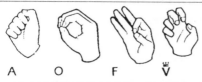

A   O   F   V̈

Examples of productive classifier forms include those listed in Figure 3, taken from Brennan (1992).

Figure 3: Productive forms involving classifiers in BSL

BODY FELL WITH A THUD   SLEIGH WINDING DOWNHILL

WASH CLOTHES (a)   WASH CLOTHES (b)

My own informal observations of discussions of classifier forms, most obviously by interested groups (eg teachers of a sign language) is that the most frequently elaborated type of example is the classic verb of motion/location such as

VEHICLE MOVES FROM SIDE TO SIDE IN DOWNWARD DIRECTION

Handling classifiers appear to receive considerably less focus. McDonald's early work provides a very useful set of examples which demonstrates all too clearly the importance of handling classifiers within productive forms.

2.2 Metaphorical morphemes

Brennan (1990a, 1990b and 1993) has suggested that there is a further set of morphemes which can play a part in the productive lexicon. These are termed metaphor morphemes. Whilst the term itself appears to be rather controversial, there is nevertheless a growing recognition that such morphemes do play a significant role within the productive lexicon. The claim is that these morphemes are not purely arbitrary: there is a metaphorical relationship between the form of the morpheme and its meaning. Examples of proposed metaphor morphemes in BSL are shown in Figure 4.

Figure 4: Proposed metaphor morphemes in BSL.

emanate	A handshape opening to s handshape
lines	s handshape
absorb	B parallel handshape closing to B closed
hold	s handshape closing to A

Examples of productive forms exploiting these morphemes are presented in Figure 5.

Figure 5: Productive forms exploiting BSL metaphor morphemes.

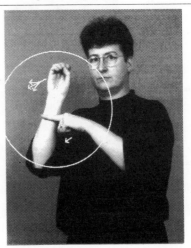

THOUGHT TRANSFER   TRANSMIT

Figure 5 (continued).

PHOTOCOPY   UNDERSTAND

   Brennan (1990a) also suggests that there is a large set of spatial metaphors in BSL.
Just as many spoken languages exploit spatial patterning, so do sign languages:
however, in the latter case these spatial metaphors are literally expressed in space. In
English, for example, notions of inferiority and superiority, are expressed through
such spatial notions as high and low: we speak of an individual or group as having
high or low status and of one individual being in a lower position (eg in a firm) than
another; in England, at least, people still speak of the upper, middle and lower
classes and of the higher echelons of power. There are, of course, hundreds of such
examples of spatial metaphor. What is being suggested here (and in earlier works) is
that these and other such metaphorical relationships are expressed more directly in
sign languages, simply because of the spatial-gestural modality. Thus the hands can
literally be placed higher or lower in respect to each other; one hand may be placed
in front of or behind the other; the hands may change places and so on. We know
that such metaphorical positioning can be exploited in BSL syntax. What is
suggested here is that it may also be exploited within the productive lexicon. Thus
the relatively new notion of advocacy is expressed in BSL in a number of different
ways: one sign makes use of two À handshapes, one moving to a position behind the
other and then both moving forward. This could be analysed as exploiting a
handshape which has a positive value within BSL signs (ie is linked with meanings
related to goodness or positive effects); the movement of the dominant hand into a
position behind the non-dominant appears to be equivalent to phrases in English
such as "I'm right behind you"; "I'm there to back you up"; "You have my full
backing". The movement forward can be seen as indicating a kind of progress:
again notice such expressions as "We can move forward on this matter"; "The
Americans are ahead of us in this area." Similarly, the notion of segregation is

shown by holding the two **B** hands together, back to back, and then the dominant hand moving away in a firm action. Again, the notion of segregation is being represented by a motivated form: it is as if one entity is pushed away from another just as one hand pushes away from the other.

2.3 Fuzzy edges

So far in this discussion, it has been implied that the distinction between the frozen and productive lexicon is clear and obvious. Of course, this is not the case. Not only is there an overlap between the two forms, such that it may not be clear how we should categorise specific forms, but there are several kinds of fuzzy edges. We are dealing with the fuzziness inherent in the traditional distinction between derivational morphology and inflectional morphology as well as the haziness of the productive frozen distinction.

Like many contrasts of this type, the derivational/inflectional contrast works well with what we might think of as the central or prototypical examples. Certain criteria have been elaborated which supposedly justify the distinction. If this distinction were absolute, we might well argue that any dictionary of the language should include the the root of a word form and some indication of the types of inflectional and derivational affixes (whether simultaneous or sequential) which could be added to this. However, we might imagine that, as with most English dictionaries, the requirement to specify all potential derivational affixes would be too onerous. The kinds of criteria that have been elaborated with respect to the traditional distinction, include the following:
• derivations provide new words (or lexemes); inflections simply provide different forms of the same word;
• inflections do not cause a change of word-class category (eg from noun to verb); derivations may cause a categorial change (eg noun to adjective);
• inflectional forms typically constitute closed sets: we do not add to them or lose items from these sets, except, typically over long periods of time;
• inflectional affixes have regular meanings; derivational affixes are more variable;
• derivational affixes occur prior to inflectional affixes: they occur nearer the root;
• inflection is productive (eg English '-ing' is applied to verbs in a very regular manner—it has high productivity); derivation is only partially productive;
• inflections are more directly relevant to syntax: eg in traditional grammar, syntax and inflections together were said to constitute grammar.

Several writers have accepted the relevance of these criteria for sign languages and have been able to demonstrate the applicability of these criteria: for example, Newport (1982) demonstrates that processes of derivational affixation occur prior to processes of inflectional derivation. However, this is to assume that we do know which is which: the argument can easily become circular.

We can illustrate some of the problems by looking at a few examples of what might be regarded as typical productive forms in BSL. Some key examples are given in Figure 6.

Figure 6: Productive forms in BSL.

RUNNING WITH HUGE STRIDES   SAUNTERING

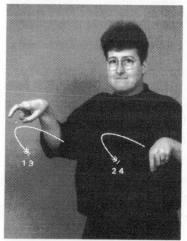 

SPIRAL OF COINS (LOCATED)   HAND OVER A SPIRAL OF COINS

What are the component parts which make up these lexemes? Can we specify the root of any of these forms, ie the central form to which all further affixes are added? Immediately we enter an area of controversy. How do we decide which is the central content component? One way of answering the question might be to say that in all of these cases we happen to be dealing with words containing a classifier component: the class of classifiers in BSL is relatively large. It is much larger, for example, than the set of aspectual inflections. Therefore it might seem appropriate to treat these forms as the central semantic components in that they cannot be said to belong to a small closed class. This might then be an appropriate criterion to exploit to make the distinction. However, it may be that we should treat these classifiers as derivational affixes. But how do we decide if these are affixes when we remain unclear about the root—after all, one of the criteria for deciding that an affix is derivational is that it occurs nearer the root than inflectional forms.

What are the candidates for inflectional forms in these exampes? We can see that the other elements of meaning within the forms include;

• marking of aspect;
• marking of manner;
• marking of subject object agreement;
• marking of location.

Treatments of aspect in BSL and other sign languages (Brennan, 1983; Bergman, 1980) demonstrate that we are dealing with a limited closed set of options, which on the whole can be said to have regular meanings. However, manner is somewhat more difficult to decide upon. Supalla's accounts of verbs of motion and location (1978, 1982, 1986) include manner morphemes within movement: ie in terms of what might be termed manner of movement: this can be illustrated by some of his glosses:

• VEHICLE-WANDER-UPWARD-ACROSS-HORIZONTAL-WIDE-STRAIGHT-SHAPE
• VEHICLE-ROTATE-ON-WIDE-STRAIGHT-SHAPE
• VEHICLE-TURN-PAST-TREE
• VEHICLE-MOVE-THRU-FOUR-HORIZONTAL-THIN-STRAIGHT-SHAPES

Given that the last of these is given the English translation of "The car crashes through a fence", it may be questioned whether the full manner information is present in the glossing: ie we might expect something like—WITH FORCE.

The notion of manner can, in any case, be interpreted somewhat more widely. It is clear that in this area, non-manual forms play a highly significant role. As illustrated in Brennan (1992), there are several non-manual markers of manner such as 'at ease/without effort' (as in SAUNTER illustration), so-called 'ee' involving stretched lips, meaning the opposite, ie 'with effort/intensity' and 'puffed cheeks', which may also mean 'with effort/intensity'. The last example illustrates the difficulty of pinning down a single regular meaning to this form: in one sense it has to be interpreted according to the meaning of the other morphemes which are being assembled. While it does seem possible to delimit a fairly restricted set of affixes, it can be difficult to narrow down the set of possibilities since we are frequently dealing with combinations of non-manual markers, often including shoulder, trunk and head movements and one or more facial components. Currently it is not even clear what we should regard as constituting a single morpheme . Is 'puckered nose' a single morpheme, meaning something like 'unpleasant'? Is tongue protrusion, 'th' a further single morpheme again meaning 'unpleasant'? Since both of these components frequently, though not always co-occur, should we regard them as jointly constituting a single morpheme? Should one be regarded as an intensifier of the other? If so, which is which? Discussions with native signers suggest that there are no clear answers to such questions at the moment. We probably need to collect much more empirical evidence before we can arrive at firm conclusions. However, this certainly means that we cannot be absolutely firm about inflectional/derivational status.

While marking of subject/object agreement involves a clearly delimited set of options, locative marking is again much more difficult to analyse in terms of a limited listing of clearly distinct forms with corresponding meanings. Do we need to distinguish between right, near right, mid right, far right etc? How many divisions would we have and to what extent are such decisions arbitrary? Again it seems that not only are we far from deciding on type of morpheme, we are also unclear about the morphemic status of such options. The detailed discussions by our students, including native signers familiar with the nature of the issues involved, suggest that whilst signers often share intuitions that 'x is significant', it can be much more difficult to tie down meanings or establish regularity of patterning.

All of the above is intended to give some hint of the dilemmas currently facing the sign language lexicographer when dealing with the productive lexicon. Of course, some of these same problems occur even for the established lexicon. Typically dictionaries list the inflectional forms that verbs, for example, can take. How do we treat manner in this context? Do we add to a BSL verb such as WORK the information that the sign can take the following x number of inflections for manner? Clearly we have the same problems as listed above. This is not to say that we should not ultimately be aiming to try to present such information. We should certainly be laying the groundwork now. However, it would be false to imply that we currently have the required data and theory to make the most appropriate decisions.

One attempt to begin the process of at least providing further information is demonstrated within the *Dictionary of BSL/English* (Brien, 1992). Here a decision was made to include information about component morphemes of productive signs in the formal 'Introduction' to this dictionary (Brennan, 1992). Other dictionaries, particularly the *Dictionary of Australian Sign Language* (Johnston, 1989) and the *Thai Sign Langauge Dictionary* (Suwanarat et al, 1986) have also attempted to give information on the classifier forms of the respective languages. Within the *Dictionary of BSL/English*, the classifier table (pp 53 - 67) provides a listing of classifier forms expressed by 38 different handshapes. An extract is given in Figure 8 (see overleaf).

Figure 8: Extract from classifier table in Brennan, 1992

Classifier handshape	**G**

Size and shape	objects which are relatively long and thin, often cylindrical: the person classifier occupies a major paradigm of its own; **cigarette**[229]**, leg, missile, penis, tube train**
Tracing size and shape	index fingers trace size, shape or outline of shapes and objects; **window** (sign 441)**, square, triangle, lightning**
Handling	holding objects on tip of index finger; **contact lens, plates** (as in spinning plates)
Instrumental	instruments with long narrow, often cylindrical, component; **compass** (sign 403)**, rowel, knitting needles, compass needle**
Touch	actions of the index finger **get at** (sign 444)**, prod, poke, press/push buttons**

229. cigarette

Classifier handshape	**Ġ**

Size and shape	objects with one long and one short extension at right angles; **walking stick, set square**
Tracing size and shape	tracing dimensions, particularly depth of items, e.g. on body; **briefs** (sign 742)**, bikini, bra, pants**
Handling	(usually combines with instrumental function) holding items with long narrow extension; **petrol** (sign 462)**, gun, electric drill, staple gun, video camera**
Instrumental	(usually combines with handling function) instruments with long narrow extensions; **gun** (sign 463)[230]**, electric drill, staple gun**
Touch	

230. gun

Classifier handshape	**Ĝ**

Size and shape	triangular or wedge-shaped objects; **beak, wedge, bow** (two hands)
Tracing size and shape	used with initial opening action to trace position and shape of objects; **ear ring, collar, cuffs**
Handling	holding small, tiny or delicate objects or relatively flat items; **pill** (sign 476)[231]**, capsule, jewellery, audiotape, paper**
Instrumental	instruments with wedge-shaped or triangular components (rare); **wedge**
Touch	

231. pill

229. ⌄ G⌀< $\overset{\times}{\underset{m}{}}$·   230. ∅ °Ġ<⊥ $\left(\begin{smallmatrix} o \\ n \\ \wedge \\ m \end{smallmatrix}\right)$ 231. B̄a> Ĝ⌀⊥ $\overset{\times}{\wedge}\left(\begin{smallmatrix} o \\ T \end{smallmatrix}\right)$ // ⌄ ĜT< $\overset{\times}{}$

This table gives some indication of the scale of potential creativeness available to the BSL signer. In the past, there has been a tendency, eg in sign language teaching, and to some extent in the available literature (eg Brennan et al, 1984) to see the classifier resource as important but limited to a relatively few handshapes and meanings. It might even be suggested that we have been giving rather too much attention to vehicles and ᴄ hand persons and not enough to the wide range of resources available and clearly exploited in the language. The ᴄ hand person classifier may turn out to be relatively uncommon as compared to examples in which the notion of 'person' is encoded by the use of other classifiers, eg 'legs' classifiers exploiting ᴄ, bent ᴄ, v, bent v and ᴀ with prominent forearm and the 'head' classifier, ᴀ. However, there is no claim that this listing is fully comprehensive. Similarly, whilst an attempt is given to give clear examples of the types of meaningful components mentioned earlier (non-manual morphemes of manner, for example), our present state of knowledge and the limitations of text dictionaries inevitably limits the nature and presentation of the relevant information. Our current work on the development of a multi-media database, SIGNBASE, and related dictionary should support future work in this area. The database should ultimately, in fact, help us to solve many of these problems in that we hope, by inputting information on a large number of productive signs, we will be able to draw out regularities of patterning. [1]

3 PRODUCTIVE VERSUS FROZEN

Some of the difficulties faced by a lexicographer in terms of distinguishing the two types of lexical item arise out of the limitations of current knowledge of the language.[2]

However, some of the kinds of difficulties are inherent in the whole process of lexicography. Compilers of major dictionary resources usually attempt to record all of the current words of the language. This will include new words which will have come into the language recently. So one of the ongoing questions for the lexicographer is; what constitutes a new word? We can illustrate the nature of the difficulty by looking at two affixes in English, -able and non-. The suffix -able is highly productive in English. As Bauer [Bauer, 1988] argues it would not be possible to make an exhaustive list of all cases of -able suffixed to a base, which is a transitive verb because "every time a new transitive verb is formed, -able can also be added to it". Thus if we create a verb from the name Thatcher as in "The Swedes have begun to Thatcherise their economic processes", we know we can add the suffix -able to this new verb as in "Swedish society is simply not Thatcherisable". Users of English have no difficulty whatsoever in understanding the way in which such a suffix operates. However, dictionary compilers make different decisions as to when to include forms with the -able ending. Similarly non- can be said to be a highly productive prefix. One

Collins English Dictionary includes a number of full entries which exploit this prefix as in *nonproductive, nonprofit-making, nonproliferation*. However, it also lists several hundred examples without full entries, i.e. simply providing the word and an indication of its syntactic classification in terms of noun, adjective and so on. These include examples such as *nonCatholic, nonintellectual, nonrecognition* and *nonverifiable*. Presumably all of these forms have been attested, i.e. the dictionary maker has included these forms precisely because they have been noted within English usage. The decision to include an item within a main entry would seem to be dependent upon some notion of the relative productivity of the item concerned. Thus the Collins lexicographers appear to have decided that *nonproliferation* is, for example, more common than *nonCatholic*. One of the difficulties faced by lexicographers is that there may be different types and levels of usage amongst individuals as opposed to the society as a whole. Thus within Catholic communities individuals may in fact use the term *nonCatholic* quite frequently, whereas their use of *nonproliferation* may be relatively rare. However, over society as a whole this situation may be reversed.

Bauer (1988) argues that "the dominating criteria distinguishing the two [individual and societal productivity] are probably widespread use in the written and spoken media and listing in dictionaries. In a pre-technological society it would probably be much harder to draw the distinction and indeed in very small speech communities there may not be any distinction to be drawn" (Bauer, 1988: 65).

One of the difficulties for the lexicographer is the very act of placing an item within the dictionary gives it a new type of status. Within the BSL lexicography we do not, of course, have written records to guide our decision making. The increasing use of BSL on a few regular television programmes does provide at least one source for attested forms. There are also considerable video resources now available of BSL usage, although these resources are scattered throughout the country and are not particularly easily accessible to the researcher. More importantly, there is currently no major project which would allow the collection of such resources and the detailed coding of signs which ideally is required. The SIGNBASE multi-media project should provide an appropriate multi-media database format but the resources for the collection of data are still very limited. Nevertheless, it is possible to observe signs being created and introduced into the language.

In recent years it has been possible to note the way in which several new signs for linguistic terminology have entered the lexicon. The three examples I will refer to here are the signs glossed as DIGLOSSIA, PIDGIN and CREOLE. In each case it could be argued that these signs were created by exploiting primarily motivated, in particular metaphorically motivated, morphemes of the language. The sign DIGLOSSIA appears to have devloped from signers referring to the two varieties within a diglossic situation, i.e. the H (high) and the L (low) varieties. Signers tended to produce forms in which two bent B hands were used, i.e. fingers together, hand bent at the major knuckles, and for the high variety to use a slight upward repeated movement with the dominant hand and for the low variety to use a slight downward repeated movement with the non-dominant hand. In discussions of diglossia various different versions of this form were seen again and again. Eventually a single sign emerged for the overall concept in which both B hands were used, the differential height in space was maintained but the non-dominant hand made contact with the forearm of the dominant hand in a sideways simple tapping motion. It could be argued that this is a classical example of a motivated form losing some element of its transparency within the refining down process. The sign PIDGIN involves two 5-hands with palms facing down and fingers pointing forward one above the other moving in an alternating side to side action. This again appears to be a motivated form indicating the mixing of two separate languages (as represented by the two hands) and the relatively unstable nature of the linguistic structure concerned (as represented by the side to side movement). This sign contrasts with the sign CREOLE which again involves the two 5-hands, with the dominant hand placed above the other, but in this case the dominant hand moves forward from a position at shoulder level, then both hands move forward in a complementary fashion. This appears to suggest movement over time (i.e. the right hand coming from the right shoulder) and the relative stability of the creole situation, i.e. the side to side movement has disappeared.

Within linguistic discussion of pidgins and creoles, these two signs now seem to be fairly widely used although a sign based on the English word *pigeon* sometimes glossed as BIRD has also been observed on many occasions. This kind of example illustrates what might be termed the cultural/political dilemma of the lexicographer. Perhaps ideally both entries should be included. If the 'bird' entry is excluded, it could be argued that the lexicographer is ignoring relatively widespread usage amongst those Deaf people who discuss the notion of pidgin sign language. The newer version may be used by a much smaller group of people although observations would suggest that once individuals become aware of the two forms they tend to prefer the newer form, at least if they are involved in sign language linguistics. Nevertheless the lexicographer can be seen to be making an evaluation or judgement as opposed simply to be recording usage. However as the Collins Dictionary examples demonstrate, lexicographers have to do this all the time.

4 THE PRAGMATICS OF PRODUCTIVITY

In this section I would like to focus on two aspects of the use of productive forms. Firstly I would like briefly to comment on the types of discourse in which productive forms occur and secondly I would like to give some attention to the pragmatic influences on the use of different combinations of formational components within productive forms.

4.1 Discourse

One of the suggestions which has been made concerning discussion of classifier based forms is that they are typically found within stories, anecdotes, informal conversation and so on. There has been a tendency, therefore, to assume that the productive lexicon can only be associated with types of discourse which can be classified as informal and perhaps, more particularly, types of discourse which can be regarded as narrative. It is suggested here that this is much too narrow a base in which to consider the productive lexicon. An examination of a wider range of texts demonstrates that in almost all cases there is some use of productive forms and in both narrative and non-narrative texts there is often considerable use of such forms. It may well be that classifier based forms are more prevalent in narrative and descriptive types of discourse, whilst metaphorical morphemes are more likely to occur within more abstract types of (possibly formal) discourse.

4.2 The nature of discourse

Interaction can be seen as an interweaving of communicative acts which rely on such features as;
• Mutual orientation: both participants being able to exploit deixis in a mutually intelligent way;
• Shared knowledge: both/all participants sharing knowledge of a domain and the mechanisms by which that knowledge can be updated;
• Shared understanding of the goals of the interaction.

I would like to suggest that a further pragmatic consideration relates to shared linguistic expectations. The signer has a built in set of expectations concerning the extent to which the addressee will share full access to the total potential of the sign linguistic system s/he is exploiting. The Deaf person is used to having to adjust to differences in access to this full potential. Thus we know, for example, from the work of Supalla and Newport that access to the true potential of the ASL morphological system can vary depending on age of aquisition/learning of ASL. So even within Deaf-Deaf interactions there is a built in requirement to adjust linguistic expectations. The suggestion I am making here is that, in formal contexts where it is not possible to monitor and to adjust to the addressees' responses in a regular way (expecially when there is a mixed audience with inevitably mixed responses), there is what we might think of as a 'default setting' with respect to the use of productive morphology. It is almost as if within the evolution of BSL, the community of signers has arrived at a particular degree of shared linguistic knowledge but that this may change and indeed is changing as the language is allowed to move into previously restricted areas (such as formal abstract discourse).

The 'default setting' can be seen as involving a particular level of productive morphology along with a set of markers or indicators as to the nature of the productive forms. Another way of putting this is to say that the meaning or content of the productive forms is cued for the addressee by particular types of linguistic indicators. These markers may include explicit lip patterns which denote English words or related versions of English words; finger spelling forms of English words which may, for example, denote the object or the action referred to in the productive form; a frozen form, i.e. an established sign, which expresses some aspect of the meaning of the productive form. In some cases, the signer may use a frozen form which shares the same English gloss as the productive form, but which actually has a different meaning in BSL (as in the MOUSE example below).

The 'default setting' and its expression can be demonstrated by examples from two sets of data. Both of these extracts come from relatively formal contexts: the first is an account of several aspects of computer technology and the second is a question asked by a native Deaf signer at a conference on bi-lingual education. The following examples are taken from the discussion of computer technology. What we can see here is that the signer not only clarifies a productive form by adding an item from the frozen lexicon, typically accompanied by lip pattern, but even interrupts the articulation of the productive form to insert the clarifying information (figure 9).

Example 1. TUNE (as in tuning a television or tuning in a video monitor).
___
The signer produces a classifier based form interrupts this with the finger spelling t-u-n-e accompanied by the lip pattern 'tune' and then continues the classifier based form.

Example 2. MOUSE (i.e. the device used with computers).
___
Again the signer produces a classifier based productive form involving the use of the handling classifier V̈ then interrupts this to produce the established sign 'mouse' (i.e. usually referring to a small mammal) accompanied by the English lip pattern for 'mouse'. He then continues to produce the productive form.

Example 3. READ.
___
The signer uses the metaphorically based form 'read' in the sense of a computer taking in the information from the disc (the grasp metaphor is used). However the signer then adds the established frozen form 'read' (making use of the V hand shape) together with the lip pattern.

In all of these cases we have what appears to be a type of clarifying process taking place. It is as if the signer is saying 'I know I have provided you with the context. I know you have some understanding of the context, but I cannot expect you to have a full understanding of what I am talking about simply from the productive forms.'.

Of course, in an example such as this, the question also arises as to whether the presenter has a teaching goal in mind also. It is common practice, for example, in computer technology to exploit English terminology even in countries where English is not the standard language. It may be that within computer technology, as within linguistics, there is a pressure on the BSL presenter to make his/her audience more bilingually aware. There is a political view that, given that Deaf people have frequently been deprived of adequate access to education, it is simply not enough to provide them with the relevant concepts in their own preferred language. Full access to information in such areas as computers and linguistics may also require some knowledge of English. Although it may seem surprising that the signer may have such aims in mind when involved in ordinary day to day interaction, there does seem to be an indication that such influences are present at least at some kind of subconscious level which influences linguistic activity. If we return to the dilemmas facing lexicographers, we need to examine the role of lip pattern or English mouthing within both frozen and productive forms. In the instances which I have just described, the signer deliberately, it appears, leaves the productive form free of the 'clutter' of a frozen label. It is as if the productive form can be understood and in a sense enjoyed in its own terms while the frozen form takes on an almost bilingual function. It was predicted on the basis of such examples that productive forms would not take lip pattern, however, this is not fully supported by the data. While in the majority of cases the lip pattern co-occurs with frozen forms, in some complex forms there is what may appear to be the remnant of a frozen form. Thus in a productive sign which we might gloss as COMPUTER FILE the signer makes use of the lip pattern 'file' simultaneously with the sign. In this instance we can say that it is merely the location and size of the sign FILE which renders it a productive form. We could argue, therefore, either that COMPUTER FILE is on its way to being a fully frozen sign or that it is influenced by the fact of a fully frozen form already existing. It is worth noting that we seem to have a kind of irony here in that what is accompanied by lip pattern, is the most established part of the lexicon. In other words that what is most fully explicit and established is being made, as it were, even more explicit .

Finally I would like to draw attention to a real example of BSL usage which demonstrates all too well both the enormous creativity of native BSL signers and the difficulty of encapsulating such creativity within dictionaries. Unfortunately within a text version of this paper it is simply impossible to present the relevant information adequately. [3] Within this extract the signer is asking a question and making a comment at a conference on bilingual education in England. The signer is discussing the need to adapt one's signing to the level of the child rather than 'signing over the child's head' (note the spatial metaphor which is used in English).

The signer suggests that just as we have to adjust the heat of an iron to suit different types of material, so we have to adjust our signing to adjust to the lingistic level of children. The whole chunk of signing incorporates a range of productive forms, sandwiched between frozen forms such as AGREE, MEET, HEAT, WOOL and SILK.

I will focus here on two small sections of the sign production. The first concerns the use of a form which might literally be translated "as if turning dials on one's chest". The signer uses two parallel V bent handshapes, ie thumb, index finger and middle finger extended and bent, placed on the chest with palm orientation towards the body and both hands simultaneously twisting downwards. The signer uses a similar sign articulated with one hand to mean "adjusting the heat dial on an iron". It could be argued that the problems raised by this type of example are comparable to those raised by Brien and Turner (this volume, P 400) with regard to their discussion of CATERPILLAR CRAWLING UP A THIN OBJECT . Does the lexicographer attempt to list all attested forms such as: turn dial on iron; turn dial on iron to the right; turn iron to the right repeatedly; turn dial on video recorder; turn dial on stereo set; turn dial on radiator; turn central heating dial etc. As well as the additional variations of the forms listed above, there are clearly numerous other attested forms and potentially occurring forms. These examples could be seen as relating directly to objects and actions: however, the earlier example relating to "turning dials on one's chest" can be seen as a metaphorical extension of this literal meaning.

The second example from this same extract is even more complex. The signer uses what seems to be a type of chaining of morphemes. He initially provides the context by the use of the frozen forms MATCH and AGREE, both with accompanying lip pattern. The sign MATCH is made with two bent B hands (ie fingers together, both hands bent at major knuckles). The hands are held with palms facing each other in front of the body and the two hands come together so that the finger tips almost touch. The signer then changes the orientation and position of the two hands so that the dominant hand is held above and behind the other, with palm facing away and the non-dominant hand is held with palm up at a much lower position. The signer then executes a sign which could be literally translated as "gradually pull towards": the image is of hauling something in with a rope. The signer then returns to the second version of MATCH with the hands moving towards the body in step-like movements so that both hands are at the same level in space. However, the signer also adds a flickering motion of the fingers at two of the stages. This flickering movement is rather difficult to translate precisely but appears to mean that signing is being produced: it can be seen as a version of the 'spread' metaphor morpheme. This whole sequence can be translated as:

"You have to adjust your signing to match the needs of the child. In that way you can raise the level of the child's signing, constantly modifying your signing so that eventually both adult and child produce mutually comprehensible signing." . The signer then is both adapting the resources of the frozen lexicon by using significant re-positioning and re-orientation of frozen signs and exploiting the potential of the productive lexicon. It is difficult to imagine how such examples can be adequately reflected in any text-based dictionary.

What does all this tell us then about pragmatics and productivity? It is suggested here that productive forms constitute a much larger proportion of signing than is often recognised, even within types of discourse that are not normally associated with creativity. Because of this it is essential that dictionaries find some way of dealing with such forms. However, full listing of attested and potential forms will never be possible, although perhaps we should endeavour to list sufficient attested examples to ensure that learners and users understand the full potential of the productive lexicon. Recognition of the importance of productive forms must work alongside a realisation that frozen forms may often play a clarifying role in discourse, functioning as cues to the meaning of the productive forms. Whilst at an individual level the signer can adjust for understanding in an ongoing way, this is less possible in certain types of formal context, where the addressees are not expected to respond. In these situations the signer appears to work on the basis of an overall view of the degree of clarification required. Such clarifiaction may also be influenced by a sense of responsibility to provide access to the spoken/written language equivalents of the productive forms.

* Mary Brennan: Deaf Studies Research Unit, Department of Sociology and Social Policy, University of Durham, Elvet Riverside 2, New Elvet, Durham DH1 3JT, England. E-mail: Mary.Brennan @ uk.ac.durham
1. More details of this project, supported under the EC TIDE programme, may be obtained from David Brien or Mary Brennan at the DSRU, University of Durham.
2. It is worth stressing that the amount of research that has been undertaken and is being undertaken with respect to BSL is extremely limited. We should not be altogether surprised at the limited nature of knowledge if we compare the thousands of individuals who work, and have worked, on English as compared to BSL. One of the major difficulties facing sign language linguistics is that many of us are working in 'applied' contexts, before theories and description have been fully elaborated: indeed in some areas work has not even begun.
3. At Salamanca it was possible to show the relevant extract from the video.
4. My thanks to Jerry Hanifin and Clark Denmark for permission to use extracts of their signing for analysis and demonstration.

Bibliography

Bauer, L. [1988] Introducing Linguistic Morphology. Edinburgh University Press, Edinburgh.

Bergman, B. [1983] Verbs and adjectives: morphological processes in Swedish Sign Language, in Kyle, J.G. and Woll, B. (eds.) Language in Sign: an International Perspective on Sign Language. Croom Helm, London.

Brennan, M. [1983]. Marking Time in British Sign Language, in Kyle, J.G. and Woll, B. (eds.): Language in Sign; an International Perspective on Sign Language. Croom Helm, London.

Brennan, M. [1990a]Word Formation in British Sign Language. University of Stockholm, Stockholm.

Brennan, M. [1990b] Productive Morphology in British Sign Language, in Prillwitz, S. and Vollhaber, T. (eds.) Current Trends in European Sign Language Research: Proceedings of the 3rd European Congress on Sign Language Research. Signum Press, Hamburg.

Brennan, M. [1992] The Visual World of BSL: An Introduction, in Brien, D. (ed.). Dictionary of British Sign Language/ English, Faber and Faber, London.

Brennan, M., Brien, D., Collins, J., Elton, F. and Turner, G. H. [1993] The Dictionary of British Sign Language/English: A Bilingual Resource. Paper presented at LASER Facilitating Bilingualism Conference, St. Albans, Hertfordshire.

Brennan, M., Colville, M.D., Lawson, L.K. and Hughes, G. [1984] Words in Hand: A Structural Analysis of the Signs of British Sign Language (second edition). Moray House College of Education, Edinburgh.

Johnston, T. [1989] Auslan Dictionary: A Dictionary of the Sign Language of the Australian Deaf Community. Deafness Resources, Australia.

McDonald, B. [1982] Aspects of the American Sign Language Predicate System. Ph.D. Thesis, University of Buffalo.

Newport, E.L. [1982] Task Specificity in Language Learning: evidence from speech perception and American Sign Language in E. Wanner and L.R. Gleitman (eds.) Language Acquisition: The State of the Art . University Press, New York and Cambridge.

Newport, E.L. and Supalla, T. [1980] The Structuring of Language: clues from the acquisition of signed and spoken Language in U. Belugi and M. Studdert-Kennedy (eds.). Signed and Spoken Language: Biological Constraints on Linguistic Form. Verlag Chemie, Berlin.

Supalla, T. [1980] Morphology of verbs of motion and location in American Sign Language, in F. Caccamise and D. Hicks (eds.) Proceedings of the Second Naitonal Symposium of Sign Language Research and Teaching. National Association of the Deaf, Silver Spring, Maryland.

Supalla, T [1982] Structure and Acquisiton of verbs of motion and location in American Sign Language, Doctoral dissertation, University of California, San Diego.

Supalla, T. [1986] The classifier system in American Sign Language, in C. Craig (ed.) *Noun Classes and Categorisation*. John Benjamins Publishing Company, Amsterdam and Philadelphia.

Supalla, T. and Newport, E.L. [1978] How many seats in a chair? The derivation of nouns and verbs in American Sign Language, in Siple, P. (ed.) *Understanding Language Through Sign Language Research*. Academic Press, New York.

Suwanarat, M. et al [1986] *Thai Sign Language Dictionary*. National Association for the Deaf in Thailand and the Human Assistance Programme, Thailand.

Lemmas, dilemmas and lexicographical anisomorphism: presenting meanings in the first BSL-English Dictionary

DAVID BRIEN AND GRAHAM H. TURNER *

1 INTRODUCTION

Critical analysis of sign dictionary volumes produced all around the world[1] shows a sub-section of sign linguists grappling with a complex set of issues as they attempt to do justice to the rich patterns of these widely misunderstood and still often misrepresented languages. Essentially, the problem for all sign lexicographers stems from the absence of orthographies (as opposed to technical notation systems) for sign languages. Monolingual dictionaries of spoken/written languages work because print allows both form and meaning to be adequately represented in the same medium. The *form* of signs can be effectively depicted using illustrations or photographs (most editors choose to annotate these with additional artwork symbolising the particular movements required in each sign). The *meaning* of signs, on the other hand, cannot straightforwardly be presented in the same format. Definitions, example sentences and usage notes laid out using illustrations or photographs would inevitably prove impracticably cumbersome[2]. The resulting compromise—meanings presented in English text—blurs the distinction between a monolingual sign language dictionary and a bilingual signed/written language dictionary in a challenging way. This paper explores the presentation of meanings in the first bilingual British Sign Language-English dictionary.

2 HISTORY OF THE DICTIONARY

It has been suggested that the last twenty five years have been the "best of quarter centuries" for Deaf people (Hacking [1990]). During this period, signed languages achieved linguistic recognition as natural languages; languages independent of spoken/written languages. This recognition has led Deaf people in many countries to redefine their situation, identifying themselves as members of a linguistic minority group rather than disabled persons. In Britain, the British Deaf Association (the national representative organisation of Deaf people) has been at the forefront of a campaign to obtain formal government recognition for British Sign Language (BSL), the signed language of the British Deaf community.

The British Deaf Association (BDA) has not confined its efforts to simply campaigning on this issue. In recent years, it has committed a significant proportion of its resources to sponsoring sign language research and training programmes. Its most long-standing commitment has been to the publication of a BSL dictionary.

Deaf people's recognition that their preferred means of communication might properly be described as a language considerably pre-dates formal linguistic recognition. At the first British Deaf and Dumb Association Congress (in Leeds back in 1890) the first resolution to be passed read as follows : "That the Congress of the British Deaf and Dumb Association indignantly protests against the imputation... that the finger and signed language is barbarous. We consider such a mode of exchanging our ideas most natural and indispensable".

3 SIGN LEXICOGRAPHY

In 1960, the American linguist William C. Stokoe published the first paper in which the basis for the linguistic analysis and recognition of signed languages was outlined (Stokoe [1960]). Five years later, together with his colleagues Dorothy Casterline and Carl Croneberg, he published the first sign language dictionary based on linguistic principles (Stokoe et al. [1965]). Entries were presented through a notation system developed for the recording of signs, which described the signs in relation to the location, configuration and movement of the hands. It provided a means to view signs as linguistic phenomena rather than as a characteristic of Deaf people which served only to confirm the severity of their disability. The extent to which our work has drawn upon the principles of organisation first developed by Stokoe and his colleagues will be readily apparent to those familiar with the *Dictionary of American Sign Language*, which represented a landmark in the study of signed languages and marked the start of sign lexicography.

In claiming such importance for the dictionary designed by Stokoe et al., it is necessary to explain why, in the twenty-five years that followed, the majority of dictionaries published were organised according to very different principles. The notated entries and limited number of illustrations did not make it readily accessible to non-linguists. However, this does not explain why the principles that informed the organisation of entries were not considered appropriate by the compilers of other sign language dictionaries. In order to do this, it is necessary to locate sign lexicography within the general debate that was taking place during this period on the role of signed languages in the education of deaf children. Although the last twenty-five years may indeed have been the 'best of quarter centuries' for Deaf people, there was (and still is) considerable resistance to implementing social and educational policies based on the linguistic recognition of signed languages such as BSL and American Sign Language (ASL), and their use by Deaf people. This was reflected in the dictionaries produced during this period.

Dictionaries are often defined as being about the words of a language; the volume edited by Stokoe et al. was about the words (i.e. the signs) of ASL. Many of the dictionaries published since 1965 have not been about the signs as used in signed languages but about signs used as (or as if they were) supplements to or images of the words of a spoken/written language, ordered according to the principles of the spoken/written language. There was usually no reference in such publications to the meanings of the signs—it was implied that these were the same as the single English word 'translation' that usually accompanied each sign. The introduction during this period of the Total Communication approach in the education of deaf children—based not on the use of signed languages, but the use of signs as a support to a spoken language—did not encourage the development of dictionaries of natural signed languages. It has only been in the last five or six years that we have seen the publication of sign language dictionaries organised on similar principles to those advocated by Stokoe and his colleagues over twenty-five years ago (see, for example, Suwanarat et al [1986]; Johnston [1989]; Radutzky [1992]).

4 THE BDA'S DICTIONARY PROJECT

When Allan Hayhurst (former General Secretary of the BDA) commenced work on the BDA's dictionary project, the work of William Stokoe was not known to him. The BDA (then as now) was engaged in seeking to bring about change in the education of deaf children. At that time, education policy was still dominated by the philosophy and practice of oralism. The main aim of the dictionary was to provide hearing parents and teachers with a reference book which would facilitate their communication with deaf children. An English word list was drawn up and signs corresponding to those words were identified. In certain cases, where it was thought a sign did not exist that corresponded to a particular English word, a sign was created or borrowed from Gestuno the then recently published collection of 'international signs'. Photographs were used to illustrate the signs with the addition of artwork to indicate the movements involved. A written description of how to produce each sign accompanied the photograph, along with the English words most commonly associated with the sign. The signs were arranged according to subject headings, e.g. family, school, travel, et cetera.

As the project neared completion, Hayhurst became acquainted with the work of Stokoe and other sign linguists. In the United Kingdom, sign language research projects had recently been established at Moray House College of Education and at the University of Bristol. The recognition by linguists that signed languages were natural languages led Hayhurst to question the value of publishing the dictionary in its then existing form—a format which he felt would advance the use of signs in combination with spoken English (Sign Supported English) rather than the signed language of the British Deaf community (BSL). He was engaged in consultations as to how the work could be revised when he died. In recognition of his enormous contribution to the dictionary, the work in its final form (Brien [1992]) is dedicated to him and the Deaf community in Britain that he served.

5 CONTRIBUTION OF THE UNIVERSITY OF DURHAM

In accordance with Allan Hayhurst's wishes it was eventually agreed that the task of reorganising the contents of the dictionary should be undertaken. In the early years, a number of those who later became consultants to the project, or members of the editorial team, contributed to the work on a part-time, voluntary basis. In later years, the development of a number of sign language projects at the Deaf Studies Research Unit at the University of Durham brought together the group that formed the editorial team.

The reorganisation of the contents was guided by the following objectives :
1. that the signs contained in the Dictionary of British Sign Language/English (DBSL/E) should be BSL signs, i.e. signs identified by Deaf informants as signs they themselves, or other Deaf people, used when communicating in BSL;
2. that the entries should be organised on linguistic principles, appropriate to a signed language;
3. that a guide to the meaning(s) of the signs (and thereby a guide to appropriate usage) be provided;
4. that the DBSL/E should be of use to both Deaf users of BSL and people wishing to learn the language.

A grant from the British Petroleum Company enabled a series of meetings to take place at which Deaf informants, recognised as fluent users of BSL, and drawn from different parts of the country, reviewed all the signs that had been collected by Hayhurst and his colleagues. The aim was to establish the BSL signs, and not the English words, as the starting point of the DBSL/E. The English words that had been assigned to each sign were removed and the Deaf informants asked to identify those which were BSL signs. Signs which they rejected according to this criterion were replaced with signs which, in their view, were BSL signs. After this had been done, they were asked to identify English words they would associate with each sign. This provided the basic database which the editorial team have drawn upon to produce the DBSL/E.

6 CONTENT OF THE DICTIONARY

The DBSL/E is in four main sections:
1. *How to use the Dictionary*
2. *The visual world of BSL: An introduction*
3. *BSL Section*
4. *English (Guide to Meaning) Section.*

The *How to use the Dictionary* section provides a detailed explanation of how the BSL and *English (Guide to Meaning)* sections are organised. In order to emphasise the status of BSL as an independent language, it was agreed that the BSL signs, categorised according to visual-gestural characteristics, should be presented on the left hand pages of the BSL section without reference to English. Each photograph of a sign is accompanied by the notation of the sign, demonstrating how signs can be recorded without recourse to English. This policy has also been followed in the Introduction where signs have been notated so that the user (should he or she be familiar with the system) does not need to identify the signs by English glosses.

The right hand pages of the BSL section provide a description in English of how to produce each sign, with a list of some of the English glosses associated with each sign. The descriptions may be seen as 'translations' of the notations. They are organised in relation to the main parameters of the signs, i.e. handshape and orientation; location, hand arrangement and contact; movement; and, where appropriate, non-manual features. In this way, non-linguists are introduced to the component parts of a sign, and gain an appreciation of the complex structure of signs.

The signs contained in the BSL section represent only a very small selection of the signs that constitute the established vocabulary of the language. The fact that the signs were originally chosen in relation to subject headings, and not formational characteristics, has resulted in certain handshape sections containing a very limited number of examples. It was not possible in the main body of the dictionary to add substantially to the collection of signs compiled by Allan Hayhurst. The glosses and reference numbers allow the user to move between the BSL section and the English (Guide to Meaning) section of the dictionary. It should be noted that the editorial team do not claim that the English words (glosses), or the meanings that are given in relation to each sign, are necessarily the only glosses and meanings appropriate to the sign. It was not possible to research the usage of each sign in natural settings. For this reason, the entries have not been described as 'definitions' but rather 'guides to the meaning' of the signs.

The English (Guide to Meaning) section seeks to serve two functions and meet the needs of two very different potential users of the DBSL/E. Insofar as the entries provide a guide to the meaning of the signs, it provides information to those seeking a sign relating to a particular meaning, and therefore will be of particular value to people learning BSL. If the dictionary is used in the opposite direction, i.e. from the BSL signs to the English words, it is hoped that it will prove of value to Deaf people studying English as a second language—in particular those attending English classes taught through BSL. In this way, we hope the DBSL/E will assist both Deaf and hearing people to advance their knowledge of a second language.

The task of writing entries for the English (Guide to Meaning) section had been started when, prior to publication, information on the first of the Collins COBUILD dictionaries became available. In writing the entries, we had attempted to use a style of English and form of presentation which would make the entries accessible to

Deaf people for whom English is a second language. The COBUILD Dictionary had been compiled especially for learners of English as a second language. Its use of complete sentences in definitions written in clear, concise English distinguished it from the other dictionaries we had consulted. We were most fortunate to be granted permission to use entries from the COBUILD dictionaries to provide the basis for the entries in the *English (Guide to Meaning)* section of this volume. As with the glosses, we have not sought to be prescriptive with regard to these entries. They represent a descriptive guide to the meanings of the signs based on usage within the Deaf community, as observed by the members of the editorial team fluent in BSL and English, our Deaf informants and consultants.

As stated earlier, in a volume of the DBSL/E's size only a small sample of the vocabulary of BSL can be included. The vocabulary of BSL, however, does not consist only of those established signs that can be listed in a dictionary. Of equal importance are the lexical resources used by fluent users of BSL to create new vocabulary. It was therefore considered essential to include information not only on examples of the established lexicon of BSL, but also on the productive lexicon—the meaningful parts of the language which are used to create new vocabulary. The *Introduction* provides the reader with a general introduction to BSL, with particular reference to the nature of the BSL words and the community of people who use the language. Further information on aspects of the productive lexicon may be found in the introductions to the handshape sections, and in the strategy used in selecting explanatorily equivalent glosses (see below).

7 COMPLETION OF THE PROJECT

Once the University of Durham had agreed to accept the project, a combination of new and existing projects undertaken within the DSRU brought together a group of people who, in addition to their other responsibilities, were able to contribute to the development of the DBSL/E. The demands of these projects (in particular the British Sign Language Tutor Training Course) were at times difficult to accommodate with work on the DBSL/E. Without such projects, however, it would not have been possible to retain staff essential to this work. In accepting responsibility for the development of the British Sign Language Tutor Training Course, the University of Durham recognised the potential importance of such a programme to the Deaf community: in addition it was realised that the Tutor Training and Dictionary projects would clearly complement each other in making a practical contribution to linguistic bridge-building between BSL-users and English-users in the United Kingdom.

The existence of trained Deaf tutors as a consequence of the Tutor Training Course has contributed significantly to changing prevailing views of BSL as a 'simple' language. However, it still appears to be believed that competence in sign language and the training of sign language tutors and interpreters can be achieved in a far shorter period of time than that required in relation to other languages. We trust that the DBSL/E will encourage a re-examination of such views.

8 STRATEGY

Producing a two-way-access bilingual dictionary like this presents many challenges, not the least of which is to find a principle for keeping the two languages balanced, or for allowing one to dominate in a controlled way. It is important to remember the larger sociolinguistic context in which the work was being undertaken: BSL is a minority language, fighting to gain recognition, to become accepted as a 'real and proper' natural language, and to achieve the status and functions that go with recognition. In this context, theorists like Ladislav Zgusta [1971] have argued that the lexicographer can legitimately and profitably start by taking the vocabulary of the established majority language (i.e. use it as a *source* language) and then find words in the minority language which can be considered equivalent (i.e. the minority language is the *target* language). Zgusta argues that it is frequently useful not to compile a monolingual dictionary at first, but rather a bilingual one, in which the minority language is the target language. The minimum for the lexicographer to do is then to describe the meanings of the lexical units of the rich, fully established source language by means of the target language.

Following such a project, as Allan Hayhurst set out to do, would have resulted in an English-led but nevertheless thereby status-enhancing dictionary. Yet beginning the undertaking with a list of English vocabulary would have meant that the very last set of BSL lexemes to emerge would be the truly idiomatic and culture-bound items. These are the very items that so clearly distinguish the BSL usage which is most open to the language's internally-evolved strengths and expressive capacities from that usage which is heavily influenced by English.

Such reasoning informed the decision to present the pattern of BSL—English equivalences as seen in the completed DBSL/E. The development of the project over time led to both paths of approach being reflected in the resulting material. The influence of English is counter-balanced by the attempt to reflect the *visual* information regularly encoded in the BSL lexicon, thus achieving a significant gain in terms of cultural sensitivity. The end result of the DBSL/E, then, is a volume intended to be explicitly *bilingual* both in principle and in the details of execution. The entries here are not described as 'definitions', but as 'guides to the meaning' of the signs, since resources did not allow usage to be researched to the extent that 'definitive' specifications could be advanced. (The very inclusion of such information nevertheless constitutes a significant advance within the field.) The single most crucial feature of these 'guides to meaning' is that—presentation as English text notwithstanding—they relate first and foremost to the BSL signs: they relate to the English word glosses only to the extent that these overlap *directly* with the signs portrayed.

In many ways, this end product is unusual within the entire lexicographical field in its strategy (though see Tomaszczyk [1983] for tentative developments in this direction). On the one hand, without glosses this would have been a relatively standard monolingual dictionary, made special by its presentation in photographic form of the selected lemmas. On the other hand, without the *Guide to Meaning*, it would be a straightforward bilingual volume in which lists of English words and phrases were offered as apparent translational equivalents of the BSL signs without further explanation. Instead, the DBSL/E includes paraphrastic 'proto-definitions', explanatory equivalents amongst the glosses, and suggestions of translational equivalents (demonstrated to function in context by example sentences representing both English and potential BSL structure). Partly by historical accident, then, the team working on the DBSL/E was given the chance to reconceptualize the balance maintained between the two languages, and thereby the relationship of BSL and English as presented in this dictionary. The more the theoretical stance led to consideration of the BSL lexicon on its own terms, the more the fit between the two languages evened out: in practice, it was considered both socio-culturally and linguistically imperative that the DBSL/E should reflect the visually-rich warp and weft of the signed lexicon.

9 RENAISSANCE OF THE VISUAL

Figure 1: SAY

⌣ GTΛ ×⊥

In the context of such a complex of potentially overwhelming (or undermining) problems, armchair lexicography might appear greatly preferable to any practice that is actually going to require an end product. However, the demand for functional reference works must be met, no matter that resources which would enable optimally elegant solutions to be sought are never available. So how has the DBSL/E begun to tackle the issues raised above?

Figure 1 shows the sign Allan Hayhurst would originally have been offered as a response to the question "what is the sign for *say*?". However, in English one can say *Clark said…*, meaning not that he expressed some comment in speech, but that he made an utterance using some form of language. So what English equivalents will be appropriate for the sign in figure 1? Does this sign mean *say* (in the sense of a signed comment), *say* (in the sense of a handwritten comment), *say* (in the sense of a printed comment), et cetera? On the basis of visual form, one would answer 'no'. Attempting to give a thoroughly descriptive account, and acknowledging the influence of manual forms of the English language on natural signed interaction, one has to answer 'yes': the DBSL/E's *Guide to Meaning* shows an attempt to cope with relevant pressures.

---

say 347

1 When you **say** something, you speak words or sign signs. *e.g. Did I hear you say you think linguistics is boring?*

2 You use **say** when you report the actual words or signs that someone has uttered. *e.g. British Deaf News reported that Clark Denmark had said 'More attended than at the old Delegates' Conferences'.*

3 You use **say** when you give an approximate report of the words or signs that someone has uttered. *e.g. He said it was an accident.*

4 To **say** something means to express an idea, fact or opinion using words or signs. *e.g. I said she should resign.*

5 If you have a **say** in something, you have the right or the opportunity to give your opinion, especially when there is a decision to be taken. *e.g. Teachers should have a say in the new curriculum.*

With two further examples, we'd like to show the attempt made in this dictionary not only to give an honest account of the English influence on BSL, but at the same time to offer the strongest possible demonstration of the inherent visual sophistication and creative vitality of everyday BSL usage that occurs elsewhere in the lexicon, far beyond the reach of any English influence. In its treatment of signs such as these, and the supplementary information given about the word-formation processes involved in their usage, the DBSL/E puts forward a powerful argument for the renaissance of the deeply-rooted visual worlds of signed languages.

First, though, a little background. The two examples can both be seen to illustrate the phenomenon of *anisomorphism*—the mismatch of meaning between languages—in lexicography. Authors like Tomaszczyk [1983] have clearly pointed out that it is common knowledge that different languages lexicalise semantic space differently. At one end of the continuum there are the rare cases of one-to-one correspondence or 'perfect equivalence'; and at the other end there are those items in one language that have no equivalent at all in the other. This does not mean that the other language cannot express the given thing; it ordinarily can, but does so differently. It is common to find *explanatory equivalents* in dictionaries for such items where no *translational equivalence* is valid.

What kind of words present these problems and receive such treatment? The first impression is that 'culture-bound' words do. For instance, a Latin-English dictionary might render *consul* as 'the highest executive dignitary of the Roman republic[3]. However, one should not get carried away with the idea that the culture-specific words of a language can readily be isolated and identified for particular attention. The notion of cultural specificity is actually very hard to deal with. Noting that similar problems crop up throughout the lexicon, Zgusta [1971] concludes that it would be plain wrong to limit the concept of anisomorphism and the discussion of it to the 'culture-bound words' only. On the contrary, anisomorphism must be expected in all lexical units. The notional systems of the two languages should not, as a matter of principle, be expected to be identical. Even in those areas where the two cultures overlap and where the material world is identical, the lexical units of the two languages are not just different labels affixed to identical notions.

Figure 2: CATERPILLAR CRAWLING UP A THIN OBJECT

G⊥ʌ ₁ₓ G̈<ʌ ⚥̂ₓ

And so to an example. Figure 2 illustrates the sign Deaf informants considered to be an equivalent of the English word *caterpillar*.

Notice that this is a product of the BSL-to-English line of approach. What happens if one looks at it from the other direction? How does one capture in a gloss what is actually visually encoded in the sign—does CATERPILLAR CRAWLING UP A THIN OBJECT cover it? Since it is conventionally associated with the English word *caterpillar*, many Deaf people also use the sign to mean just that, and that fact is reflected in the DBSL/E entry that does indeed include the simple gloss CATERPILLAR for this item. The longer gloss is also included; for this is the element-by-element truth about what is actually visually salient within this sign as used in more usual interaction by native signers.

Figure 3: SQUEEZE TOOTHPASTE FROM A TUBE ONTO A TOOTHBRUSH

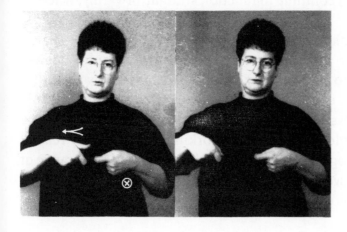

Figure 3 gives an exactly parallel example. Originally proposed as "the sign for *toothpaste*", informants suggested that—in terms of its visual content—it should more accurately be glossed as SQUEEZE TOOTHPASTE FROM A TUBE ONTO A TOOTHBRUSH. This gloss appears in the DBSL/E's *Guide to Meaning* section.

Analyses and theoretical frameworks for such deconstruction and reconstruction of meaningful elements within signs have been developed by McDonald [1982, 1983, 1985] and fine-tuned to a significant level by Brennan [1990a, 1990b, 1992]. The

DBSL/E has begun to address the question of how best such dramatic accounts of the authentic, utterly embedded and rich content of these languages for the eye can be reflected in reference works. Successor volumes in the UK and elsewhere will be keenly studied for further development of these initial reconceptualisations. Some of the implications for teaching and learning signed languages will be explored in other work from the Durham University team (Brennan et al. [1993]).

10 RECONSIDERING THE LEMMA

It is possible, of course, that sign language dictionaries will find themselves being overhauled entirely in the attempt to reorganise their contents around the visual logic of the languages themselves. What scope is there for reorganisation? After all, what one puts in dictionaries are simply the words (or signs) of the language. This might, for a start, invite sign lexicographers to go back to their definition of *word* and rethink it in the sign linguistics context: the possibilities raised by the simultaneous elements of many signed constructions obviously need careful attention, since some traditional criteria of *wordhood* continue to function straightforwardly, whereas others are more problematic.

Or it might invite them to look at dictionaries involving other languages—Bantu languages like Swahili, for instance—which also have complex, dense morphological structure; and to note that they do indeed include comparable sub-lexical units as independent entries. Recent work (e.g. by Bwenge [1989]) demonstrates—somewhat reassuringly—that Swahili lexicographers have not by any means solved all the problems and are still working through many related issues. The complex morphological structure of Swahili includes a wide range of affixes. A sense of this can be given by considering the morphological elements of a word like *umetukutanisha* ('it has caused us to meet'):

u	subject
me	present tense perfect aspect
tu	object
kut	verbal root 'meet'
an	reciprocal
ish	causative
a	declarative

How does one go about listing these in the dictionary? Without repetition on a huge scale throughout the dictionary, the lexicographer will be making the assumption that the user can bring together all of the appropriate elements for himself or herself and go on to create grammatically acceptable multimorphemic forms. Whatever one does include in the lexicon, making explicit the lexical and morphological relationship between the 'root' forms and the various affixes remains a problem. Recognition of affixational morphology as a property of the lexicon requiring more accessible and thorough presentation in dictionaries—building upon and applying the analytical frameworks developed by Engberg-Pedersen [1993; see especially chapter 8] and others—could help learners both 'diagnose' when working from their second to their first language and to 'generate' (i.e. produce well-formed idiomatic lexical items) when going from first to second language.

11 FUTURES

The production of dictionaries of spoken/written languages has been transformed in recent years through the use of modern computer technology. The twenty-five years of sign linguistic research have, of course, quite closely coincided with a similar period of dramatic technological evolution. It is salutary to recall that the computer which landed Neil Armstrong on the moon was about as powerful as that of a modern washing machine! Modern technology has enabled lexicographers to create databases which store and allow detailed sorting of millions of examples of actual language use. This sorting process has provided quantifiable evidence of usage which permits the production of dictionaries based on naturally-occurring data of a breadth and depth never previously envisaged. This is not to say that lexicography becomes a straightforward mechanical exercise: on the contrary, a great deal of interpretation of this new mass of data is required. One consequence of description and analysis on this scale has been a recognition of the importance of collocational patterning in the identification of semantic specifications (Sinclair [1991]).

The DBSL/E editorial team developed their analysis of signs within a descriptive linguistic framework but did not have such a database of usage from which entries could be extracted. In contemplating how this approach could be applied to sign lexicography, one is forced to recognise that the equivalent systems programming is as yet insufficiently advanced to allow the creation of appropriately structured databases. In order to carry out such analysis one would need not only to compile a highly compressed databank of samples of sign usage, but also to create a software facility which would enable recognition of the significant elements of signs, and patterns in the construction of signed utterances, in the same way that current programmes allow lexicographers to identify and analyse the structures of spoken/ written languages. Only through such developments will it prove possible to undertake, for example, collocation studies of signed languages in the same way that is now possible for spoken/written languages. The Deaf Studies Research Unit at the University of Durham (in conjunction with the Dutch Foundation for the Deaf and Hard-of-Hearing Child, BSL Computer Consultancy and Pin Drop Productions) has begun to make explicit—though very much initial—steps in this direction with the development of its SIGNBASE project under the European Community's TIDE programme.

Like all known lexicographers throughout human history, the editorial team of the DBSL/E were not, of course, satisfied with the results of all their efforts. There is much scope for improvement and for development of the strategies employed. Much of the room for manoeuvre depends upon the format of future dictionaries. Traditionally one of the most complex questions for discussion among lexicographical logisticians has been *But how will they know where to look it up?* Dictionaries produced using current CD-ROM and computer technology seductively suggest that they might render this problem negligible, by offering search possibilities that will allow users to find items by following formational pathways without needing to know the feature analyses which allow them to do this (i.e. the on-screen look-up may be conducted in the user's first language, but the internal search is driven by theoretically-rooted analytical inventories). Paper dictionaries have no such luck.

What is more challenging in the light of our argument above, though, is the notion that two specific theoretical leaps may optimise the functional value of sign dictionaries. Firstly, with respect to bilingual dictionaries, comes the suggestion that strict division between source and target languages will not enhance equally the presentation of both lexical sets, and that it would be both culturally responsible and practically useful to do this by maintaining a most careful balance in allowing each of the two languages to drive the dictionary engine from time to time. In order to do this, of course, and still to accommodate the most culture-bound items of vocabulary, both translational and explanatory equivalents are likely to be necessary.

Secondly, and of equal relevance to bilingual and monolingual work, the suggestion that reassessment of the nature of the lemma in sign-bearing dictionaries would be beneficial presents a significant challenge. Do sign linguists need to rework their notion of the signed word, and can this be done effectively? If sub-lexical elements can legitimately be isolated for lexicographic purposes, for which items is this strategy feasible? And what additional information about their functional and structural behaviour, their lexical and syntactic patterning, would have to be included in order to give the user all the tools he or she needs before beginning to use the items generatively?

From small beginnings (e.g. Teuber et al. [1980]), digital sign lexicography is now progressing rapidly, such that a clutch of current projects aim to create CD-ROM and/or computer-based dictionaries of signed languages—including dictionaries of BSL (see reference to the SIGNBASE project, above); ASL (Wilcox and Stokoe [forthcoming]; Stokoe [1993a, 1993b]), Japanese Sign Language (Kanda, [this volume]), Australian Sign Language (Adam Schembri [personal communication]), Finnish Sign Language (Malm [this volume]) and German Sign Language (Schulmeister [1990]; Prillwitz [1990]). Nevertheless, every single one of the issues raised above in relation to the optimal presentation of the signed language itself, and its relationship with the surrounding spoken/written language, will remain equally pertinent to these scholars and scientists. Impressive as the multimedia technological prowess may be in terms of *form*, it will be equally important for us all to avoid taking a step back, post-DBSL/E, in terms of *content*. We must seek to ensure that the dictionaries which take us into the 21st century do not offer semantically incomplete representations which fail to take adequate account of the visual sophistication so characteristic of natural signed languages.

Footnotes

* David Brien and Graham H. Turner: Deaf Studies Research Unit, Department of Sociology and Social Policy, University of Durham, Elvet Riverside 2, New Elvet, Durham DH1 3JT, Durham, England.

1 See Carmel [1992] for a useful, though somewhat incomplete and inconsistent—due to difficulties in data collection—checklist of sign language dictionaries, demonstrating that the number of such volumes published has been growing almost geometrically since 1940.

2 Using the size of photographs in the DBSL/E, the present 230 pages of 'guides to meanings' would take over 20,000 pages (and this for a mere 1739 BSL sign entries) to lay out using illustrations or photographs without text.

3 The explanatory equivalents are liable to be lengthy and somewhat complex: to such an extent that Zgusta's [1971] advice is that the lexicographer should not despair if s/he finds that it is not possible to give all the detailed information on them in a dictionary: s/he cannot, after all, be expected to insert long encyclopedic articles with detailed descriptions of another culture.

Bibliography

Brennan, M. [1990a] *Word Formation in British Sign Language*. University of Stockholm, Stockholm.

Brennan, M. [1990b] Productive morphology in British Sign Language, in Prillwitz, S. and Vollhaber, T. (eds.) *Current Trends in European Sign Language Research*. Signum Press, Hamburg.

Brennan, M. [1992] The Visual World of BSL: An Introduction, in Brien, D. (ed.) *Dictionary of British Sign Language/English*. Faber and Faber, London.

Brennan, M., Brien, D., Collins, J., Elton, F. and Turner, G. H. [1993] The Dictionary of British Sign Language/English: A Bilingual Resource. Paper presented at LASER *Facilitating Bilingualism* Conference, St. Albans, Hertfordshire.

Brien, D. (ed.) [1992] *Dictionary of British Sign Language/English*. Faber and Faber, London.

Bwenge, C. [1989] Lexicographical treatment of affixational morphology: a case study of four Swahili dictionaries, in James, G. (ed.) *Lexicographers and their works*. University of Exeter, Exeter.

Carmel, S. J. [1992] A Checklist of Dictionaries of National Sign Languages of Deaf People, in *Sign Language Studies*, 76.

Engberg-Pedersen, E. [1993] *Space in Danish Sign Language: The semantics and morphosyntax of the use of space in a visual language*. Signum Press, Hamburg.

Hacking, I. [1990] Signing, in *London Review of Books*, 5 April.

Johnston, T. [1989] *Auslan Dictionary: A Dictionary of the Sign Language of the Australian Deaf Community*. Deafness Resources, Australia.

McDonald, B. [1982] *Aspects of the American Sign Language Predicate System*. Unpublished PhD Thesis, University of Buffalo.

McDonald, B. [1983] Levels of Analysis in Sign Language Research, in Kyle, J. G. and Woll, B. (eds.) *Language in Sign: An International Perspective on Sign Language*. Croom Helm, London.

McDonald, B. [1985] Productive and frozen lexicon in ASL: an old problem revisited, in Stokoe, W. C. and Volterra, V. (eds.) *SLR'83: Proceedings of the 3rd International Symposium on Sign Language Research*. Linstok Press, Silver Spring, MD.

Prillwitz, S. [1990] Development of a Computerized Sign Language Dictionary with Animated Pictures, in Edmondson, W. H. and Karlsson, F. (eds.) *SLR'87: Papers from The Fourth International Symposium on Sign Language Research*. Signum Press, Hamburg.

Radutzky, E. [1992] *Dizionario bilingue elementare della lingua italiana dei segni*. Edizioni Kappa, Roma.

Schulmeister, R. [1990] A Computer Dictionary with animated Signs for the Special Field of Computer Technology, in Prillwitz, S. and Vollhaber, T. (eds.) *Current Trends in European Sign Language Research*. Signum Press, Hamburg.

Sinclair, J. [1991] *Corpus, Concordance, Collocation*. Oxford University Press, Oxford.

Stokoe, W. C. [1960] *Sign language structure (Studies in Linguistics: Occasional paper 8)*. University of Buffalo, Buffalo, NY.

Stokoe , W. C. [1993a] Unabridged—Two Recent Dictionaries, in *Sign Language Studies*, 78.

Stokoe , W. C. [1993b] Dictionary Making: Then and Now, in *Sign Language Studies*, 79.

Stokoe, W. C., Casterline, D. C. and Croneburg, C. G. [1965] *A Dictionary of American Sign Language on Linguistic Principles*. Gallaudet College Press, Washington, DC; (Revised 1976) Linstok Press, Silver Spring, MD.

Suwanarat, M. et al. [1986] *Thai Sign Language Dictionary*. National Association of the Deaf in Thailand/Human Assistance Programme, Thailand.

Teuber, H. et al. [1980] A Computerized Lexicon of American Sign Language: The DASL in FORTRAN, in *Sign Language Studies*, 29.

Tomaszczyk, J. [1983] On bilingual dictionaries: The case for bilingual dictionaries for foreign language learners, in Hartmann, R. R. K. (ed.) *Lexicography: Principles and Practice*. Academic Press, London.

Wilcox, S. and Stokoe, W. C. [forthcoming] Multimedia Dictionary of American Sign Language, in Coninx, F and Elsendoorn, B. A. G. (eds.) *Interactive Learning Technology for the Deaf*. Springer-Verlag, Berlin.

Zgusta, L. [1971] *Manual of Lexicography*. Mouton, Den Haag.

A computer dictionary of Japanese Sign Language

KAZUYUKI KANDA *

1 HARDWARE SYSTEM

Our idea of a computer dictionary of Japanese Sign Language is to be realized by a computer database on a floppy disk with the related pictures and short movies stored on the optical disk. The devices we use are NEC PC 98 which is the most popular personal computer in Japan and Panasonic TQ 3200, the optical reader-writer, connected to the computer NEC PC 98 through its RS 232c connector as in Fig.1.

Figure 1.

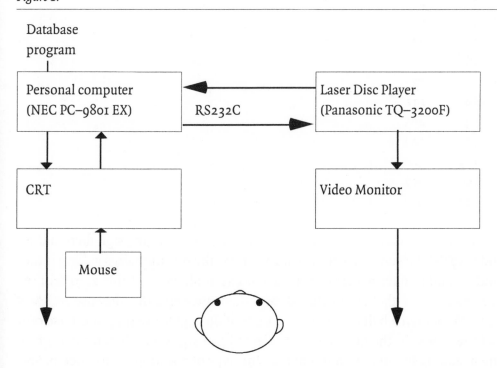

Our attempt is to offer the people in Japan the computerized data of JSL which are easy for both Deaf and Hearing to handle and to access. The computer NEC PC 98 is very popular, and the database software d-Base III plus we use is popular, too. But the optical device is still expensive and is not popular yet. We plan to publish this dictionary by the floppy disks and the laser disk or the CD disk in the future since an

LD player or a CD reader is cheaper and is already popular now. But because of the high cost of printing the LD, we chose to use the optical disk device for our experiment. We recorded the JSLsigns by a native signer on the S-VHS videotape and transmitted them to the optical disk.

2 LEXIS

About 4,000 signs in total are listed on Watashitachi-No-Shuwa (Our Signs) published by Japanese Federation of the Deaf in their 10 volumes of the books. It has many new signs which are not well accepted yet by Japanese Deaf society. Kanda [1988] collected 19 kinds of JSL dictionaries and counted 9,703 signs among them, which are less than 10% of the whole, and are listed on the six or more books out of the 19 (Table 1).

Table 1.: Frequency of common signs

Books	Signs	Total
17	2	2
16	4	6
15	18	24
14	18	42
13	31	73
12	59	132
11	73	205
10	77	282
8	129	511
7	156	667
6	242	909

It means that JSL has a great variety of signs as far as we see the sign dictionaries. In Kanda [1988], he sent 100 people (in 10 places) the questionaires asking if they use, understand or have never seen the 909 signs as shown in Table 2. 91% of the people replied and of them more than 80% of them answered that they use 70.8% of the signs. More than a half of them use 92.9% of the signs and they don't use only 0.7% of the signs. In the next step, he selected 100 signs which had the highest agreement among the signers and sent the same type of questionairs to 1,000 people in 50 places all over the country. 63.3% answered that 96 signs are used by more than a half of them. This means that Japanese signers feel most of the signs quite common and that most dictionaries do not list the proper lexis. Then our computer dictionary in the final stage would contain about 900 signs which were proved to be common above. This paper is a trial of 10 signs which shows its idea and its phonological and morpholigical structure as in Table 3; single handed or two handed signs, symmetrical or non-symmetrical hands, movement or hold, directional or non-directional signs, and simple or complex signs.

Table 2.: Result of questionaires

Questionaires: 100 persons				
Answered: 91 persons (91%)				
Answerer	*Use*	*Ustd*	*Dfrt*	*NUse*
100–90%	50.8	0	0	0
89–80%	20	0	0	0
79–70%	10.8	0	0	0
69–60%	7.8	0	0.1	0
59–50%	3.5	0.1	0.5	0
49–40%	3.3	0.5	0.6	0
39–30%	1.6	2.5	1.7	0
29–20%	1.1	11.3	4.8	0
10–10%	0.9	23.6	9.8	0.8
9–0%	0.2	62.1	82.5	99.2

Table 3.

	Hold	*Non-Directional*	*Directional*	*Compound*
Single Handed	MAN	MASTER-OF-CEREMONY	COMMUTE	DEAF
Double Handed (symmetrical)	HOUSE	GREETING	MEET	PEOPLE
Double Handed (non-symmetrical)	NAME	ISLAND	POPULAR	

3 STRUCTURE OF THE DATABASE

In our d-Base III plus database, there are three kinds of files, phonological representations, morphological informations and lexical informations with weak forms, sample sentences, etc. Those files are related under a single lexical items with a code number to access to the picture or the short movie stored in the optical disk as in Fig.2 (see overleaf).

The general database includes all the informations in one file consisting of six subfiles, the three phonological files, the morphological file, the lexical file and the sample sentences.

For example, a structure of the phonological representation file 1 of our database is as in Table 4(see overleaf). Each lexical entry has its code number in the field 8(Pictcode), sign in the field 1(Sign), Japanese translation in the field 2(Japanese), English translation in the field 3(English), the number on Our Signs in the field 7(OurSigns) and the phonological representations in the field 4, 5 and 6. Our Signs

Figure 2.: Relational Database Files

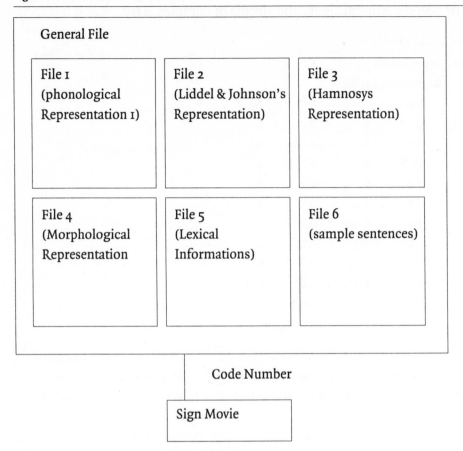

Table 4.: Database structure of File 1.

N°.	Fields	Type	Columns
1	JAPANESE	Symbol	8
2	JAPANESE	Symbol	8
3	ENGLISH	Symbol	8
4	HANDSHAPE	Symbol	16
5	LOCATION	Symbol	8
6	MOVEMENT	Symbol	16
7	OURSIGNS	Number	6
8	PICTCODE	Number	4
	Total		74

is a name of the dictionary publised by Japanese Federation of the Deaf. The user of our database can check the illustration of the sign on Our Signs when s/he has no access to our optical disk. The phonological representation in File 1 is transcribed by the notational system of Kanda(1992, only his symbols in Table 5) which seems to fit

Japanese users best. For universal or international users, we adopted Liddell & Johnson[1989] for File 2 and Hamnosys V1.2. for File 3. The former is more phonetic, the latter is easier to handle. We think each of these three notational systems has its own merit. As in Table 5, Kanda[1992] analyzed JSL signs into three components; Hand Posture Component including hand configurations, orientations of palm, wrist and finger tips, local movement and relations of two hands, Space Component including space, distance and bodypart, and Movement Component including path movement, mode of movement and movement of two hands. Handconfigurations and their symbols are shown in Appendix 1.

Table 5.: Symbols in Kanda (1992).

I. Hand Posture Component

1. Hand Configurations:

1, 2, 3, 4, 5, C, 7, イ, ウ, I, オ, カ, キ, ケ, コ, サ, セ,

タ, チ, ツ, テ, ヌ, ネ, メ, モ, ヤ, ラ, ル, レ, ロ, 2B, 3B, 4B,

5B, ヲB, ルB, レB, 5A, ウA, ルA, レA, ルP, 姉, 薬

佐, 燕, 八, 婆 (48)

2. Orientations:

Palm Orientation, Wrist Orientation

ipsilateral, contralateral

R, L, U, D, F, B

3. Local Movement:

Part: Finger, Wrist, Elbow

Movement: ro(tation), be(nt), ex(tend), op(en), cl(ose), wg (wiggling), tw(ist), co(unt), ru(b)

4. Hand Relation:

idn (identical), alt(ernative), cro(ss), con(tact), lin(k), right/left

II. Space Component

1. Space: NS (Neutral Space), UP (Upper Space), DU (Lower Space), RU, LU, FU, BU

2. Distance: C, P, M, D

3. Body part: HD, FA, FH, EY, NO, MO, EA, NK, TH, TN, CK, CN, TM, BR, BL, SH, UA, EL, WD, WV, LA, HB, HP, HA, FG

III. Movement

1. Path: planes (HP, VP, SP, MP, UP), orientations (R, L, U, D, F, B), ST(amping)

2. Mode: big, sml, fas, slo, * (repeat)

3. Two Hands: {x (right)/y (left)}, con(tact), nco, cro(ss)

IV. Others

Sign boundary: {,}, Translation boundary: 「, 」, Simultaneous: /, Serial: +

Table 6. Morphological Structure database (File 4).

1. AISATSU, GREETING={#CL人(MAN)/#CL人(MAN)/#BEND

2. AU, MEET={[#CL人(MAN)/#CL人(MAN)/#REP]+[X/Y/#APP]}

3. IE, HOUSE={#IE(HOUSE)}

4. KAYOU, COMMUTE={[[#CL男(MAN)/#GO]+[X/#COME]]*2}

5. NAMAE, NAME={#拇印(THUMB-PRINT)/#平板(BOARD)/#REP}

6. NINKI, POPULAR={#人(MAN)/#多数(MANY)/#APP}

7. OTOKO, MAN={#CL男(MAN)/#REP}

8. ROUASHA={#ROUA,DEAF+#SHA,PEOPLE}={#EAR-CLOSE+#MOUSE-CLOSE} + {#男女(COUPLE)
   /#男女(COUPLE)/#MANY}

9. SHIKAI, MASTER OF CEREMONY={#司会(MC)}

10. SHIMA, ISLAND={#/水(WATER)/#塊(LOAF)}

In the morphological representation file(Table 6), morpheme boundaries are shown by initial "#" marks. The serial combination mark "+" shows that two morphemes are combined linearly and the simultaneous combination mark "/" shows that two morphemes are combinedsimultaneously. "{ }" marks shows its hierarchical construction of a sign. For example as in Table 4, No.9 SHIKAI (Master of Ceremony) is made of a single morpheme so that it is shown as {#SHIKAI}. No.7 OTOKO(man) is made of two morphemes, a classifier #CL:man and a representer morphome #REP, thus OTOKO=#CL:man/#REP. No.4 KAYOU(commute) is described as {{#CL:man/#GO}+{x/#COME}}*2 which means that a classifier #CL:man moves go forth(GO) and bak(BACK) twice. "x" substitutes the former #CL and "*" shows repetition. No.8 ROUASHA(Deaf people) is a complex sign of ROUA(Deaf) and SHA(people). They are separated into two items ROUASHA 1 and ROUASHA 2.

In the morphological information file, directionality (whether the verb is directional or not) is marked. When it is directional, some examples of the inflected form are shown by the phonological symbols and the pictures on the optical disk. For example, No.2 AU(meet) inflects in an accordance with the persons. The ten signs above are the typical examples of directional and non-directional signs, simple and complex signs.

In the lexical information file(File 5), other Japanese translations, if any, and the synonyms are listed. Some sample sentences are listed in the forms of signs and symbols in File 6 with pictures on the optical disk.

Our attempt would show you our general idea about a computer dictionary of JSL and its structure of our database which includes only ten items of the typical examples in this paper. But it will be expanded to 100 in the next stage, 900 in the final stage.

The computer dictionary has a peculiar character that a user can look into the dictionary both from a spoken language and from a sign language. In our system, the user can check its real action on the movie which benefits the users who are not familiar with the transcriptions by the symbols. For those users, we plan to create some programs to display the pictures and the symbols together on the same CRT screen, although they are displayed on the separate monitor at this moment. When they would like to find a meaning of a sign, for example, the handconfigurations in the Appendix I are shown on the first screen, and a user selects one from them by using a mouse or by the keyboard, then it turns to the next screen, the local movement is to be shown by some illustrations. In the third step, s/he selects a location on a body and a distance and so on. At this stage the computer will research up several candidates. If the user would go farther to the next stage of movement, s/he would find a single or only a few candidates. It is easier to find a sign from Japanese. All s/he has to do is to key-in a Japanese word.

For more advanced users, needless to say, the database provides a lot of information they need.

This is the beginning of 10 signs level. We will expand the lexis to 100 signs in the next stage, 200, 400, 600 and 900 signs in the last. In this primary stage, our goal is to check if the system and its hardware apparatus would work well. Some example printout of File 1 and File 4 are shown in Appendix 2.

Footnotes

---

* Kazuyuki Kanda: Chukyo University, Japan

Appendix 1.

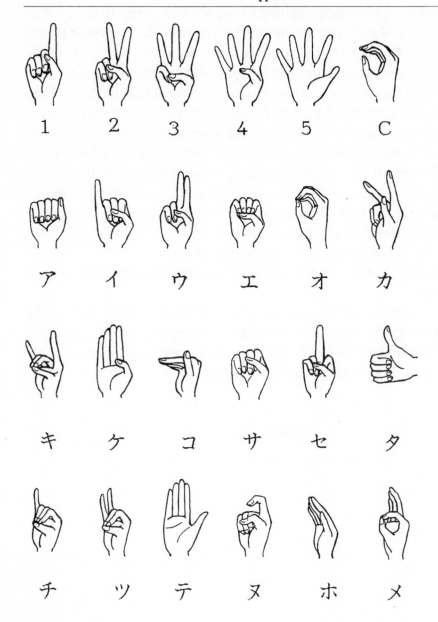

1　　2　　3　　4　　5　　C

ア　イ　ウ　エ　オ　カ

キ　ケ　コ　サ　セ　タ

チ　ツ　テ　ヌ　ホ　メ

Appendix 1 (cxontinued).

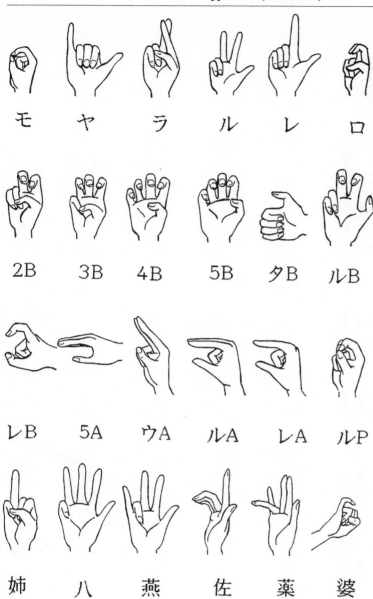

| モ | ヤ | ラ | ル | レ | ロ |

| 2B | 3B | 4B | 5B | タB | ルB |

| レB | 5A | ウA | ルA | レA | ルP |

| 姉 | 八 | 燕 | 佐 | 薬 | 婆 |

Appendix 2.

SIGN	JAPANESE	ENGLISH	HANDSHAPE	LOCATION	MOVEMENT	OURSIGNS	CODE	MORPHOLOGICAL STRUCTURE
AISATSU	挨拶	GREETING	1Pcbeidn	NS	ST	1–33	1	{#CL人/#CL人}/#BEND
AU	会う	MEET	1Pcidn	NS	L/R		2	{#CL人/#CL人}/#REP+(X)/#APP
IE	家	HOUSE	テPDc,con	NS	ST	1–80	3	{#CL平板/#CL平板}/#REP
KAYOU	通う	COMMUTE	タ	BRP+BRM	(F+B)*2	5–136	4	{(#CL男/#GO)+(X/#COME)}*2
NAMAE	1名前	NAME	タ/テ	HPC	ST	3–174	5	{#CL小丸/#CL平板}/#REP
NINKI	人気	POPULAR	5/タ	BRP	B	5–173	6	{#CL人/#CL多}/#APP
OTOKO	男	MAN	タ	NS	ST	1–16	7	#CL男/#REP
ROUASHA1	ろうあ	DEAF	テPU/サ	EAC+MOC	SP	1–31	8	#EAR-CLOSE+#MOUTH-CLOSE
ROUASHA2	○○者	PEOPLE	サPBroidn	NS	R/L	1–31	8	{#CL人々/#CL人々}/#MANY
SHIKAI	司会	MC	ㅌPF	US+RS	R+D	1–71	9	#司会
SHIMA	島	ISLAND	5Bc/テ	FL	C/a	10–89	10	#CL水/#CL塊

*** 合計 *** *** *** *

Bibliography

Kanda, K. [1988]. *Nihon Shuwa Hogen Chosa*. Shuwa kaihatsunotameno zogohoni kansuru hokokusho, pp. 3–24 Zennihon Roa Renmei. (*Research on JSL Dialect. Report for Developing New Signs*, pp. 3–24. Japanese Federation of the Deaf).

— [1992]. Nihon shuwa oninron. *Shuwagakukenkyu* 12. Nihonshuwagakkai. (JSL Phonology. *Japanese Journal of Sign Linguistics* 12. Japanese Association of Sign Linguistics.)

Kanda, K., Atari, H. and Fukuda, Y. [1992]. *Nihon shuwa densi jisho*. (*JSL Computer Dictionary*). Paper presented at the 18th Annual Meeting of Japanese Association of Sign Linguistics.

Liddell, S. and Johnson, R. [1989]. American Sign Language: The Phonological Base. *Sign Language Studies* 64.

Prillwitz, S. et al. [1989]. *HamNoSys Version* 2.0. Signum Press, Hamburg.

The Dictionary of New Zealand Sign Language user requirements survey [†]

DAVID MOSKOVITZ *

Abstract

What do potential users of a sign language dictionary want? How do they think they will use a dictionary? What information do they want in a dictionary? What do they think of existing dictionaries for other sign languages? How can this information be taken into account in making a sign language dictionary?

This paper describes the planning, method, and results of a survey of deaf and hearing potential users of the Dictionary of New Zealand Sign Language. The survey, conducted in 1991 in New Zealand's three main cities, canvassed user requirements for a sign language dictionary. These requirements will shape the format and content of the dictionary.

1 INTRODUCTION

A project to make a dictionary of New Zealand Sign Language (NZSL) began in July 1991 at Victoria University of Wellington, New Zealand. The dictionary project is overseen by a National Editorial Board (NEB) of four representatives from the New Zealand Association of the Deaf (NZAD) and three representatives from Victoria University. The project has funds of approximately NZ$250,000 (excluding printing and distribution costs) to last three years.

Three staff currently work part time on the project. The Technical Editor (the author) is responsible for computer automation, project planning and budgeting, survey design, and ensuring that the methodology and content of the dictionary are consistent with current work in sign linguistics. The Compilation Editor, Pat Dugdale, is responsible for collecting signs and writing the text of the dictionary entries. The Managing Editor, Graeme Kennedy, is responsible for fundraising, and overall project management. One staff member is hard of hearing, one totally deaf, and one hearing.

The project was established with an explicit mission "to produce an accurate record of signs which would be generally acceptable and satisfy user requirements." In order to better understand what the potential users of the dictionary wanted, the Editors conducted a survey.

1.1 why survey?

But why survey potential users? With much less time and expense, the Editors could have simply outlined perceived requirements, and proceeded to make the dictionary accordingly. A number of dictionaries have been published for the sign languages of other countries, and the Editors could have chosen one or more of these as a model.

The most important reason for performing a survey was to get direct input from potential users on what they wanted in a dictionary. There was not enough time or money in the budget to allow for the making of mistakes in this area, which would affect the entire dictionary making process from sign collection to final publication. The Editors were aware that in the past, deaf people have not had their fair say in many matters that affect them, and in the present case deserved a say in the description of their own language.

Secondly, without asking users what they wanted, it would have been difficult to determine how much and which information to include. There are many different types of dictionary, and many different uses for dictionaries. There are many different pieces of information that can end up in a dictionary entry, but one would not necessarily want to include all of them for reasons of cost, space, and ease of use. Each member of the dictionary staff had their own opinion about which information was important.

Furthermore, the availability of funds for sign lexicography is limited. After the time and money runs out for the project, it may not be possible to continue working on new, different purpose editions. Therefore, the Dictionary should cover as large a group of potential users as possible.

Finally, the Editors wanted to minimise future criticism about the usefulness of the dictionary, or its form or content. Information from a survey would enable the delivery of a product that the potential users had a hand in specifying.

1.2 the New Zealand deaf community

The following brief description of the New Zealand situation will help the reader better understand the potential users of the dictionary.

Although no official census data are available on the subject of deafness, The Hearing Report [New Zealand Board of Health 1984] estimates that there are about 6,700 profoundly or totally deaf people in New Zealand, out of a total population of 3.3 million.

The first deaf school was established in 1880 at Sumner near Christchurch. Gerrit Van Asch, a teacher of the deaf from Holland, was appointed to run the school, establishing a long tradition of Oralism. The predominance of Oralism lasted until the mid-1970's, when Australasian Signed English (ASE) was introduced into the curricula at the deaf schools. There are currently two residential deaf schools in New Zealand: the original school at Sumner, and another school at Kelston near Auckland.

In general, public awareness of deafness is poor. Government departments generally do not have TTY's or NZSL trained staff. There is no relay service. NZSL has no official status, although it has been recognised as an endemic language in the discussion of a possible National Languages Policy. Until 1985, there were no trained interpreters; there are now four, and a permanent interpreter training programme is being established this year. Some introductory NZSL classes are run by local Deaf Clubs, high schools, and polytechnics. However, without extensive teacher training or an NZSL curriculum, proficiency gained through these classes is limited. These problems are only just beginning to be addressed.

1.3 research into nzsl and the deaf community

The problems of public awareness and lack of services are related to the lack of descriptive research into NZSL and the Deaf community. Very few papers have been published to date. The Hearing Report (op. cit.) devotes a chapter to describing pathological and social problems of profound deafness and available government services, as well as making some recommendations for improving services for Deaf people. Pat Dugdale [1989] conducted a feasibility study of interpreters for deaf people. Marianne Collins-Ahlgren's [1989] Ph.D. thesis provides a thorough overview of linguistic aspects of NZSL; NZSL word formation processes are described in detail in Collins-Ahlgren [1990].

At the time of writing, in addition to the dictionary project, three projects are known by the authors to be underway further describing NZSL and the Deaf community. David Moskovitz is working on a statistical analysis of the NZSL lexicon at Victoria University, Sue Townshend is writing a thesis on the history of Deaf education in New Zealand from a Deaf perspective at Massey University, and Leila Monaghan is working on describing gender variation in NZSL through UCLA. This body of research is hardly comprehensive. The Dictionary of NZSL will augment the body of data available on NZSL, and promote the status and acceptance of NZSL as a language.

2 METHOD
2.1Potential Users of the Dictionary

In order to determine the user requirements of the dictionary, the potential users had to be identified. The Editors divided the potential users into the following user categories:

Group 1. Deaf persons, their families and close hearing friends.

Group 2. Hearing persons with frequent contact with the Deaf Community, including interpreters and NZAD staff, as well as deaf and hearing people involved in teaching or learning NZSL and interpreter training.

Group 3. Service providers to the Deaf community, including government departments, the legal system, educational institutions, and medical workers. Workmates, employers and employees of deaf people are also included in this group.

Group 4. Others, including linguists, and casual acquaintances of deaf people, and other interested persons.

Given these categories, the National Editorial Board was asked to assign weightings to each group to determine the relative importance of the input from those groups. Figure 1 shows the resulting weightings (referred to below as the NEB weightings) normalised to add up to 100.

Figure 1: Relative weightings of user groups.

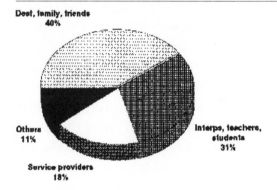

Deaf, family, friends
40%

Others
11%

Interps, teachers, students
31%

Service providers
18%

2.2 sampling method

In order to focus on the more important groups, but still get quality information from all groups, the editors decided to take a representative sample from the more important groups 1 and 2, and a selective sample from groups 3 and 4.

For group 1, deaf people and their families and close friends, the deaf clubs in Auckland, Wellington, and Christchurch were asked to provide lists of deaf volunteers to participate in the survey. The editors requested that each list of volunteers contain at least twice the number of required respondents, and that there be approximately equal numbers of people from each of three age groups: 25 or younger, 26-50, and 51 or older, and equal numbers of each gender. Volunteers were not required to be members of the deaf club. A random sample was then taken from each location proportional to its estimated deaf population, stratified by age group. The editors attempted to make interview appointments with all of the selected volunteers. Where it was not possible to make an appointment, volunteers from the cross-classification (location X age group) were randomly chosen from the remaining pool. The 60 deaf respondents amounted to just under one percent of the estimated total deaf population of New Zealand.

From the selected sample, one person from each cross-classification was randomly chosen to nominate a hearing family member to participate in the survey. From the same sample, another person from each cross-classification without reselection from the previous group was chosen to nominate a close hearing friend to interview.

For group 2, those with frequent contact with deaf people, all four interpreters were asked to participate, along with the person responsible for establishing a Sign Language interpreter training programme. Random samples were taken from the NZAD communicator (untrained voluntary ad-hoc interpreter) list, the NZAD staff list, a list of NZSL teachers with at least two years experience. Each of the selected teachers was then asked to supply a list of names of NZSL students who had completed at least one year of instruction, from which a random sample was taken.

For group 3, service providers, NZAD was asked to provide names of people from each area who were known to have occasional contact with deaf people. Selected deaf people were asked to provide the names of workmates.

For group 4, two linguists were asked to participate, Wellington Deaf Society was asked to provide names of other interested hearing persons, and selected deaf people were asked to provide names of casual acquaintances.

Table 1 summarises the number of survey respondents by group, location, and deaf/hearing status.

Table 1: Number of respondents by group, location, and deaf status

		Auckland		Christchurch		Wellington		Totals
Group	Category	Deaf	Hearing	Deaf	Hearing	Deaf	Hearing	
1	Deaf	30		21		9		60
	Family		5		3		2	10
	Friends		5		3		2	10
2	Interpreters		2		1		1	4
	Communicators		5		3		2	10
	NZAD Staff		2		2		2	6
	NZSL Teachers	2		1		2		5
	NZSL Students		5		3		2	10
	Interp. Training		1					1
3	Social Welfare						2	2
	Labour						2	2
	Medical						2	2
	Police						2	2

Table 1. (continued): Number of respondents by group, location, and deaf status

Group	Category	Auckland Deaf	Auckland Hearing	Christchurch Deaf	Christchurch Hearing	Wellington Deaf	Wellington Hearing	Totals
	Justice						2	2
	Workplace						2	2
	Educators	I		I			2	4
4	Linguists						2	2
	Acquaintances						2	2
	Others						2	2
	Totals	32	26	22	16	II	31	138

All of the interviews were performed face-to-face and one-on-one to get as much accurate information as possible from the respondents. Interviewing times ranged from less than half an hour to over two hours, and averaged slightly less than an hour. Each interview was carried out in the same manner by one of three interviewers. The only difference in the interviews was that some were performed in NZSL, and some in English. The survey forms were filled in by the interviewers immediately upon receiving the information from each question. Respondents were given the opportunity to ask for clarification of the survey questions, and to change previous answers after further thought.

2.3 Information requirements

The information requested in the survey falls into the following broad categories:
1. Interview control information: Respondent's age and geographical region, date of interview etc.
2. Usage: How and why the dictionary would be used.
3. Organisation: How the entries should be ordered, and whether the information would be sought more frequently from Sign to English or English to Sign.
4. Entry contents: What information should be included in each entry.
5. Special terms: Any special areas of interest for which words and signs should be entered.
6. Dictionary comparison: Samples of nine different sign language dictionaries were shown, comments elicited on features liked and disliked.
7. Supplementary information: What background information should be provided in appendices.
8. Graphics: What type of pictures were preferred.
9. Physical: The physical size and cost of the dictionary.
10. Comments: Any other comments the respondent wished to make.
A sample completed survey form appears as Appendix 1.

The interviewing process took three part-time interviewers three weeks to complete. The Editors analysed the answers to the open questions, categorised the responses, and coded the forms. The information was then entered into a SAS (1985) database and analysed.

3 RESULTS AND ANALYSIS
3.1 Normalisation

Each response to each closed or categorised question was given a point value to adjust for the number of survey respondents in each user category and the weighting given to the user category by the NEB. The point value was equal to the NEB weighting divided by the number of respondents in that category. Thus, for a single answer multiple choice question with no missing responses, if all respondents in a particular group gave the same answer, the total point value for that answer would be equal to the NEB weighting of the group. Disregarding missing data, the point values add up to 100, with the following exceptions: for some questions, respondents could answer more than once, and for other questions, the respondents could answer either positively or negatively. For these questions, the total point values do not necessarily add up to 100.

The responses to the three open questions that were not categorised were compiled separately. These are discussed below.

3.2 Reasons for wanting the Dictionary

The answers to the open questions "Why do you want a dictionary of NZSL?" and "How would you use a dictionary of NZSL?" were analysed, and then classified in the following categories:

• Learning aid: to improve own NZSL vocabulary and/or skills.
• Reference: to look up words and signs (except while conversing).
• Communication aid: to assist during communication with deaf or hearing people, e.g. pointing to an entry, quickly looking up a sign or word, et cetera.
• Teaching aid: to help teach other people NZSL.
• Language resource: to have available a large body of signs.
• NZSL status: to improve the status of NZSL, and show others that it is a living language with a large number of signs.
• Interest: to browse for enjoyment; interest in seeing other people's signs.
• Deaf awareness: to make people more aware of Deaf people and their language.
• Standardise NZSL: to provide a standard vocabulary so that people will tend to use more of the same signs.
• Needed in work: to improve ability to communicate with deaf clients.
• English reference: to be able to look up English words when unsure of spelling or meaning.

• Language record: to have a record of the current signs of NZSL.

• Supplementary information: to learn more about the Deaf world through supplementary information that could be included in the dictionary as appendices. Figure 2 summarizes the responses.

Figure 2: *Reasons for wanting a dictionary of NZSL*

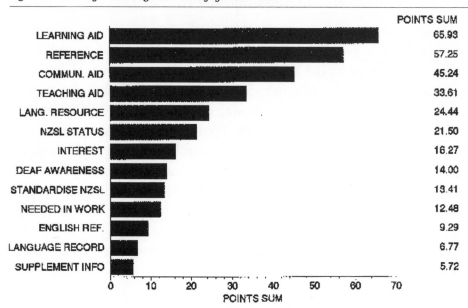

	POINTS SUM
LEARNING AID	65.93
REFERENCE	57.25
COMMUN. AID	45.24
TEACHING AID	33.61
LANG. RESOURCE	24.44
NZSL STATUS	21.50
INTEREST	16.27
DEAF AWARENESS	14.00
STANDARDISE NZSL	13.41
NEEDED IN WORK	12.48
ENGLISH REF.	9.29
LANGUAGE RECORD	6.77
SUPPLEMENT INFO	5.72

It is significant that the most popular reason people want the dictionary is specifically to learn NZSL; furthermore, the top four categories, or about two thirds of the responses, all involve some aspect of acquiring new vocabulary. This has serious implications for the dictionary: it must be usable by a naive person, and be easy to learn from.

3.3. Organisation method

Should the dictionary be organised alphabetically, by handshape, by concept group, or by some other method? Figure 3 shows the responses to this question. Almost half of the responses favour an alphabetical approach. Many respondents felt that alphabetical organisation was quick, easy, and familiar.

This English bias is supported by the question, "In which direction would you use the dictionary most, English to Sign or Sign to English?" Figure 4 shows that almost 90% would use English to Sign more. This is probably due at least in part to the low status of NZSL; both hearing and deaf people consider it something to be translated into rather than translated from. The cynical person would say that hearing people are used to telling deaf people what to do (and not necessarily paying attention to the responses), and deaf people are used to being talked at but not listened to. With time, these expectations should change. However, this overwhelming bias necessitates planning the first edition of the Dictionary of New Zealand Sign Language to be directional from English to NZSL.

Figure 3: Organisation method.

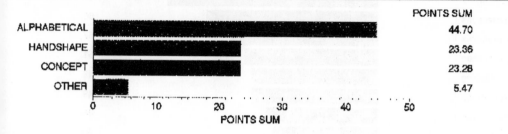

Figure 4: Direction of most frequent use.

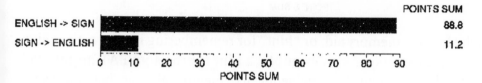

3.4 Information in each entry

Question 17 in the survey gives respondents a list of information items that could be included in each entry, and asks them to specify which are important, and which are not needed. Points were accumulated for positive answers, and subtracted for negative answers. Respondents could say they were unsure or had no opinion in which case points were neither added nor subtracted. The interviewers explained each information item very briefly, and added more detail if they believed the respondents did not fully understand. Figure 5 (overleaf) shows the results.

Two information items received negative scores: English phonetics, and identification of other sign languages that are known to use the same sign. These will be excluded from the dictionary. The rest of the information items all received positive scores.

English grammar (part of speech) will probably not be included in the dictionary, except where it would help clarify different senses of the same word form. This information can be found in any dictionary of English.

Some respondents did not want regional variants of signs to be included in the dictionary. Typically, these respondents wished there to be one New Zealand Sign Language, with a uniform lexicon that would be used throughout the country. The NEB and editorial staff feel strongly that because regional variation is an important aspect of NZSL, it should be described in the dictionary.

Figure 5: Information in each entry.

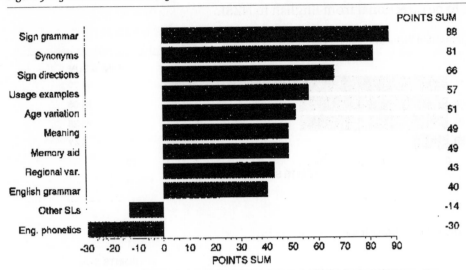

The inclusion of a memory aid, or "hint" for remembering how to make a sign, raises some controversy. As an example, a hint for the sign EAT might read, "bringing food to the mouth". Some people like memory aids, as they supposedly help people remember the sign. The validity of this assertion would be an interesting topic for further research. Some people dislike memory aids as they tend to reinforce the iconic nature of many signs, and in some cases suggest folk etymologies. The extent to which sign languages are iconic and how iconicity affects the linguistic status of a language are questions beyond the scope of this paper. The editors have not yet resolved how to deal with this issue.

The meaning of the English word, or definition, can be found in any dictionary of English. This information will probably be included only where it would clarify different senses of the same word form. As English words, especially frequently used words, tend to have several meanings, definitions will probably be included in many entries.

Age variation is another important phenomenon worth describing in NZSL. Young signers and old signers have many signs unique to their age group. The young signers tend to use more ASE or modified ASE signs. Unfortunately, due to constraints of time and funding, age variation information will not be included in the entries of the Dictionary of New Zealand Sign Language.

To get statistically reliable information on age variation, twice the number of deaf informants would be required, and the dictionary would take almost twice as long to produce. When faced with the difficult decision to either collect information on age variation, or halve the number of entries in the dictionary, the examination of age variation had to be postponed. This is unfortunate, as the dictionary making process would be ideal for collecting data to study this interesting phenomenon.

The rest of the information items all received general acceptance from a majority of respondents, and will be included in the dictionary. These are: examples of how to use the English word in context, English instructions on how to perform the sign, synonyms, and sign grammar, e.g. directionality, optional one- or two-handedness, etc.

3.5 Dictionary comparison

Respondents were asked to look at nine dictionary samples. Each dictionary sample consisted of three photocopied A4 pages. Table 2 shows the sources of the samples. Each sample was labelled with a code so that the respondent would not know which country the dictionary was from.

Table 2: Sources of dictionary samples

Label	Code	Source
ASL-Costello	AL	Costello (1983)
ASL-Sternberg	AS	Sternberg (1981)
Auslan	AU	Johnston (1989)
BSL	BS	Brien˚ (1990)
Canadian	CA	Bailey* (1990)
Dutch	DU	N.S.D.S.K.* (1990)
Gestuno	GE	British Deaf Association (1975)
NZSL Intro	LE	Levitt (1985)
Thai	TH	Sunwanarat et al. (1990

* - Indicates draft pages from works in progress.

The respondents were then asked to state which they liked, and why, as well as which they did not like, and why not. Respondents could say they liked or did not like as many of the samples as they wished; often they liked some features and disliked others in a particular sample.

Responses were classified into the following categories: pictures, complexity (or simplicity); quantity of information, words / text, general (e.g. "I don't know, I just like it"), layout / size, facial expression, organisation (Alphabetical, Concept groups, or Handshape), arrows, print size, synonyms, phonetics, hints, and glosses.

3.5.1 Feature significance

In order to analyse which features of the sample dictionaries respondents thought were significant, all of the responses, either positive or negative, were assigned one normalised point, and tallied by feature category. Figure 6 shows the overall scores by feature category. Those features that drew the most comment should be given the most careful consideration in the Dictionary of New Zealand Sign Language.

Figure 6: Significance of features.

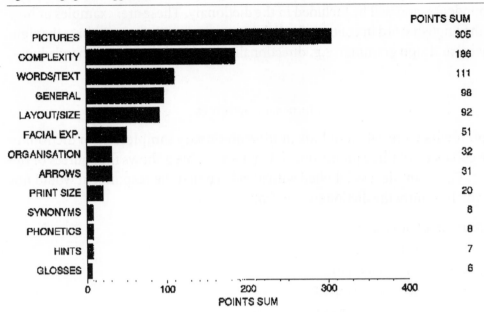

The following subsections describe the responses by feature. For every reason a respondent stated for liking a sample, a positive normalised point was scored; for every reason stated for not liking a sample, a negative normalised point was scored. For each feature, the points were accumulated by dictionary sample.

3.5.2 Pictures

Clearly, the quality of the pictures in a sign language dictionary is of primary importance. Pictures that are too simple, too detailed, do not show sufficient hand or face information, are blurred, or the wrong size detract from the usability of a dictionary. The picture contains more information than any other item in an entry; it is at once a lexeme and a guide to producing manual and non-manual aspects of the sign. For a sign dictionary to be successful, it must have good pictures.

Respondents tended to feel strongly about whether line drawings or photographs better suited a dictionary. This is discussed below. ASL-Costello compromised between large detailed drawings (like Thai and Canadian) and small simplified drawings (such as Auslan and ASL-Sternberg). Respondents liked the ASL-Costello drawings best of all the samples. The Dutch photographs were clear and detailed, with subjects in neutral clothing. Of the photographs, these were the best liked. The other dictionaries with photographs (Gestuno, NZSL Intro, and BSL) all had smaller photos with less visible facial expression. It should be noted that the only pages available for the BSL dictionary were poor quality photocopies, lowering the clarity of the photographs.

Figure 7: Comparison of pictures.

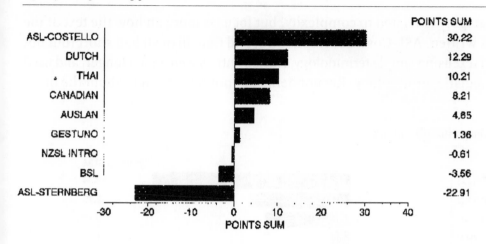

3.5.3 Complexity (Information quantity)

The quantity and presentation of information in a dictionary is also very important in the minds of the users. Almost all of the responses in this category were negative, indicating that the samples were either too complex or too simple. Respondents only made positive comments about the complexity of ASL-Costello and Canadian. In general, respondents thought that NZSL Intro, Dutch, Gestuno and Thai were too simple, and that ASL-Sternberg, Auslan, and BSL were too complex. When making a dictionary, it is important to exclude information that may be superfluous, and to avoid linguistic jargon. Entries should be concise. It is also important to include enough information for the dictionary to be useful.

Figure 8: Comparison of complexity.

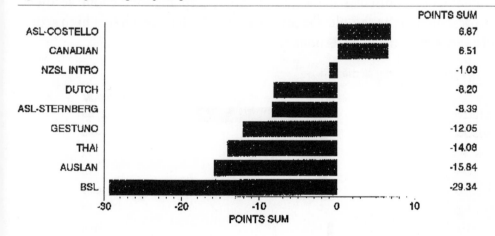

3.5.6 Words / Text

This category is related to complexity, but focuses more on how the text of the entries is written. ASL-Costello, NZSL Intro, and Canadian all had short (but not minimal) text using simple terminology. Auslan entries were much longer, and used some linguistic terminology. Respondents did not feel strongly about the other samples.

Figure 9.: Comparison of words/text.

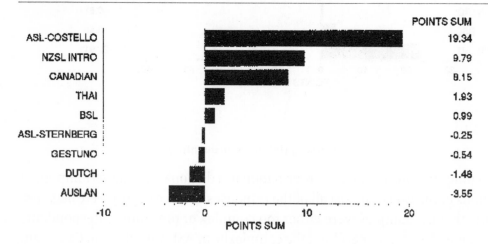

3.5.7 General

This category was used for circumstances where people said they liked a sample, but did not specifically state why. This "gut feeling", or first reaction, should not be dismissed as being the product of a respondent who did not care enough to go into detail, but rather recognised as an indication of the acceptance of the total aesthetic package presented in the sample. Once again, ASL-Costello received a high score. BSL had a very strong negative response.

Figure 10.: Comparison of general reaction.

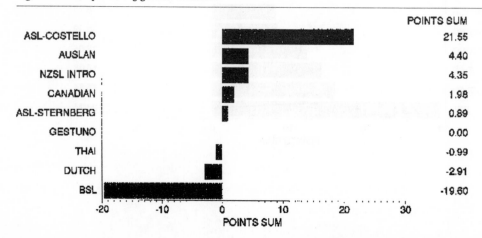

3.5.8 Layout / size

Comments about how the information was presented on the page or the size of the entries were recorded in this category. Yet again, respondents liked the ASL-Costello layout best; Dutch was also rated positively. Auslan entries were thought to be too crowded on the page with small pictures, while Thai was considered too sparse. People did not understand how to connect the various bits of information from different pages and columns in the BSL sample, the text page of which was laid out in table format.

Figure 11.: Comparison of layout/size.

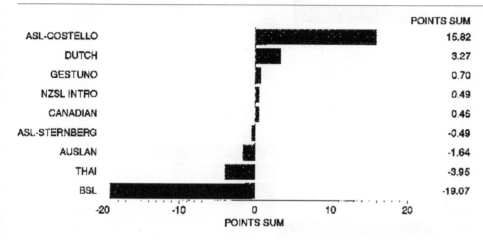

	POINTS SUM
ASL-COSTELLO	15.82
DUTCH	3.27
GESTUNO	0.70
NZSL INTRO	0.49
CANADIAN	0.45
ASL-STERNBERG	-0.49
AUSLAN	-1.64
THAI	-3.95
BSL	-19.07

3.5.9 Facial expression

Facial expression can be central to sign production, particularly in mulitchannel signs, and is often difficult to explain in text. The crisp photographs of the Dutch sample helped give it the top score in this category, while the large line drawings of Thai and Canadian gained positive comments for them. The small Auslan drawings do not show facial expression. ASL-Sternberg often omitted the face completely from the drawings. (Table 12, see overleaf.)

3.5.10 Organisation

Organisation refers to the method used in the dictionary samples to organise the information. Responses in this category amounted to just over three percent of the total responses, indicating marginal significance. All responses bar one were to non-alphabetical methods, despite the overwhelming preference for alphabetical organisation when specifically asked (see figure 3). ASL-Costello used a concept grouping and Auslan used handshapes, both with alphabetical indexes. BSL was organised by handshape, with text and photos on different pages, with an alphabetical dictionary of English as an appendix.

Figure 12.: Comparison of facial expression.

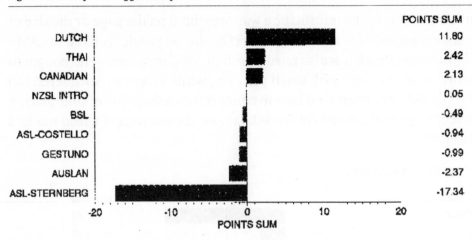

Figure 13.: Comparison of organisation method.

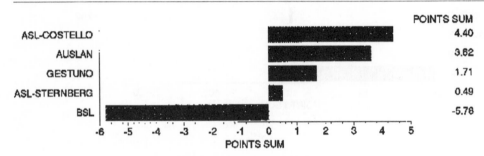

3.5.11 Arrows

The arrows on the pictures drew some response, but only at a marginally significant level. The striking fat arrows of the Canadian sample were most favoured.

Figure 14.: Comparison of arrows.

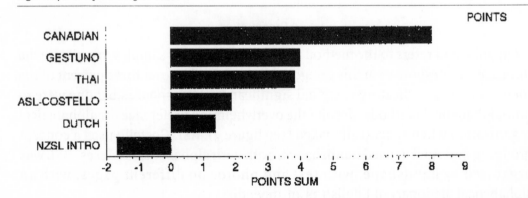

All of the remaining categories (print size, synonyms, phonetics, hints, and glosses) received less than three percent of the responses. It would be difficult, therefore, to glean any reliable information from them.

3.6 Summary by individual dictionary sample

The ASL-Costello dictionary was the most popular by a margin of well over four to one over its nearest rival. This sample scored highest in the categories of pictures, complexity, words/text, general, layout/size, and organisation. This is five out of the top five categories, and six out of the eight significant categories. It did not score bottom in any category. This overwhelming response influenced the Editors of the Dictionary of New Zealand Sign Language to emulate the format of ASL-Costello to a large degree.

The Canadian, Dutch, and NZSL Intro samples all received positive scores, while Thai, Gestuno, and Auslan received mildly negative responses.

ASL-Sternberg suffered badly from its pictures, scoring bottom in the categories of pictures and facial expression. It scored negatively in several other categories. BSL scored worst, with lowest scores in the categories of layout/size, general, organisation, and complexity. It also scored negatively in pictures and facial expression, but it should be noted that the sample pages were poor quality photocopies, as mentioned above.

Figure 15.: Summary comparison of dictionary samples.

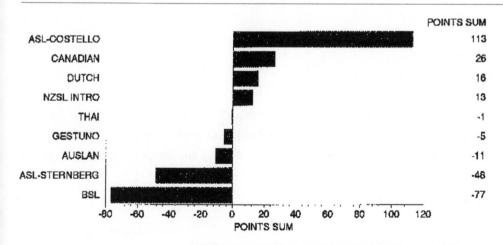

3.6.1 Line drawings versus photographs

After having a chance to view the dictionary samples, users were then asked, in question 22, "What kind of pictures would you like to see in the dictionary?" Figure 16 shows the responses.

Figure 16.: Preferred picture type.

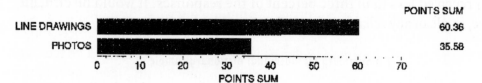

Line drawings were preferred over photographs by almost two to one. This is backed up by the comparison of pictures in the different sample dictionaries above, where the samples with line drawings were generally more popular than those with photographs. Line drawings make it difficult to show detailed facial expression well; this can be mitigated through written instructions and detail insets where necessary. Line drawings can cut down on the amount of 'visual noise', leaving a clear abstraction of how to produce the sign without any extraneous information.

3.6.2 Physical size

How big should the dictionary be? During the survey questioning, respondents were given four sample books in brown paper covers. They were labelled as follows (approximate dimensions in centimetres):

Table 3: Book size samples

Label	Height	Width	Thickness
Square	26	22	2
Textbook	23	16	4
Pocket	18	11	2
Landscape	16	23	2

In retrospect, in planning the survey, the Editors erred in not offering an A4 size book as a choice. Many respondents specifically asked for an A4 size book in their comments at the end of the survey. Figure 17 shows the responses for the given samples.

Figure 17.: Preferred book size.

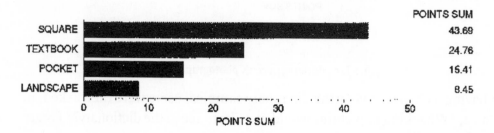

3.6.3 Cost

When planning a product, it is worthwhile finding out what the market is willing to pay for it. The Editors did not want to produce a book that would be priced out of reach of the people it is meant to serve. The cost will influence, but not dictate, the ultimate size of the dictionary, cover type, and paper quality. It seems that the NZ$40-60 range would satisfy over 80% of the potential users.

Figure 18.: Preferred book cost.

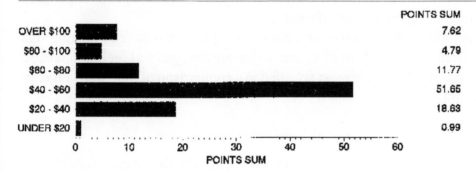

	POINTS SUM
OVER $100	7.62
$80 - $100	4.79
$80 - $80	11.77
$40 - $60	51.65
$20 - $40	18.63
UNDER $20	0.99

POINTS SUM

3.6.4 Special words and signs

While collecting signs for the dictionary, in addition to using videotaped conversations as source data, the Editors will use a 'word net', or checklist of important concepts to include in the dictionary. Sources for the word net include the Council of Europe vocabulary threshold list, the Australian merged word list (Victorian Deaf Society 1987), Nation's list of the 1000 most frequently used words, Orsman's list of NZ unique words, and indexes from several other sign language dictionaries. In question 18 in the survey, the potential users were given the chance to specify any special terms they wanted to see included in the dictionary. These terms and subject areas were compiled, and will be included in the sign collection process.

3.6.5 Supplementary information

Respondents were also asked what information other than entries they would like to see included in the dictionary. Common responses fell into the following broad categories: communication modes, strategies, and systems; Deaf culture; effects of deafness; history of the Deaf community; ow to make contact with the Deaf community; index of deaf organisations; NZSL as a unique language; NZSL structure and grammar; and where to go to learn NZSL.

The Editors could write several other books given the above list. The supplementary information will be necessarily brief.

4 CONCLUSION

4.1 Summary of survey results

The survey provided useful information which will strongly influence the form and content of the Dictionary of New Zealand Sign Language. The identified potential users clearly want the following things: a dictionary to assist learning and for quick reference; alphabetical order; line drawings rather than photographs; information in each entry about sign grammar, synonyms, how to produce the sign, usage examples, and age variation; a larger book in the NZ$40-60 price range, and a large amount of supplementary information.

The users thought that pictures were the most significant feature of existing sign language dictionaries, followed by entry complexity, general feel, and layout. Costello (1983) was by far the most favoured in a comparison of nine sign language dictionary samples.

4.2 Validity of survey results

Do the respondents really know what they want, and did they successfully express this in the survey? One could argue that the surveyed respondents do not know enough about sign linguistics, lexicography, or even NZSL to make educated judgements about how best to make a dictionary, and that responses to a survey could have been made hastily in an unconsidered way.

While it is true that the majority of respondents were not expert NZSL users, and that only three trained academics were surveyed, the ultimate use of the dictionary must be taken into account when considering these facts. The first Dictionary of New Zealand Sign Language must satisfy the requirements of a very wide range of users, many of whom are not expert NZSL users, and very few of whom are trained academics. As an analogy, when a building is designed, the architect gets information from people who will be using the building about how and why they will be using the building, shows them different examples of building types, and uses her experience and research skills to meet those requirements. The people requesting the building are not necessarily architects or familiar with the building trade, and may not have even been in a building of that type before. Like the architect, the Editors got information from potential users about how and why they would want to use a dictionary, and presented them with several alternative models to choose from.

Every effort was made by the survey team to get accurate, detailed information from potential users about what they wanted. When asking questions, the surveyors did not rush respondents, and made sure they understood the questions before responding. The editors consider the information from the survey invaluable, and will contribute greatly toward delivering a dictionary that will be generally acceptable and satisfy user requirements.

4.3 Application of survey results

The editors used the information from the survey to design a trial format for the Dictionary of New Zealand Sign Language, and a prototype system for collecting, analysing, and recording NZSL signs.

After the results from the survey were analysed, the editors drew up requirements for a computer system to support the work of the dictionary. An Apple Macintosh 2ci with 12 megabytes of memory, and a 510 megabyte hard disk was purchased, as well as a scanner and laser printer. Adobe Streamline and Illustrator will be used to process line drawings, and Fourth Dimension will be used to store all lexicographical information. The system is flexible enough so that should funding become available after the completion of the first edition, the editors could produce further editions easily, using other ordering methods, or including different subsets of information.

Footnotes

† The Dictionary of New Zealand Sign Language is funded by the J.R. McKenzie Trust, the Ministry of Education, the NZ Lottery Grants Board, the Oticon Foundation, the Roy McKenzie Foundation, Telecom Corporation of New Zealand Limited, and the V.U.W. Internal Grants Committee. Additional financial support for this paper came from the National Foundation for the Deaf and the V.U.W. English Language Institute Research Fund.
* David Moskovitz: Victoria University of Wellington, New Zealand.

Bibliography

Bailey, C.S. [1990]. *Personal communication to Pat Dugdale.*

Brien, D. [1990]. *Personal communication to Pat Dugdale.*

British Deaf Association [1975]. *Gestuno: International Sign Language of the Deaf.* BDA, Carlisle.

Collins-Ahlgren, M. [1989]. *Aspects of New Zealand Sign Language.* Unpublished doctoral dissertation, Victoria University of Wellington.

Costello, E. [1983]. *Signing: How to Speak with Your Hands.* Bantam Books, New York.

Dugdale, P. [1989]. *Report on the Feasibility Study for the Training of Interpreters for Deaf People.* Unpublished manuscript, National Foundation for the Deaf, Inc., Auckland.

Johnston, T. [1989]. *Auslan Dictionary.* Deafness Resources Australia Ltd., Petersham, NSW.

NSDSK [1990]. *Personal communication to Pat Dugdale through P.M.H. de Korte.*

Levitt, D. [1985]. *Introduction to New Zealand Sign Language*. New Zealand Association of the Deaf, Auckland.

New Zealand Board of Health [1984]. *The Hearing Report: Findings and Initial Recommendations of the Board of Health Committee on Hearing*. P.D. Hasselberg, Government Printer, Wellington.

SAS Institute, Inc. [1985]. *The Statistical Analysis System, Release 6.04*. SAS Institute, Inc. Cary, North Carolina.

Sternberg, M. [1981]. *American Sign Language: A Comprehensive Dictionary*. Harper and Row, New York.

Sunwanarat, M. et al. [1990]. *The Thai Sign Language Dictionary*. The National Association of the Deaf in Thailand, Bangkok.

Bibliography

Aarons, D., Bahan, B., Kegl, J. and Neidle, C. [1992a]. Clausal structure and a tier for grammatical marking in American Sign Language. *Nordic Journal of Linguistics* 15:2, pp. 103–142.

Aarons, D., Bahan, B., Kegl, J., and Neidle, C. [1992b]. *Tense and Agreement in American Sign Language.* Paper presented at the Fourth International Conference on Theoretical Issues in Sign Language Research, San Diego, CA.

Aarons, D., Bahan, B., Kegl, J. and Neidle, C. [in press]. Lexical tense markers, to appear in: Ahlgren, I. and Bergman, B. (eds) *Sign, Gesture, and Space.* Lawrence Erlbaum, Hillsdale, NJ.

Adone, D. [1992]. *Empty Categories in Mauritian Creole Child and Adult Grammar.* Paper to the Dept. of General Linguistics, University of Amsterdam, June 1992.

Ahlgren, I. [1990]. Deictic pronouns in Swedish Sign Language, in: Fischer, S. and Siple, P. (eds) *Theoretical Issues in Sign Language Research Vol. 1: Linguistics.* Academic Press, New York.

Ahlgren, I. and Bergman, B. [1990]. Preliminaries on narrative discourse in Swedish Sign Language structure, in: Vollhaber, T. (ed) *Current Trends in European Sign Language Research. Proceedings of the Third European Congress on Sign Language Research,* pp. 261–267. Signum-Verlag, Hamburg.

Akmajian, A., Steele, S. and Wasow, T. [1979]. The category AUX in Universal Grammar. *Linguistic Inquiry* 10:1, pp. 1–64.

Angelini, N., Borgioli, R., Folchi, A. and Mastromatteo, M. [1991]. *I Primi 400 Segni.* La Nuova Italia, Firenze.

Appel, R. and Muysken, P. [1987]. *Language Contact and Bilingualism.* Edward Arnold, London.

Atkinson, J. [1984]. *Our Master's Voices: The Language and Body Language of Politics.* Methuen, London.

Atkinson, J. and Heritage, J. (eds) [1984]. *Structures of Social Action: Studies in Conversation Analysis.* Cambridge University Press, Cambridge.

Bailey, C.S. [1990]. Personal communication to Pat Dugdale.

Baker, C. [1977]. Regulators and turn-taking in American Sign Language discourse, in: Friedman, L. (ed)*On the Other Hand: New Perspectives on American Sign Language,* pp. 215-236. Academic Press, New York.

Baker, C. and Cokely, D. [1980]. American Sign Language: A Teacher's Resource Text on Grammar and Culture. T.J. Publishers, Inc., Silver Spring, MD.

Baker, M. [1988]. *Incorporation: A Theory of Grammatical Function Changing.* University of Chicago Press, Chicago.

Baker-Shenk, C. [1983]. A Microanalysis of the Nonmanual Components of Questions in American Sign Language. Ph.D. dissertation, University of California, Berkeley.

Baker-Shenk, C. [1985]. Nonmanual behaviors in sign languages: methodological concerns and recent findings, in: Stokoe, W. and Volterra, V. (eds) SLR'83: Sign Language Research, pp. 175–184. Linstok Press, Silver Spring, MD.

Barnes, S., Gutfreund, M., Satterley, D. and Wells, G. [1983]. Characteristics of adults' speech which predict children's language development. Journal of Child Language 10, pp. 65–84.

Bates, E., Begnini, L., Bretherton, I., Camaioni, L. and Volterra, V. [1979]. The Emergence of Symbols: Cognition and Communication in Infancy. Academic Press, New York.

Battison, R. [1978]. Lexical Borrowing in American Sign Language. Linstok Press, Silver Spring, MD.

Bauer, L. [1988] Introducing Linguistic Morphology. Edinburgh University Press, Edinburgh.

Bellugi, U. and Fisher, S. [1972]. A comparison of sign language and spoken language: rate and grammatical mechanisms. Cognition: International Journal of Cognitive Psychology 1, pp. 173–200.

Bellugi, U., Lillo-Martin, D., O'Grady, L. and Van Hoek, K. [1990]. The development of spatialized syntactic mechanisms in American Sign Language, in: Edmondson, W.H. and Karlsson, F. (eds) SLR'87: Papers from the Fourth International Symposium on Sign Language Research, pp. 16–25. Signum Press, Hamburg.

Bendixen, B. [1975]. Eye Behaviors Functioning in American Sign Language. Manuscript.

Bergman, B. [1983] Verbs and Adjectives: Morphological Processes in Swedish Sign Language, in Kyle, J.G. and Woll, B. (eds.) Language in Sign: an International Perspective on Sign Language. Croom Helm, London

Bergman, B. and Wallin, L. [1985]. Sentence structure in Swedish Sign Language, in: Stokoe, W. and Volterra, V. (eds) Proceedings of the Third International Symposium on Sign Language Research 1983, pp. 217–225. Linstok Press, Silver Spring, MD.

Berman, R. [1990]. On acquiring an (S)VO language: subjectless sentences in children's Hebrew. Linguistics 28, pp. 1135–1166.

Bickerton, D. and Odo, C. [1976]. Change and variation in Hawaiian English. General Phonology and Pidgin Syntax Vol.1. Social Sciences and Linguistics Institute, University of Hawaii.

Blankenstijn, C. and Bogaerde van den, B. [1989]. Hand in Hand. Tweetalige Aspecten in het Taalaanbod van Drie Dove Moeders aan hun Horende Kinderen. Master thesis, Institute for General Linguistics, University of Amsterdam, Amsterdam.

Bochner, J.H. and Albertini, J.A. [1988]. Language varieties in the deaf population and their acquisition by children and adults, in: Strong, M. (ed). Language Learning and Deafness, pp. 3–48. Cambridge University Press, Cambridge.

Boden, D. and Zimmerman (eds) [1991]. Talk and Social Structure. Polity Press, Cambridge.

Bogaerde, B. van den and Mills, A.E. [in press]. Word order in input to children: data from SLN, in: *ISLA Working Papers* .

Borer, H. [1988]. On the parallelism between compounds and constructs. *Yearbook of Morphology* 1, pp. 45–66.

Borer, H. [in press]. Parallel Morphology. MIT Press, Cambridge, Mass.

Bos, H., Alons, L., Emmerik, W. et al. [1988]. Persoons- en Locatiemarkering.:*Een Onderzoek naar Acht Directionele Werkwoorden in de Nederlandse Gebarentaal*. Verslag van de Onderzoeksgroep 'Gebarentaal'. Institute for General Linguistics, University of Amsterdam.

Bos, H., Alons, L., Emmerik, W. et al. [1989]. Gebarentalen van doven en de taalkundige theorie: enkele grammaticale kenmerken van gebarentalen. *Tijdschrift voor Taal- en Tekstwetenschap* 9:1, pp. 1–19.

Bos. H. [1990]. Person and location marking in Sign Language of the Netherlands: some implications of a spatially expressed syntactic system, in: Prillwitz, S. and Vollhaber, T. (eds) *Current Trends in European Sign Language Research*., pp. 231—246. Signum Press, Hamburg.

Boyes-Braem, P. [1973]. Acquisition of the Handshape in American Sign Language: A Preliminary Analysis. Unpublished paper. Centre for Sign Language Research, Basel.

Boyes-Braem, P. [1981]. *Features of the Handshape in American Sign Language*. Ph.D. Dissertation, University of California at Berkeley.

Boyes-Braem, P. [1984]. *Sign Structure*. Paper presented at the International Sign Language Workshop, Bristol, United Kindom, September 1984.

Boyes-Braem, P. [1990]. Einführung in die Gebärdensprache und ihre Erforschung. Signum-Verlag, Hamburg.

Boyes-Braem, P., Fournier, M.L., Rickli, F., Corazza, S., Franchi, M.L. and Volterra, V. [1989]. Une comparaison des techniques pour exprimer des roles semantiques et des relations locatives dans les langues des signes suisse-française et italienne, in: Querinmont, S. and Loncke, F. (eds) *Etudes Européennes en Langues des Signes*, pp. 111–140. EDIRSA, Brussels.

Brennan, M., Colville, M.D. and Lawson, L.K. [1980] *Words in Hand: A Structural Analysis of the Signs of British Sign Language*. Moray House College of Education, Edinburgh.

Brennan, M. [1983]. Marking time in British Sign language, in: Kyle, J. and Woll, B. (eds) *Language in Sign: An International Perspective on Sign Language*, pp. 3–10. Croom Helm, London.

Brennan, M. [1986]. Linguistic perspectives, in: Tervoort, B.T. (ed) *Signs of life: Proceedings of the Second European Congress on Sign Language Research*, pp. 1–16. Publications of the institute nr. 50, University of Amsterdam.

Brennan, M. [1990a]. Word Formation in British Sign Language. Ph.D. dissertation, University of Stockholm.

Brennan, M. [1990b]. Productive Morphology in British Sign Language. Focus on the Role of Metaphors, in: Prillwitz, S. and Vollhaber, T. (eds). *Current Trends in European Sign Language Research*, proceedings of the 3rd European Congress on Sign Language Research, pp. 205–228. Signum Press, Hamburg.

Brennan, M. [1992] The Visual World of BSL : An Introduction , in Brien, D. (ed.). *Dictionary of British Sign Language/English*, Faber and Faber, London.

Brennan, M., Brien, D., Collins, J. Elton, F. and Turner, G.H. [1993]. *The Dictionary of British Sign Language/English : A Bilingual Resource.* Paper presented at LASER Facilitating Bilingualism conference, St. Albans, Hertfordshire.

Brennan, M, Colville, M.D. Lawson, L.K. and Hughes, G. [1984] *Words in Hand: A Structural Analysis of the Signs of British Sign Language (Second Edition)*, Moray House College of Education, Edinburgh.

Brien, D. (ed.) [1992]. *Dictionary of British Sign Language/English.* Faber and Faber, London.

Bretherton, I. and Bates, E. [1984]. The development from 10 to 28 months: differential stability of language and symbolic play, in: Enide, R.N. and Harmon, R.J. (eds) *Continuities and Discontinuities in Development.* Plenum, New York.

Brien, D. [1990]. Personal communication to Pat Dugdale.

British Deaf Association [1975]. *Gestuno: International Sign Language of the Deaf.* BDA, Carlisle.

Bruner, J. [1974]. The ontogenesis of speech acts. *Journal of Child Language* 2, pp. 1–19.

Button, G. and Lee, J. (eds) [1987]. *Talk and Social Organisation.* Multilingual Matters, Avon.

Bwenge, C. [1989]. *Lexicographical Treatment of affixational morphology: a case study of four Swahili Dictionaries*, in, James, G. (ed.). *Lexicographers and their Works.* University of Exeter, Exeter.

Caccamise, F. (ed) [1978] *Proceedings of the Second National Symposium on Sign Language Research and Teaching.* National Association of the Deaf, Silver Spring, MD.

Cameracanna, E. and Corazza, S. [1989]. Time Lines in Italian Sign Language. Paper presented at The Deaf Way—An International Festival and Conference on the Language, Culture and History of Deaf People. Washington, DC, July 1989.

Cameracanna, E., Corazza, S., Pizzuto, E. and Volterra, V. [1991]. Terms for Spatio-Temporal Relations in Italian Sign Language (LIS): What They Can Tell Us About Iconicity in Sign and...Speech. Paper presented at the Colloquium on Iconicity in Language, University of Rome 'La Sapienza', Rome, 3–4 October 1991.

Carmel, S.J. [1992] A Checklist of Dictionaries of National Sign Languages of Deaf People, in Sign Language Studies, 76.

Carter, M. [1981]. The Acquisition of British Sign Language (BSL): A First Analysis. Unpublished paper. Centre for Deaf Studies, University of Bristol.

Chinchor, N. [1978]. The Structure of the NP in ASL: Argument from Research on Numerals. Unpublished manuscript, Brown University, Providence.

Chomsky, N. [1965]. Aspects of the Theory of Syntax. MIT Press, Cambridge, Mass.

Chomsky, N. [1981]. Lectures on Government and Binding. Foris Publications, Dordrecht.

Chomsky, N. [1986]. Barriers. MIT Press, Cambridge.

Chomsky, N. [1989]. Some notes on economy of derivation and representation. MIT Working Papers in Linguistics, pp. 43–74.

Cicourel, A.V. [1974]. Cognitive Sociology. Penguin, London.

Clahsen, H. and Muysken, P. [1986]. The availability of universal grammar to adult and child learners: a study of the acquisition of German word order. Second Language Research 2, pp. 93–119.

Coerts, J. [1990]. The analysis of interrogatives and negations in Sign Language of the Netherlands, in: Prillwitz, S. and Vollhaber, T. (eds) Current Trends in European Sign Language Research, pp. 265–277. Signum Press, Hamburg.

Coerts, J. [1992]. Nonmanual Grammatical Markers: An Analysis of Interrogatives, Negations and Topicalisations in Sign Language of the Netherlands. Ph.D. dissertation, Institute for General Linguistics, University of Amsterdam.

Coerts, J. [in press]. Constituent order in Sign Language of the Netherlands, in: ISLA Working Papers .

Coerts, J., Mills, A. and Bogaerde van den, B. [1990]. Language Input, Interaction and the Acquisition of Sign Language of the Netherlands. Paper related to poster presentation at the 4th European Conference of Developmental Psychology. Stirling, Scotland, August 1990.

Cogen, C. [1977]. On the aspects of time expressions in ASL, in: Friedman, L.A. (ed) On the Other Hand: New Perspectives on ASL. Academic Press, New York.

Cokely, D. and Baker, C. [1980]. American Sign Language: A Student Text Units 1-9. T.J. Publishers,Silver Spring, MD.

Collins-Ahlgren, M. [1989]. Aspects of New Zealand Sign Language. Unpublished doctoral dissertation, Victoria University of Wellington.

Comrie, B. [1985]. Tense. Cambridge University Press, Cambridge.

Corazza, S. [1990]. The morphology of classifier handshapes in Italian Sign Language (LIS), in: Lucas, C. (ed) *Sign Language Research: Theoretical Issues*, pp. 71–82. Gallaudet University Press, Washington, DC.

Corazza, S. and Volterra, V. [1987]. Configurazioni, in: Volterra, V. (ed) *La Lingua Italiana dei Segni: La Comunicazione Visivo-Gestuale dei Sordi*, pp. 9–22. Il Mulino, Bologna.

Corazza, S. and Volterra, V. [1988]. La comprensione di lingue dei segni 'straniere', in: De Mauro, T., Gensini, S. and Piemontese, M.E. (eds) *Dalla Parte del Ricevente: Percezione, Comprensione, Interpretazione*, pp. 73–82. Bulzoni, Roma.

Costello, E. [1983]. Signing: How to Speak with Your Hands. Bantam Books, New York.

Cummins, J. [1976]. The influence of bilingualism on cognitive growth: a synthesis of research findings and explanatory hypotheses. *Working Papers on Bilingualism* 19, pp. 121–129.

Cummins, J. [1984]. *Bilingualism and Special Education: Issues in Assessment and Pedagogy*. Multilingual Matters, Clevedon.

Davis, J. [1989]. Distinguishing language contact phenomena in ASL interpretation, in: Lucas, C. (ed) The Sociolinguistics of the Deaf Community, pp. 85–102. Academic Press, San Diego.

Davison, A. [1984]. Syntactic markedness and the definition of sentence topic. *Language* 60, pp.797–846.

Deuchar, M. [1983]. Is British Sign Language an SVO language? in: Kyle, J. and Woll, B. (eds) *Language in Sign: An International Perspective on Sign Language*, pp. 69–76. Croom Helm, London.

Deuchar, M. [1984]. *British Sign Language*. Routledge and Kegan Paul, London.

Di Sciullo, A.M. and Williams, E. [1987]. On the Definition of Word. Monographie Linguistic Inquiry 14. MIT Press, Cambridge, Mass.

Dik, S.C. [1978]. Functional Grammar. North Holland Publishing Company, Amsterdam.

Dik, S.C. [1989]. *The Theory of Functional Grammar Part I: The Structure of the Clause*. Foris Publications, Dordrecht.

Dubuisson, C. et al. [1991]. Les mouvements de tête dans les interrogatives en langue des signes québécoise. *Revue Québécoise de Linguistique* 20:2, pp. 93–122.

Dugdale, P. [1989]. Report on the Feasibility Study for the Training of Interpreters for Deaf People. Unpublished manuscript, National Foundation for the Deaf, Inc., Auckland.

Ebbinghaus, H. and Hessmann, J. [1990]. German words in German Sign Language, in: Prillwitz, S. and Vollhaber, T. (eds) *Current Trends in European Sign Language Research*. Signum Press, Hamburg.

Edge, V.L. and Herrmann, L. [1977]. Verbs and the determination of subject in American Sign Language, in: Friedman, L.A. (ed) *On the Other Hand: New Perspectives on American Sign Language*. Academic Press, New York.

Edmondson, W. [1981]. Sign language in an unfavourable setting: a perspective, in: Woll, B., Kyle, J.G. and Deuchar, M. (eds) *Perspectives on British Sign Language and Deafness*, pp. 204–217. Croom Helm, London.

Edmondson, W.H. and Karlsson, F. (eds) [1990]. SLR '87: Papers from the Fourth International Symposium on Sign Language Research. Signum Press, Hamburg.

Engberg-Pedersen, E. [1986]. The use of space with verbs in Danish Sign Language, in: Tervoort, B.T. (ed) *Signs of life: Proceedings of the Second European Congress on Sign Language Research*, pp. 32-41. Publications of the institute nr. 50, University of Amsterdam.

Engberg-Pedersen, E. [1991]. *Lærebog i Tegnsprogsgrammatik*. Døves center for Total Kommunikation, Copenhagen.

Engberg-Pedersen, E. [in press]. Simultaneous syntactic constructions, in: Brennan, M. and Turner, G. (eds) *Word Order Issues in Sign Language: Working Papers*. International Sign Linguistics Association, Durham, England.

Everitt, B.S. [1986]. The Analysis of Contingency Tables. Chapman and Hall, London.

Fant, L. [1977]. Sign Language. Joyce Media Inc., Northridge, CA.

Fein, G.A. [1978]. Play revisited, in: Lamb, M. (ed): Social and Personality Development. Holt, Renehart and Winston, New York.

Fève-Tagger, N. [1991]. La question en langage gestuel, in: Kerbrat-Orecchioni, C. (ed) *La Question*, pp. 189–200. Presses Universitaires de Lyon, Lyon.

Fischer, S. [1975]. Influences on word order change in American Sign Language, in: Li, C.N. (ed) *Word Order and Word Order Change*, pp. 3–25. University of Texas Press, Austin.

Fischer, S. [1990]. The head parameter in ASL, in: Edmondson, W.H. and Karlsson, F. (eds) SLR'87: Papers from the Fourth *International Symposium on Sign Language Research*, pp. 75–85. Signum Press, Hamburg.

Fischer, S. and Gough, B. [l972]. Some unfinished thoughts on FINISH. Manuscript, Salt Institute for Biological Studies, La Jolla, California.

Fischer, S. and Janis, W. [1990]. Verb sandwiches in American Sign Language, in: Prillwitz, S. and Vollhaber, T. (eds) *Current Trends in European Sign Language Research*, pp. 279–293. Signum Press, Hamburg.

Fischer, S. and Siple, P. (eds) [1990]. *Theoretical Issues in Sign Language Research Vol 1: Linguistics*. Academic Press, New York.

Fisher, K. [1980]. A theory of cognitive development: the control and construction of hierarchies of skills. *Psychological Review* 87, pp. 477–531.

Friedman, L. [1975a]. The manifestation of subject, object and topic in the American Sign Language, in: Li, C.N. (ed) *Subject and Topic*, pp. 125–128. Academic Press, New York.

Friedman, L. [1975b]. Space, time, and person reference in American Sign Language. *Language* 51:4, pp. 940–961

Friedman, L. [1977]. On the Other Hand: New Perspectives on American Sign Language. Academic Press, New York.

Friedman, L. and Battison, R. [1973]. *Phonological Structures in American Sign Language*. NEH Grant Report AY821873136.

Frishberg, N. [1985]. Dominance relations and discourse structures, in: Stokoe, W. and Volterra, V. (eds) *SLR '83: Sign Language Research*, pp. 79–90. Linstok Press, Silver Spring, MD.

Frishberg, N. and Gough, B. [l973]. Time on Our Hands. Paper presented to 3rd Annual California Linguistics Meeting. Stanford, California.

Gee, J.P. and Goodhart, W. [1985]. Nativization, linguistic theory, and deaf language acquisition. *Sign Language Studies* 49, pp. 291–342.

Gee, J.P. and Kegl, J.A. [1983]. Narrative/story structure, pausing, and American Sign Language. Discourse Processes 6, pp. 243–258.

Geluykens [1988]

Gillis, S. and Verlinden, A. [1988]. Nouns and verbs in early lexical development: effects of input frequency? *Antwerp Papers in Linguistics* 54, University of Antwerp.

Goodwin, C. and Goodwin, M. [1987]. Concurrent operations on talk: notes on the interactive organisation of assessments. *IPRA Papers in Pragmatics* 1:1, pp. 1–54.

Gregory, S. [1985]. *Deaf Infants and Their Mothers: The Development of Their Communication Skills*. Paper presented to the International Congress on Education of the Deaf. Manchester, England.

Grimes, J. E. [1975]. The thread of discourse. Janua Linguarum Series Minor 207. Mouton, Amsterdam.

Groot, C. de [1981]. The structure of predicates and verb agreement in Hungarian, in: Daalder, S. and Gerritsen, M. (eds) *Linguistics in the Netherlands 1981*, pp. 149–158. North-Holland Publishing Company, Amsterdam.

Grosjean, F. and Lane, H. [1977]. Pauses and syntax in American Sign Language. Cognition 5, pp. 101–117.

Hacking, I. [1990]. Signing, in *London Review of Books*, 5 April.

Hakulinen, A. (ed) [1989]. Kieli 4: Suomalaisen Keskustelun Keinoja I. Yliopistopaino, Helsinki.

Hall, S. [1983]. Train—gone—sorry: the etiquette of social conversations in American Sign Language. *Sign Language Studies* 41, pp. 291–309.

Hannay, M. and Vester, E. [1987]. Non-restrictive relatives and the representation of complex sentences, in: Auwera, J. v.d. and Goossens, L. (eds) *Ins and Outs of the Predication. Functional Grammar Series 6*, pp. 39–51. Foris Publications, Dordrecht.

Harder, R. and Knoors, H. [1987]. Consolidation of method or future changes? Use of signs in the education of the deaf in the Netherlands, in: J. Kyle (ed) *Sign and School: Using Signs in Deaf Children's Development*, pp. 109–119. Multilingual Matters, Clevedon.

Harris, M., Clibbens, J., Chasin, J. and Tibbitts, R. [1989]. The social context of early sign language development. *First Language 9*, pp. 81–97.

Harris, M., Clibbens, J., Tibbitts, R. and Chasin, J. [1987]. Communication between deaf mothers and their deaf infants, in: Griffiths, P., Mills, A. and Local, J. (eds) *Proceedings of the Child Language Seminar*. University of York, York.

Hedberg, T. [1989]. Name signs in Swedish Sign Language. Paper presented at The Deaf Way, Gallaudet University, Washington, DC.

Hedberg, T. [1992]. Name signs in Swedish Sign Language: their formation and use, in: *Equality and Self-Reliance: Proceedings of the XI World Congres of the World Federation of the Deaf.*

Heny, F. and Richards, B. (eds) [1983]. *Linguistic Categories: Auxiliaries and Related Puzzles; Vol 1: Categories.;Vol 2: The Scope, Order, and Distribution of English Auxiliary Verbs*. D. Reidel Publishing Company, Dordrecht.

Heritage, J. [1984]. *Garfinkel and Ethnomethodology*. Polity Press, Cambridge.

Heritage, J. [1989]. Current developments in conversation analysis, in: Roger, D. and Bull, P. (eds) *Conversation.*, pp. 21–47. Multilingual Matters, Clevedon.

Holm, J. [1988]. *Pidgins and Creoles Vol. 1 and 2*. Cambridge University Press, New York.

Huang, C.T. [1982]. *Logical Relations in Chinese and the Theory of Grammar*. Ph.D. Dissertation, Massachusetts Institute of Technology, Cambridge, MA.

Huang, C.T. [1984]. On the distribution and reference of empty pronouns. *Linguistic Inquiry 15*, pp. 531–574.

Humphries, T., Padden, C. and O'Rourke, T. [1980]. *A Basic Course in American Sign Language*. T.J. Publishers, Silver Spring, MD.

Hyams, N.M. [1986]. *Language Acquisition and the Theory of Parameters*. D. Reidel Publishing Company, Dordrecht.

Hyams, N.M. [1992]. A reanalysis of null subjects in child language, in: Weissenborn, J., Goodluck, H. and Roeper, T. (eds) *Theoretical Issues in Language Acquisition: Continuity and Change in Development*, pp. 249–268. Lawrence Erlbaum Associates, Hillsdale, NJ.

Hyams, N.M. and Wexler, K. [1991]. *On the Grammatical Basis of Null Subjects in Child Language*. Paper to NIAS, Wassenaar, March 1991.

Ichida, Y. [1991]. Elementary grammar of sign language, in: Ogawa, J. (ed) *Foundations of Sign Interpreting*, pp. 138–150. Dai-ich Hoki, Tokyo. (In Japanese).

Jacobowitz, E.L. and Stokoe, W. [1988]. Signs of tense in ASL verbs. *Sign Language Studies* 60.

Jacobs, S. [1992]. Coda talk column. Coda Connection 9:1 (February), pp. 1–3.

Jaegli, O. and Safir, K.J. [1989]. The null subject parameter and parametric theory, in: Jaegli, O. and Safir, K.J. (eds) *The Null Subject Parameter*, pp. 1–44. Kluwer Academic Publishers, Dordrecht.

Jefferson, G. [1985]. An exercise in the transcription of laughter, in: Dijk, T. van (ed) *Handbook of Discourse Analysis Vol 3*. Academic Press, London.

Jeffrey, D. and McConkey, R. [1976]. An observation scheme for recording children's imaginative doll play. *Journal of Child Psychology and Psychiatry* 17, pp. 189–197.

Johnson, R.E. [1991]. Sign language, culture and community in a traditional Yucatec Maya village. *Sign Language Studies* 73, pp. 461–478.

Johnson, R.E. and Erting, C. [1989]. Ethnicity and socialization in a classroom for deaf children, in: Lucas, C. (ed) *The Sociolinguistics of the Deaf Community*, pp. 41–84. Academic Press, San Diego.

Johnson, R.E. and Massone, M.I. [1992]. Números y numerales en la Lengua de Señas Argentina, in: Massone, M.I. and Machado, E.M. *Lengua de Señas Argentina: Análisis y Vocabulario Bilingüe*. Edicial, Buenos Aires.

Johnston, T. [1987]. *A General Introduction to Australian Sign Language*. Tafe National Centre for Research and Development, Australia.

Johnston, T. [1989]. *Auslan Dictionary: A Dictionary of the Sign Language of the Australian Deaf Community*. Deafness Resources Australia Ltd., Petersham, NSW.

Kanda, K. [1988]. *Nihon Shuwa Hogen Chosa*. Shuwa kaihatsunotameno zogohoni kansuru hokokusho, pp. 3–24 Zennihon Roa Renmei. (*Research on JSL Dialect*. Report for Developing New Signs, pp. 3–24. Japanese Federation of the Deaf).

Kanda, K. [1992]. Nihon shuwa oninron. *Shuwagakukenkyu* 12. Nihonshuwagakkai. (JSL Phonology. *Japanese Journal of Sign Linguistics* 12. Japanese Association of Sign Linguistics.)

Kanda, K., Atari, H. and Fukuda, Y. [1992]. *Nihon shuwa densi jisho*. (JSL Computer Dictionary). Paper presented at the 18th Annual Meeting of Japanese Association of Sign Linguistics.

Kantor, R. [1980]. The acquisition of classifiers in American Sign Language. *Sign Language Studies* 28, pp. 193–208.

Kay, P. and Sankoff, G. [1974]. A language-universals approach to pidgins and creoles, in: DeCamp, D. and Hancock, I.F. (eds) *Pidgins and Creoles: Current Trends and Prospects*. Georgetown University Press, Washington, DC.

Kegl, J. [1976]. Pronominalization in ASL. Manuscript.

Kegl, J. [1985]. Locative Relations in American Sign Language Word Formation, Syntax, and Discourse. Ph.D. Dissertation, Massachusetts Institute of Technology. Distributed by MIT Working Papers in Linguistics, Cambridge, MA.

Kegl, J. [1986]. Clitics in American Sign Language, in: Borer, H. (ed) Syntax and Semantics: The Syntax of Pronominal Clitics Vol. 19, pp. 285–309. Academic Press, New York.

Kegl, J. [1987]. Coreference relations in American Sign Language, in: Lust, B. (ed) Studies in the Acquisition of Anaphora Vol. II, pp. 135–170. D. Reidel Publishing Company, Dordrecht.

Kegl, J. [1990]. Predicate argument structure and verb-class organization in the ASL lexicon, in: Lucas, C. (ed) Sign Language Research: Theoretical Issues, pp. 149–175. Gallaudet University Press, Washington, DC.

Kegl, J. and Schley, S. [1986]. When is a classifier no longer a classifier? in: Nikiforidou, V., VanClay, M., Niepokuj, M. and Feder, D. (eds), Proceedings of the Twelfth Annual Meeting of the Berkeley Linguistics Society, pp. 425–441.

Kerbat-Orecchioni, C. (ed) [1991]. La Question. Presses Universitaires de Lyon, Lyon.

Klima, E. and Bellugi, U. [1979]. The Signs of Language. Harvard University Press, Cambridge, MA.

Knoors, H. [1989]. Verwerving van congruentie in Nederlandse Gebarentaal door dove kinderen zonder primair gebarentaalaanbod (Acquisition of verb agreement in Sign Language of the Netherlands by deaf children without primary sign language input), in: Hagen, A.P.M. van and Knoors, H. (eds) Onderwijs aan Doven, pp. 29–42. Swets and Zeitlinger, Lisse.

Knoors, H. [1990]. De gebaarruimte benoemen: benoeming van abstracte punten door late gebarentaalverwervers. (Localisation: nominal establishment by late learners of sign language). Van Horen Zeggen 30: 4, pp. 156–163.

Knoors, H. [1992]. Exploratie van de Gebarenruimte: Een Onderzoek naar de Verwerving van Ruimtelijke Morfosyntactische Gebarentaalstructuren door Dove Kinderen met Horende Ouders (Exploration of the Signing space: A Study into the Acquisition of Spatial Morphosyntactic Sign Language Structures by Deaf Children with Hearing Parents). Eburon Publishers, Delft.

Koopman, H. and Lefèbre, C. [1981]. Haitian Creole pu., in: Muysken, P. (ed) Generative Studies on Creole Languages, pp. 201–223. Foris Publications, Dordrecht.

Kyle, J. [1990]. The Deaf community: custom, culture and tradition, in: Prillwitz, S. and Vollhaber, T. (eds) Sign Language Research and Application. Signum Press, Hamburg.

Kyle, J. and Ackerman, J. [1990]. Signing for infants: Deaf mothers using BSL, in: Edmondson, W.H. and Karlsson, F. (eds) SLR '87: Papers from the Fourth International Symposium on Sign Language Research. Signum Press, Hamburg.

Kyle, J. and Allsop, L. [1981]. Deaf People and the Community. Final Report to the Nuffield Trust. University of Bristol, Bristol.

Kyle, J. and Woll, B. [1985]. Sign Language: The Study of Deaf People and Their Language . Cambridge University Press, Cambridge.

Kyle, J., Ackerman, J. and Woll, B. [1987]. Early mother-infant interaction: language and pre-language in deaf families, in: Griffiths, P., Mills, A. and Local, J. (eds) Proceedings of the Child Language Seminar. University of York, York.

Laudanna, A. [1987]. Ordine dei segni nella frase, in: Volterra, V. (ed) La Lingua Italiana dei Segni: La Comunicazione Visivo-Gestuale dei Sordi, pp. 211–230. Il Mulino, Bologna.

Laudanna, A. and Volterra, V. [1991]. Order of words, signs and gestures: a first comparison. Applied Psycholinguistics 12, pp. 135–150.

Lebeaux, D. [1987]. Comments on Hyams, in: Roeper, T. and Williams, E. (eds) Parameter Setting, pp. 23–40. D. Reidel Publishing Company, Dordrecht.

Levinson, S.C. [1983]. Pragmatics. Cambridge University Press, Cambridge.

Levitt, D. [1985]. Introduction to New Zealand Sign Language. New Zealand Association of the Deaf, Auckland.

Liddell, S. [1978]. Nonmanual signals and relative clauses in ASL, in: Siple, P. (ed) Understanding Language through Sign Language Research, pp. 59–90. Academic Press, New York.

Liddell, S. [1980]. American Sign Language Syntax. Mouton, The Hague.

Liddell, S. [1990]. Four functions of a locus: reexamining the structure of space in American Sign Language, in: Lucas, C. (ed) Sign Language Research: Theoretical Issues, pp. 176–198. Gallaudet University Press, Washington, DC.

Liddell, S. [1992]. Discrete and Continuous in Four Classes of ASL Signs. Paper presented at Theoretical Issues in Sign Language Research Conference IV, 5–8 August, 1992.

Liddell, S. and Johnson, R. [1989]. American Sign Language: The Phonological Base. Sign Language Studies 64.

Lillo-Martin, D. [1986]. Two kinds of null arguments in American Sign Language. Natural Language and Linguistic Theory 4, pp. 415–444.

Lillo-Martin, D. [1990]. Parameters for questions: evidence for wh-movement in ASL, in: Lucas, C. (ed) Sign Language Research: Theoretical Issues, pp. 211–222. Gallaudet University Press, Washington, DC.

Lillo-Martin, D. [1991a]. Anaphora in American Sign Language: Reference, Binding, and Logophoricity. Handout from talk presented November 8, 1991 at the University of Massachusetts, Amherst, MA.

Lillo-Martin, D. [1991b]. Universal Grammar and American Sign Language. Kluwer, Dordrecht.

Lillo-Martin, D. [1992]. Comments on Hyams and Weissenborn: on licensing and identification, in: Weissenborn, J., Goodluck, H. and Roeper, T. (eds) *Theoretical Issues in Language Acquisition: Continuity and Change in Development*, pp. 301–308. Lawrence Erlbaum Associates, Hillsdale, NJ.

Lillo-Martin, D. and Fischer, S. [1992]. Overt and Covert Wh-Questions in American Sign Language. Paper presented at the Fourth International Conference on Theoretical Issues in Sign Language Research, San Diego, CA.

Lillo-Martin, D. and Klima, E. [1990]. Pointing out differences: ASL pronouns in syntactic theory, in: Fischer, S. and Siple, P. (eds), *Theoretical Issues in Sign Language Research Vol. 1: Linguistics*, pp. 191–210. University of Chicago Press, Chicago.

Lillo-Martin, D., Bellugi, U., Struxness, L. and O'Grady, M. [1985]. The acquisition of spatially organized syntax. *Papers and Reports on Child Language Development* 24, pp. 70–77 Department of Linguistics, Stanford University.

Livingston, S. [1983]. Levels of development in the language of deaf children: ASL grammatical processes, Signed English structures, semantic features. *Sign Language Studies* 40, pp. 193–284.

Loew, R. [1984]. *Roles and Reference in American Sign Language: A Developmental Perspective*. Unpublished doctoral dissertation, University of Minnesota.

Loncke, F. [1984]. On the interface between sign phonology and kinesiology, in: Loncke, F., Boyes-Braem, P. and Lebrun, Y. (eds) *Recent Research on European Sign Languages*, pp. 129–137. Swets and Zeitlinger BV, Lisse.

Loncke, F. [1990]. Modaliteitsinvloed op Taalstructuur en Taalverwerving in Gebarencommunicatie. *(Influence of Modality on Language Structure and Language Acquisition in Sign Communication)* Ph.D. Dissertation, Vrije Universiteit, Brussels.

Loncke, F., Boyes-Braem, P. and Lebrun, Y. (eds) [1984]. Recent Research on European Sign Languages. Swets and Zeitlinger BV, Lisse.

Loncke, F., Quertinmont, S. and Ferreyra, P. [1990]. Deaf children in schools: more or less native signers? in: Prillwitz, S. and Vollhaber, T. (eds) *Current Trends in European Sign Language Research*, pp. 163–178. Signum Press, Hamburg.

Loncke, F., Hoiting, N., Knoors, H. and Moerman, D. [1988]. Native and non-native language acquisition: the case of signing deaf children, in: Besien, F. van (ed) *First Language Acquisition*. ABLA-papers 13. Gent-Antwerpen.

Longacre, R. E. [1983]. The Grammar of Discourse. Plenum Press, New York.

Lowe, M. and Costello, A. [1976]. A Manual for Symbolic Play Test. NFER, London.

Lucas, C. (ed) [1989]. The Sociolinguistics of the Deaf Community. Gallaudet University Press, Washington, DC.

Lucas, C. (ed) [1990]. *Sign Language Research: Theoretical Issues*. Gallaudet University Press, Washington, DC.

Maestas y Moores, L. [1980]. Early linguistic environment: interactions of deaf parents with their infants. *Sign Language Studies* 26, pp. 1–13.

Mallinson, G. and Blake, B.J. [1981]. Language Typology: Cross-Linguistic Studies in Syntax. North-Holland Publishing Company, Amsterdam.

Mandel, M. [1977]. Iconic devices in American Sign Language, in: Friedman, L.A. (ed) On the Other Hand: New Perspectives on American Sign Language, pp. 57–107. Academic Press, New York.

Marmor, G.S. and Petitto, L. [1979]. Simultaneous communication in the classroom: how well is English grammar represented? Sign Language Studies 23, pp. 99–136.

Massone, M.I. and Machado, E.M. [1992]. Lengua de Señas Argentina. Análisis y Vocabulario Bilingüe. Edicial, Buenos Aires.

Mazuka, R., Lust, B., Wakayama, T. and Snyder, W. [1986]. Distinguishing effects of parameters in early syntax acquisition: a cross-linguistic study of Japanese and English. Papers and Reports on Child Language Development. Stanford University, pp. 73–82.

McCawley, J. [1988]. The Syntactic Phenomena of English. University of Chicago Press, Chicago.

McCune-Nicholich, L. [1981]. Toward symbolic functioning: structure of early pretend games and potential parallels with language. Child Development 52, pp. 785–797.

McCune-Nicholich, L. [1982]. Combinatorial competency in play and language, in: Pepler, D.J. and Rubin, K.H. (eds) The Play of Children: Current Theory and Research. Karger, Basel.

McCune-Nicholich, L. and Fenson, L. [1984]. Methodological issues in studying early pretend play, in: Yawkey, T.D. and Pellegrini, A.D. (eds) Child's Play: Development and Applied. Lawrence Erlbaum, Hillsdale, NJ.

McDonald, B. [1982] Aspects of The American Sign Language Predicate System. Ph.D. Thesis, University of Buffalo.

McDonald, B. [1983]. Levels of Analysis in Sign Language Research, in Kyle, J.G. and Woll, B. (eds.). Language in Sign; an International Perspective on Sign Language. Croo Helm, London.

McDonald, B. [1985] Productive and frozen lexicon in ASL: an old problem revisited, in Stokoe, W.C. and Volterra, V. (eds.). SLR:'83: Proceedings of the 3rd International Symposium on Sign Language Research. Signum Press, Hamburg.

McIlvenny, P. [1991]. Some thoughts on the study of sign language talk, in: Sajavaara, K. et al. (eds) Communication and Discourse across Cultures and Languages, pp. 187–202. AFinLA Yearbook 1991. Publications de L'Association Finlandaise de Linguistique Appliqueé, Jyväskylä University.

McIntire, M. [1977]. The Acquisition of American Sign Language Hand Configurations. Sign Language Studies 16, pp. 247–266.

McIntire, M. [1982]. Constituent order and location in American Sign Language. *Sign Language Studies* 37, pp. 345–386.

McNeill, D. [1985]. So you think gestures are nonverbal? *Psychological Review* 92:3. American Psychological Association.

Meadow, K. [1977]. Name signs as identity symbols in the Deaf community. *Sign Language Studies* 16, pp. 237–246.

Meier, R. [1990]. Person deixis in American Sign Language, in: Fischer, S. and Siple, P. (eds) *Theoretical Issues in Sign Language Research Vol 1: Linguistics*. Academic Press, New York.

Miles, D. [1988]. *British Sign Language: A Beginner's Guide*. BBC Books, London.

Miller, C. [1991]. Une théorie prosodique de la phonologie des langues des signes. *Revue Québécoise de Linguistique Théorique et Appliquée* 10:1, pp. 21–55.

Miller, C. [1992]. *Constructions Simultanées et Signes Complexes en Langue des Signes Québécoise*. Manuscript.

Mills, A. and Bogaerde van den, B. [1990]. Functions and forms of bilingual input: children learning a sign language as one of their first languages, in: Prillwitz, S. and Vollhaber, T. (eds) *Current Trends in European Sign Language Research*. Signum Press, Hamburg.

Mills, A. and Bogaerde van den, B. [1991]. *Input and Interaction in Deaf Families*. Paper presented at the 16th Boston Conference on Language Acquisition, October 1991.

Mills, A. and Coerts, J. [1989]. *Uit de Eerste Hand*. Onderzoeksverslag van de werkgroep 'Adults' input to children learning sign'. Institute for General Linguistics, University of Amsterdam.

Mindess, A. [1990]. What name signs can tell us about Deaf culture. Sign Language Studies 66, pp. 1–24.

Moerman, M. [1988]. Talking Culture: Ethnography and Conversation Analysis. University of Philadelphia Press, Philadelphia.

Mohay, H., Luttrell, R. and Milton, L. [1991]. *How Much, How Often and in What Form Should Linguistic Input Be Given to Deaf Infants?* Paper presented at the Australia and New Zealand Conference for Educators of the Deaf, Surfers Paradise, Queensland. Unpublished manuscript.

Moody, B. [1983]. La Langue des Signes. Tomes 1, 2, 3. International Visual Theatre, Vincennes.

Moody, W. [1987]. International gestures, in: Van Cleve, J.V. (ed) *Gallaudet Encyclopedia of Deaf People and Deafness*. McGraw-Hill Book Company Inc., New York.

Moody, W. [1989]. La communication internationale chez les sourds. *Réeducation Orthophonique* 17.

Morris, D. [1977]. *Manwatching*. Harry N. Abrahams Inc., New York.

Mühlhäusler, P. [1986]. Pidgin and Creole Linguistics. Basil Blackwell, Oxford.

Nadeau, M. [1989]. Morpho-Syntaxe de la Langue des Signes Québécoise : Un Début d'Analyse. Unpublished paper presented at the Associaton Canadienne-Française pour l'Avancement des Sciences (ACFAS), Montréal.

Nadeau, M. [in press]. Y-a-t-il un ordre des signes en LSQ? in: Dubuisson, C. and Nadeau, M. (eds) *Etudes sur la Langue des Signes Québécoise*. Presses de l'Université de Montréal, Montréal.

New Zealand Board of Health [1984]. The Hearing Report: *Findings and Initial Recommendations of the Board of Health Committee on Hearing*. P.D. Hasselberg, Government Printer, Wellington.

Newport, E.L. [1982]. Task Specificity in Language Learning: Evidence from Speech perception and American Sign Language, in Wanner, E. and Gleitman, L.R. (eds.). *Language Acquisition, the State of the Art*. University Press, New York and Cambridge.

Newport, E. [1984]. Constraints on learning: studies in the acquisition of American Sign Language. *Papers and Reports on Child Language Development* 23, pp. 1–22. Department of Linguistics, Stanford University.

Newport, E. and Supalla, T. [1980]. The Structuring of Language: clues from the acquisition of signed and spoken language, in Bellugi, U. and Studdert-Kennedy, M. (eds.). *Signed and Spoken Language: Biological Constraints on Linguistic Form*. Verlag Chemie, Berlin.

NSDSK [1990]. *Personal communication to Pat Dugdale through P.M.H. de Korte*.

Padden, C. (ed) [1986]. *Proceedings of the Fourth National Symposium on Sign Language Research and Teaching*. National Association of the Deaf, Silver Spring, MD.

Padden, C. [1981]. Some arguments for syntactic patterning in American Sign Language. *Sign Language Studies* 32, pp. 239–259.

Padden, C. [1983]. *Interaction of Morphology and Syntax in American Sign Language*. Ph.D. Dissertation, University of California, San Diego.

Padden, C. [1986]. Verbs and role-shifting in ASL, in: Padden, C. (ed) *Proceedings of the Fourth National Symposium on Sign Language Research and Teaching*, pp. 44–57. National Association for the Deaf, Silver Spring.

Padden, C. [1988]. *Interaction of Morphology and Syntax in American Sign Language*. Garland, Outstanding Dissertations in Linguistics (based on Padden [1983]), New York.

Padden, C. [1990]. The relation between space and grammar in ASL verb morphology, in: Lucas, C. (ed) *Sign Language Research: Theoretical Issues*, pp. 253–272. Gallaudet University Press, Washington, DC.

Petitto, L.A. and Bellugi, U. [1988]. Spatial cognition and brain organization: clues from the acquisition of a language in space, in: Stiles-Davis, J., Kritchevsky, M. and Bellugi, U. (eds) *Spatial Cognition: Brain Bases and Development*, pp. 299–326. Lawrence Erlbaum, Hillsdale, NJ.

Petronio, K. [1991a]. A focus position in ASL, in: Bobalijik, J. and Bures, T. (eds) *Papers from the Third Student Conference in Linguistics*. MIT Working Papers, Cambridge, Mass.

Petronio, K. [1991b]. A focus position in ASL. MIT Working Papers in Linguistics, pp. 211–226.

Piaget, J. [1946]. *La Formation du Symbole Chez L'Enfant*. Delachaux and Niestlé, Neuchatel.

Pilleux, M. [1991]. Negation in Chilean Sign Language. Signpost, winter 1991.

Pimiä, P. [1990]. Semantic features of some mouth patterns in Finnish Sign Language, in: Prillwitz, S. and Vollhaber, T. (eds) *Current Trends in European Sign Language Research*. Signum Press, Hamburg.

Pimiä, P. and Rissanen, T. [1987]. *Kolme Kirjoitusta Viittomakielestä (Three Studies of Sign Language)* . Department of General Linguistics Pub. No. 17, University of Helsinki.

Pinsonneault, D. [1991]. Verb Echos in LSQ (Langue des Signes Québécoise). Paper presented at the ISLA Workshop on Word-order Issues in Sign Language, Durham.

Pizzuto, E. [1986]. The verb system of Italian Sign Language, in: Tervoort, B.T. (ed) *Signs of Life: Proceedings of the Second European Congress on Sign Language Research*, pp. 17–31. Publications of the institute nr. 50, University of Amsterdam.

Pizzuto, E. [1987]. Aspetti morfosintattici, in: Volterra, V. (ed) *La Lingua Italiana dei Segni: La Comunicazione Visivo-Gestuale dei Sordi*, pp. 179–209. Il Mulino, Bologna.

Pizzuto, E., Giuranna, E. and Gambino, G. [1990]. Manual and non-manual morphology in Italian Sign Language: grammatical constraints and discourse structure, in: Lucas, C. (ed) *Sign Language Research: Theoretical Issues*, pp. 83–102. Gallaudet University Press, Washington, DC.

Poizner, H., Klima, E. and Bellugi, U. [1987]. *What the Hands Reveal about the Brain*. MIT Press, Cambridge, Mass.

Pollock, J.Y. [1989]. Verb movement, universal grammar, and the structure of IP. Linguistic Inquiry 20:3, pp. 365–424.

Preisler, G. [1983]. *Deaf Children in Communication: A Study of Communicative Strategies Used By Deaf Children in Social Interactions*. Trydells Tryckeri, Laholm.

Prillwitz, S. and Vollhaber, T. (eds) [1990]. *Current Trends in European Sign Language Research*. Signum Press, Hamburg.

Prillwitz, S. et al. [1989]. *HamNoSys Version 2.0*. Signum Press, Hamburg.

Prillwitz, S. [1990] Development of a Computerized Sign Language Dictionary with Animated Pictures, in Edmonson, W.H. and Karlsson, F. (eds.). *SLR'87: Papers from the 4th International Symposium on Sign Language Research*. Signum Oress, Hamburg.

Prinz, P.M. and Prinz, E.A. [1985]. If only you could hear what I see: discourse development in sign language. *Discourse Processes* 8, pp. 1–19.

Psathas, G. (ed) [1990]. *Interaction Competence*. University of America Press, Washington, DC.

Psathas, G. and Anderson, T. [1990]. The 'practices' of transcription in conversation analysis. *Semiotica* 78:1/2, pp. 75–99.

Radutzky, E. [1990]. *Dizionario bilingue elementare della lingua italiana dei segni*. Edizioni Kappa, Rome.

Rissanen, T. [1985a]. *Viittomakielen Perusrakenne (The Basic Structure of Sign Language)*. Department of General Linguistics Pub. No. 12, University of Helsinki.

Rissanen, T. [1985b]. ViittomakielenPerusrakenne. Helsingin yliopisto, Yleisen kielitieteen laitos.

Rizzi, L. [1982]. *Issues in Italian Syntax*. Foris Publications, Dordrecht.

Romaine, S. [1988]. Pidgin and Creole Languages. Longman, New York.

Romaine, S. [1989]. Bilingualism. Basil Blackwell, Oxford.

Romano, C. [1991]. Mixed headedness in American Sign Language. MIT Working papers in Linguistics, pp. 241–254.

Romeo, O. [1991]. *Dizionario dei Segni*. Zanichelli, Bologna.

Rondal, J., Henrot, F. and Charlier, M. [1986]. Le Langage des Signes. Mardaga, Brussels.

Roy, C.B. [1989]. Features of discourse in an American Sign Language lecture, in: Lucas, C. (ed) *The Sociolinguistics of the Deaf Community*. Academic Press, New York.

Sacks, H. [1989]. Harvey Sacks: Lectures 1964-1965. Special Issue edited by G. Jefferson in *Human Studies* 12:3/4.

Sacks, H., Schegloff, E. and Jefferson, G. [1978]. A simplest systematics for the organisation of turn taking for conversation, in: Schenkein (ed) *Studies in the Organisation of Conversational Interaction*, pp. 7–55. Academic Press, New York.

Sandler, W. [1989]. Phonological Representation of the Sign: Linearity and Nonlinearity in American Sign Language. Foris Publications, Dordrecht.

SAS Institute, Inc. [1985]. The Statistical Analysis System, Release 6.04. SAS Institute, Inc. Cary, North Carolina.

Schermer, G.M. [1990]. *In Search of a Language: Influences from Spoken Dutch on Sign Language of the Netherlands*. Doctoral Dissertation, University of Amsterdam. Eburon Publishers, Delft.

Schermer, G.M., Fortgens, C., Harder, R. and Nobel, E. de (eds) [1991]. *De Nederlandse Gebarentaal. (Sign Language of the Netherlands)*. Van Tricht, Twello.

Schermer, T. and Koolhof, C. [l990]. The reality of time-lines: aspects of tense in the Sign Language of the Netherlands (SLN), in: Edmondson, W.H. and Karlsson, F. (eds) *SLR '87: Proceedings of the Third European Congress on Sign Language Research*, pp. 295–305. Signum Press, Hamburg.

Schulmeister, R. [1990]. A Computer Dictionary with Animated Signs for the Special Field of Computer Technology, in Prillwitz, S. and Vollhaber, T. (eds.). *Current Trends in European Sign Language Research*. Signum Press, Hamburg.

Shore, C., Bates, E., Bretherton, I., Beeghly, M. and O'Connell, B. [1990]. Vocal and gestural symbols: similarities and differences from 13 to 28 Months, in: Volterra, V. and Erting, C.J. (eds) *From Gesture to Language in Hearing and Deaf Children*. Springer-Verlag, New York.

Sinclair, J. [1991]. *Corpus, Concordance, Collocation*. Oxford University Press, Oxford.

Siple, P. (ed) [1978]. *Understanding Language through Sign Language Research*. Academic Press, New York.

Slobin, D.I. [1975]. The more it changes... on understanding language by watching it move through time. Papers and Reports on *Child Language Development* 10, pp. 1–30. Department of Linguistics, Stanford University.

Smith, W.H. [1990]. Evidence for suxiliaries in Taiwan Sign Language, in: Fischer, S.D. and Siple, P. (eds) *Theoretical Issues in Sign Language Research Vol 1: Linguistics*, pp. 211-228. University of Chicago Press, Chicago.

Steele, S.M. [1973]. *The Positional Tendencies of Modal Elements and Their Theoretical Implications*. Ph.D. dissertation. University of California, San Diego.

Steele, S.M. [1978]. The category AUX as a language universal, in: Greenberg, J.H., Ferguson, C.A. and Moravcsik, E.A. (eds) *Universals of Human Language.Vol. 3: Word Structure*, pp. 7–45. Stanford University Press, Stanford, CA.

Steele, S.M., Akmajian, A., Demers, R., Jelinek, E., Kitagawa, C., Oehrle, R. and Wasow, T. [1981]. An encyclopedia of AUX: a study in cross-linguistic equivalence. *Linguistic Inquiry Monographs* vol. 5. MIT Press, Cambridge, Mass.

Sternberg, M. [1981]. *American Sign Language: A Comprehensive Dictionary*. Harper and Row, New York.

Steyaert, M. and Loew, R. [1978]. *The Referential Function of Multiple Markers in American Sign Language*. Paper presented at the Annual Meeting of the Linguistic Society of America.

Stokoe, W.C. [1960]. Sign language structure: an outline of the visual communication system of the American deaf. *Studies in Linguistics Occasional Paper* 8. University of Buffalo.

Stokoe, W.C., Casterline, D. and Croneberg, C. [1965]. A Dictionary of American Sign Language on *Linguistic Principles*. Linstok Press, Silver Spring, MD.

Stokoe, W.C. [1993a] Unabridged—Two Recent Dictionaries, in *Sign Language Studies*, 78.

Stokoe, W.C. [1993b] Dictionary Making: Then and Now, in *Sign Language Studies*, 79.

Strong, M. and Charlson, E.S. [1987]. Teachers' strategies for using simultaneous communication. *Teaching English to Deaf and Second-Language Students* 4:1, pp. 21–24.

Sunwanarat, M. et al. [1990]. *The Thai Sign Language Dictionary*. The National Association of the Deaf in Thailand, Bangkok.

Supalla, S. [1986]. *Manually Coded English: An Understanding of Modality's Role in Signed Language Development*. Paper presented at the Theoretical Issues in Sign Language Research Conference, Rochester, 13–16 June 1986.

Supalla, S. [1990]. The arbitrary name sign system in American Sign Language. *Sign Language Studies* 67, pp. 99–126.

Supalla, S. [1992]. *The Book of Name Signs*. Dawn Sign Press, San Diego.

Supalla, T. [1978]. Morphology of verbs of motion and location in American Sign Language, in Caccamise, F. (ed) *Proceedings of the Second National Symposium on Sign Language Research and Teaching*. National Association of the Deaf, Silver Spring, MD.

Supalla, T. [1982]. *Structure and Aquisition of Verbs of Motion and Location in American Sign Language*. Ph.D. Dissertation, University of California, San Diego.

Supalla, T. [1986]. The classifier system in American Sign Language, in: Craig, C. (ed) *Noun Classes and Categorization*, pp. 181–214. John Benjamins, Philadelphia.

Supalla, T. and Newport, E.L. [1978]. *How many seats in a chair? The derivation of nouns and verbs in American Sign Language*, in Siple, P. (ed.). Understanding Language Through Sign Language Research. Academic Press, New York.

Supalla, T. and Webb, R. [1992]. Structure of International Sign Language. Manuscript, University of Rochester.

Sutton-Spence, R. and Woll, B. [in press]. The status and functional role of fingerspelling in BSL, in: Marschark, M. and Clark, D. (eds) *Psychological Perspectives on Deafness*. Lawrence Erlbaum Associates, Hillsdale, NJ.

Sutton-Spence, R., Woll, B. and Allsop, L. [1990]. Variation and recent change in fingerspelling in British Sign Language. *Language Variation and Change* 2, pp. 313–330.

Suwanarat, M. et al [1986]. *Thai Sign Language Dictionary*. National Association for the Deaf in Thailand and the Human Assistance Programme, Thailand.

Swisher, M.V. [1984]. Signed input of hearing mothers to deaf children. *Language Learning* 34:2, pp. 69–85.

Swisher, M.V. [1986]. *Conversational Interaction between Deaf Children and Their Hearing Mothers: The Role of Visual Attention*. Paper presented at the Conference on Theoretical Issues in Sign Language Research. Rochester, NY.

Swisher, M.V., Christie, K. and Miller, S.L. [1989]. The Reception of Signs in Peripheral Vision. *Sign Language Studies* 63, pp. 99–125.

Takkinen, R. [1988]. *Kereemipoikkeavuudet Kuuron Lapsen Viittomakielessä 2v 3kk–3v 4kk Iässä. Tapaustutkimus. ProGradu-Tutkielma*. Helsingin yliopisto, Fonetiikan laitos.

Tervoort, B.Th. [1968]. You me downtown movie fun. *Lingua* 21, pp. 455–465.

Teuber, H. et al [1980] A Computerized lexicon of American Sign Language: the DASL in FORTRAN, in *Sign Language Studies, 29*.

Tomaszczyk, J. [1983] On bilingual dictionaries: The case for bilingual dictionaries for foreign language learners, in Hartmann, R.R.K. (ed.).*Lexicography, Principles and Practice*. Academic Press, London.

Traugott, E.C. [1978]. On the expression of spatio-temporal relations in language, in: Greenberg, J.H. (ed) Universals of Human Language Vol. 3, pp. 369–400. Stanford University Press, Stanford, CA.

Viittomakielen Kuvasanakirja (Sign Language Picture Dictionary). [1973/1977/1988]. Kuurojen Liito r.y., Helsinki.

Vogt-Svendsen, M. [1990]. Eye gaze in Norwegian Sign Language interrogatives, in: Edmondson, W.H. and Karlsson, F. (eds) SLR '87: *Papers from the Fourth International Symposium on Sign Language Research*, pp. 153-162. Signum Press, Hamburg.

Volterra, V. (ed) [1987]. *La Lingua Italiana dei Segni: La Comunicazione Visivo-Gestuale dei Sordi*. Il Mulino, Bologna.

Volterra, V., Laudanna, A., Corazza, S., Radutzky, E. and Natale, F. [1984]. Italian Sign Language: the order of elements in the declarative sentence, in: Loncke, F., Boyes-Braem, P. and Lebrun, Y. (eds) *Recent Research on European Sign Languages*, pp. 19–48. Swets and Zeitlinger BV, Lisse.

Wallin, L. [1987]. *Non-Manual Anaphoric Reference in Swedish Sign Language*. Supplement for Research on Sign Language, Video report 2. University of Stockholm, Institute of Linguistics, Stockholm.

Weissenborn, J. [1990]. Functional categories and verb movement: the acquisition of German syntax reconsidered, in: Rothweiler, M. (ed) *Spracherwerb und Grammatik: Linguistische Untersuchungen zum Erwerb von Syntax und Morphologie. Linguistische Berichte: Sonderheft 3*.

Weissenborn, J. [1992]. Null subjects in early grammars: implications for parameter-setting theories, in: Weissenborn, J., Goodluck, H. and Roeper, T. (eds) *Theoretical Issues in Language Acquisition: Continuity and Change in Development*, pp. 269–300. Lawrence Erlbaum Associates, Hillsdale, NJ.

Werner, H. and Kaplan, B. [1963]. *Symbol Formation*. Wiley, New York.

Whinnom, K. [1971]. Linguistic hybridization and the 'special case' of pidgins and creoles, in: Hymes, D. (ed) *Pidginization and Creolization of Language*. pp. 91–115. Cambridge University Press, Cambridge.

Wilbur, R. [1979]. American Sign Language and Sign Systems. University Park Press, Baltimore, MD.

Wilbur, R. [1983]. Discourse structure in American Sign Language conversations. *Discourse Processes* 6, pp. 225–241.

Wilbur, R. [1987]. *American Sign Language: Linguistic and Applied Dimensions*. Second edition. College-Hill Press, Boston.

Wilbur, R. [1991]. Intonation and focus in American Sign Language, in: No, Y. and Libucha, M. (eds) ESCOL '90. Ohio State University Press, Columbus, OH.

Wilbur, R. and Petitto, L. [1983]. Discourse structure of American Sign Language conversations; or, how to know a conversation when you see one. *Discourse Processes* 6, pp. 225–241.

Wilcox, S. and Stokoe, W.C. [forthcoming] Multimedia Dictionary of American Sign Language, in Coninx, F. and Elsendoorn, B.A.G. (eds.). *Interactive Learning Technology for the Deaf.* Springer-Verlag, Berlin.

Woll, B, [1981]. Question structure in British Sign Language, in: Woll, B., Kyle, J. and Deuchar, M. (eds) *Perspectives on British Sign Language and Deafness*, pp. 136-149. Croom Helm, London.

Woll, B. [1990]. International perspectives on sign language communication. *International Journal of Sign Linguistics* 1:2. International Sign Linguistics Association.

Woll, B. [1991]. *Recent Variation and Change in BSL.* Report to the Economic and Social Research Council. Centre for Deaf Studies, Bristol.

Woll, B., Kyle, J. and Deuchar, M. (eds) [1981]. *Perspectives on British Sign Language and Deafness.* Croom Helm, London.

Woodward, J. [1973]. Some characteristics of Pidgin Sign English. *Sign Language Studies* 3, pp. 39–46.

Woodward, J. and Markowicz, H. [1975]. *Some Handy New Ideas On Pidgins and Creoles: Pidgin Sign Languages.* Paper presented at Conference on Pidgin and Creole Languages, Honolulu, Hawaii.

World Federation of the Deaf [1992]. *Equality and Self-Reliance: Proceedings of the XI World Congres of the World Federation of the Deaf.*

Yau, S and He, J. [1989]. How deaf children in a Chinese school get their name signs. *Sign Language Studies* 65, pp. 305–322.

Zgusta, L. [1971]. *Manual of Lexicography.* Mouton, Den Haag.

Zimmer, J. [1989]. Toward a description of register variation in American Sign Language, in: Lucas, C. (ed) *The Sociolinguistics of the Deaf Community*, pp. 253–272. Academic Press, San Diego, CA.

Zimmer, J. and Patschke, C. [1990]. A class of determiners in ASL, in: Lucas, C. (ed), *Sign Language Research: Theoretical Issues*, pp. 201–210. Gallaudet University Press, Washington, DC.